America and the New Global Economy
Part II

Professor Timothy Taylor

THE TEACHING COMPANY ®

PUBLISHED BY:

THE TEACHING COMPANY
4151 Lafayette Center Drive, Suite 100
Chantilly, Virginia 20151-1232
1-800-TEACH-12
Fax—703-378-3819
www.teach12.com

ISBN 1-59803-482-0

Timothy Taylor

Managing Editor, *Journal of Economic Perspectives*

Timothy Taylor is managing editor of the prominent *Journal of Economic Perspectives*, a position he has held since 1986. The journal is produced at Macalester College and published by the American Economic Association, and it is the most widely distributed and read journal of academic economics in the world. Professor Taylor graduated from Haverford College, where he majored in Economics and Political Science. He holds a Master's degree in Economics from Stanford University.

Professor Taylor has produced several courses for The Teaching Company, including *Economics* (now in its 3rd edition), *History of the U.S. Economy in the 20th Century*, and *Legacies of Great Economists*. In 2007 Professor Taylor published *Principles of Economics*, the first textbook that is available as a free, advertising-supported download from Freeload Press. From the late 1980s to the late 1990s, he wrote op-eds on economic subjects for the *San Jose Mercury-News*. He has published articles on globalization, the new economy, Medicare reform, and outsourcing.

Professor Taylor has edited a wide range of books and reports, including books on school reform, airline deregulation, and pensions for the Brookings Institution; a history of the chemical industry; and the World Bank's 1999/2000 *World Development Report*. He has consulted with the Social Security Administration and the Federal Reserve on the organization and content of their regular reports.

Professor Taylor received the award for excellent teaching in a large class (more than 30 students) given by the Associated Students of Stanford University. At the University of Minnesota, he was named a Distinguished Lecturer by the Department of Economics and voted Teacher of the Year by the Master's degree students at the Hubert H. Humphrey Institute of Public Affairs.

Table of Contents
America and the New Global Economy
Part II

America and the New Global Economy

Scope:

The global economy has become more interconnected than ever before. More goods and services are produced in one country and sold in other countries. More people migrate between countries. More investors around the world are sending their funds to other countries. These stronger economic connections have helped to bring greater prosperity to billions of people around the world.

But the tightening of these connections can bring tensions, too. In the 1950s and 1960s, other countries were interesting to most Americans mainly for their cultures or as occasional tourist destinations. For practical business affairs, a typical American worker or firm of this time could essentially ignore China, India, Mexico, Brazil—indeed, most of the world. But in the first decade of the 21st century, many U.S. workers and firms compete directly with workers and firms from these and other countries every day, in selling both within the United States and within other national boundaries. As consumers and savers, Americans also face choices about buying products from around the world and whether some portion of their retirement plans are invested in far-off and, perhaps, poorly understood countries. What happens in the rest of the world economy now matters to all of us in a direct and immediate way—and the intensity of the global interconnections and potential conflicts is only growing over time.

This course begins with an overview of the development of the global economy since 1950, including the rise of globalization and the diminishing relative importance of the U.S. economy. The main body of the course is divided into two broad sections: first, a tour of the global economy one region or country at a time, then lectures on a number of global economic issues. The focus is primarily on the last few decades, although some lectures will dip back to the 1950s or even earlier and other lectures will consider projections well into the 21st century.

Our tour of the global economy circles the world, beginning with the United States. We move from Western Europe to Eastern Europe and Russia; then on to Asia, with stops in Japan, the East Asian "tiger" economies, China, and India; to the Middle East; to sub-Saharan Africa; and finally, to Latin America.

The lectures for each region or country are usually divided by key moments in time. For example, the first lecture on Western Europe considers the decades of rapid growth in the 1950s and 1960s and the period of strong productivity and low job growth in the 1970s and 1980s, while the second and third lectures discuss how Europe's economy has developed since economic union in the early 1990s and monetary union since 1998. For Eastern Europe and Russia, the discussion begins with a review of the old economy of the Soviet Union, how it functioned and how it failed. Then, a follow-up lecture looks at the experience of these countries as they move from Communism to Capitalism. By the end of this global tour, you should have developed a familiarity with major economic events and issues from all around the world during the last few decades.

The second broad section of the course then considers a series of topics and issues that affect the global economy. The topics begin with the basics of economic globalization, including trade in goods and services, international financial investment, and international migration. Next, the lectures tackle such topics as population growth, poverty, food, urbanization, gender equality, quality of governance, and global climate change. As one example, global population is expected to increase from its current level of roughly 6 billion to about 9 billion in 2050 but then to level off. As another example, about 1 billion people—one in six people in the world—live in extreme poverty, which is defined among economists as living on income of less than $1 a day. These lectures will describe trends, suggest possible causes, and consider policy challenges for such important topics.

These issues aren't the kinds of crises that flare up one month and are resolved the next. As a result, these topics (with the exception of global climate change) are not usually in the newspaper headlines. But they represent fundamental realities that will shape the future course of the world economy. Of course, these lectures on various topics draw freely on the background knowledge of countries and regions around the world that was developed in the earlier lectures.

The concluding lecture asks how globalization might proceed in the future. Because the U.S. economy remains by far the largest in the world, it is commonly and not without some reason perceived as the face of economic globalization. That said, different parts of the world are experiencing globalization in their own distinctive contexts; the causes and consequences of globalization look rather different depending on where you are standing. The gap between those with high and low incomes around the world has widened over the last century, in part because of globalization. However, in the last few decades, the gap has stopped widening and has even, by some measures, started to shrink. During the 21st century, globalization may well contribute to convergence—rather than divergence—of incomes between the top and bottom, as lower-income countries grow at a faster rate than the United States. In all likelihood, the process of globalization has only just begun.

Lecture Thirteen
China's Gradualist Economic Reforms

Scope:

In the 1950s, China's economy was extremely poor. A series of highly disruptive and sometimes harebrained economic policies during the Great Leap Forward and the Cultural Revolution produced shortages and even famine but not economic growth. In the late 1970s, however, China began a gradualist approach to economic reform. A common practice was to require that existing producers, from farmers to factories, still fill their quotas from the central planners, but if they produced more, they could sell the extra at a prevailing market rate. New companies were also allowed to start. Through the 1990s, price controls in the economy were phased out and the role of state-owned companies was reduced. This gradualist approach to economic reform has worked extremely well for China's economic growth, but it is not clear that this approach can be readily applied in other countries.

Outline

I. Mao Zedong proclaimed a Great Leap Forward for China in the late 1950s, but in reality, China's economy was stagnant for several decades before it started market-oriented economic reforms in the late 1970s.

   A. From the 1950s to the 1970s, under the leadership of Mao Zedong, China was embroiled in a series of chaotic initiatives, including the Great Leap Forward and the Cultural Revolution. These policies led to stagnation and widespread poverty at best and mass starvation at worst.

   1. During the Great Leap Forward, China's stated goal was to shift from an agricultural society to an industrial one. But this goal was often pursued in harsh and even nonsensical ways; for example, forcibly shifting farmers away from their land led to mass starvation in the early 1960s.

   2. China's economy established one new pattern during this time that was economically helpful: dramatically increasing its rate of investment. After the Sino-Soviet split in 1960, however, little technical or industrial

expertise was available to make this investment productive.

3. China's Cultural Revolution in the second half of the 1960s spawned extreme anti-foreign and anti-intellectual sentiment. Both domestic education and expertise and foreign expertise were often under violent assault.

B. In the late 1970s, China began a series of economic reforms that have led to spectacular economic growth and marked increases in the standard of living. If this pattern of growth continues, China's economy will be the largest in the world in roughly a decade.

1. China's economy has grown about 9% a year from the reforms in the late 1970s up to the late 2000s. Population over this time has increased by about 30%.

2. Thus, the average person in China has seen a more than 20-fold increase in the standard of living over the last three decades. Poverty rates have plummeted, and ownership of consumer goods has skyrocketed.

II. China's economic changes in the late 1970s were sometimes described in overblown terms, but in retrospect, the changes were modest and gradual, especially when compared to the rapid sweeping away of the central planning apparatus in such economies as Russia or India.

A. China's economic reforms were undertaken by a Communist Party securely in power. The changes did not include privatizing all state-run companies and involved relatively modest reductions in price controls. The approach was one of gradualism, not wide-ranging reform.

B. Until the late 1970s, China's farmers worked in collectives. They had little incentive to produce more, and they didn't.

1. In 1978, the central government allowed farmers increased freedom as long as they met their basic agricultural quotas. Some sought other sources of income and were able to buy their share of production from other farmers.

2. The result was a boom in farm output, markets in agricultural products, and farmers leaving the land to seek jobs in other sectors.

C. The formerly rural workforce moved to work in township and village enterprises, typically small- or medium-sized firms, often engaged in light manufacturing of consumer goods, and owned by collectives or local governments. These enterprises grew explosively, leading the path away from state-owned production.

D. In the old Communist system, foreign trade and investment were discouraged. In recent years, however, thousands of companies have been allowed to import and export, and foreign investors have been welcomed.

E. China's early economic reforms generated additional growth for fundamentally different reasons from the growth generated by Japan or the East Asian tigers. China's early surge of growth wasn't a result of increases in education, levels of investment, or government intervention but about stepping aside to allow economic progress.

III. Another wave of economic reforms followed in the later part of the 1980s and into the 1990s, including the phasing out of price controls and a reduction in the relative importance of state-owned companies.

A. Price controls were phased out in China's economy in a process that started early in the reforms but picked up considerable speed by the late 1980s and the first half of the 1990s. By 2003, most prices for producers, for retail sales, and in agriculture were set by markets rather than by government.

B. There was considerable concern over selling or privatizing state-owned enterprises. Over time, the government allowed many of these firms to keep some of their profits and begin to operate partly in the market economy. Under this pressure, many of the state-owned firms have made progress toward a market orientation.

IV. Some countries wonder if China's economic approach might work for them. However, China's distinctive position may be difficult for other countries to copy.

A. China's neighbors, Taiwan and Hong Kong, have close ties to China and to the rest of the world, thus easing China's integration into the world economy.

B. China's government before the reforms was repressive in many ways, but its interference in the economy was fairly limited. Compared to the Soviet economy, for example, it had less involvement in setting prices.

C. China's Communist Party has never seriously had to fear losing power during the economic reforms.

D. China's economy had been so strangled by political control and the people were so poor that reform was ardently welcomed.

Suggested Readings:

OECD, *China in the World Economy: The Domestic Policy Challenges.*

Perkins, "Completing China's Move to the Market."

————, "History, Politics, and the Sources of Economic Growth: China and the East Asian Way."

Questions to Consider:

1. What was China's economy like before the economic reforms of 1978?

2. What is meant by saying that China has practiced "gradualist" economic reform?

3. Where might it be easier or harder to copy China's path to economic reform?

Lecture Thirteen—Transcript
China's Gradualist Economic Reforms

Mao Zedong proclaimed a Great Leap Forward for China in the late 1950s, but economically speaking, that was a disaster. In reality, China's economy was stagnant for several decades before it started market-oriented economic reforms in the late 1970s, and since then, China's economy has taken such an enormous jump that "Great Leap Forward" seems wholly inadequate to describe it.

Let's start off by looking back to the time of the 1950s to the 1970s, when China was under the leadership of Mao Zedong. During that time, China was embroiled in one chaotic episode after another, including the Great Leap Forward and the Cultural Revolution. From an economic point of view, these policies led to stagnation and widespread poverty at best and mass starvation at worst. After all, the late 1950s are when Mao Zedong was pushing his Great Leap Forward, his attempt to transform China's society from fundamentally agricultural to heavy industry. He imagined he was sort of following what the Soviet Union had done in the 1930s.

It's a little hard to tell the story here as an economist, because China's economic history from the 1940s up through most of the 1970s has very [few] decent economic statistics. An example of the statistical issues here is that the official Chinese government statistics report that agricultural output for China doubled in 1958 in a single year. It seems really unlikely that agricultural output doubled at a time when China was forcibly shifting farmers away from their land in a way which is going to later cause mass starvation in the early 1960s.

Mao's goal of shifting from agriculture to manufacturing was pursued in many harsh and sometimes even nonsensical ways. For example, tens of millions of people were transferred to work on dams and roads; mostly, they were supposed to build these by unaided manpower, without machines. There were also somewhat bizarre projects where they were going to create steel and cement industries by producing in small backyard furnaces. Meanwhile, the social and economic changes were killing the farmers in a literal sense, leading to widespread famine and maybe 20 million or more dead by the early 1960s.

However, there was one pattern that started during this early portion of the Communist era that has continued since then and that later on did prove useful for economic growth. China had historically been a low-saving, low-investment country in the first half of the 20th century, typically investing maybe 5% of GDP. But soon after the Communists took over in 1949, they forcibly pushed up national investment and savings rates, up to 20% and 30% of GDP, very high levels by world standards, and rates of investment, as we'll see, have gone even higher since then in the 1990s and into the 2000s. In fact, this high level of investment probably helps explain why even in the face of the chaos of the Great Leap Forward, there was at least some economic growth during this period at all.

Another big difficulty for China in the early 1960s was the big split between the Soviets and the Chinese that occurred in 1960. The Soviet Union had been supplying a lot of the technological and industrial expertise that China needed, and it took years to train enough Chinese folks to really fully replace them.

The second half of the 1960s in China is the Cultural Revolution, a sort of mob rule enforced by public violence and harsh prison labor camps—heavily anti-foreign, heavily anti-intellectual. This was a time when suggesting that any foreigners might have any useful knowledge of technology or industry that might help in Chinese manufacturing could literally get you killed. Schools barely functioned from about 1958 to about 1978 in China. Universities were largely shut down. Skilled workers, like doctors and engineers, were often sent out to do harsh manual labor.

Compared to the astonishingly high standards of social and economic dislocation from the Great Leap Forward and the Cultural Revolution, the Chinese economy did settle down a little in the early and mid-1970s, although sometimes this was called the time of the "three nothing enterprises." And what, you may ask, is a three nothing enterprise? "Three nothing enterprise" means no administration, no management, and no regulations. During this time, the entire notion of accurate economic statistics is still somewhat laughable. Even basic statistics like population are disputed by a hundred million people or so; for detailed economic statistics like GDP, I mean, forget it. This is a time when intellectuals and experts were being shipped off to hard labor in rural areas or sometimes just killed. You didn't have a whole lot of people volunteering to be government statisticians.

In recent years, of course, some very smart scholars have been digging back through the available evidence, trying to piece together the history of China's economy in the 1950s and 1960s and 1970s. From a historical perspective, this strikes me as really important work, but for the purposes of these lectures, China from the 1950s through the 1970s is, in a way, the prehistoric era; it's not our main focus here. Because what happens in 1978 is that China begins a remarkable series of economic reforms, starting just an extraordinary economic run over the last several decades, a world-changing run, to sustain economic growth this high for this long. I mean, I've been watching this happen during my professional life as an economist, and even after watching it for several decades, I can still barely believe it's happening.

China's economy has often been growing at 8% or 9% per year. And, again, just think about what growth rates like that a moment. At a growth rate of 9%, whatever the economy is will double in eight years. In very rough terms, China's per-person economic growth since about 1980 is similar to the amount of U.S. economic growth from the U.S. Civil War up to the present.

It seems quite possible that China will become, with continued growth, the largest overall economy in the world in the next couple of decades, even with, you know, varied disputes about exactly how to compare the sizes of different economies. I'm not saying it will have the highest income on a per-person basis. It should still be well behind the United States and many other high-income countries in that way. But since China has about 1.3 billion people in the late 2000s, it has more than four times the population of the United States. World Bank estimates in 2008 were that the standard of living in China is about 10% of the U.S. level. When China reaches the point where the average standard of living is 25, 30% of the U.S. level, then the overall size of China's economy will be larger than that of the U.S. economy.

China's really rapid economic growth has translated into substantial gains for the standard of living for its citizens. Back in 1980, China had maybe 60% of its population—that is to say, 600 million people or so—who were living on less than $1 a day. That $1 a day is the definition of global poverty which is typically used by the World

Bank to compare across countries, and the reason for setting it at that level is $1 a day is roughly enough to cover the costs of just basic subsistence. We'll talk more about this poverty line later on in the lecture on global poverty, but the World Bank estimates that poverty in China declined from 64% of China's population in 1981, to 33% of China's population in 1990, to 10% of China's population by 2004. And by the end of the first decade of the 21st century, they should be well under 10%, measured by that $1-a-day poverty line. This is just an enormous gain in human welfare. I mean, I'm not the biggest guy for superlatives, and yes, China has all sorts of economic and political issues—we'll talk more about them—but it's just a fact that this period of rapid economic growth for China is the largest and fastest movement out of mass poverty that we've ever seen in all of human history. It's a remarkable event.

In 1985, almost no one in China had a refrigerator, or a washing machine, or a color TV in their house. By 2003, about half had refrigerators and washing machines, and well over 90% had color TVs. From 1985 to 2003, the number of students in higher education was up by a multiple of 5 in China. Phone lines increased by a multiple of 9. Paved roads increased by a multiple of 5. Sewage lines increased by a multiple of 6. Public transit vehicles increased by a multiple of almost 6. These are just extraordinary changes happening across the economy.

The focus of this lecture is to describe how China's economic reforms unfolded, starting in the late 1970s and then up through the 1980s and into the 1990s. The following lecture will then consider the challenges facing China's economy as it attempts to sustain this extremely rapid growth into the future.

Thinking about what happened in China's economic reforms, [let's] start in the late 1970s. A simpleminded description would go something like this. It would be: China gave up Communist central planning and turned to the free market. And like most sort of simpleminded descriptions, this isn't totally wrong, but it really fails to capture what was maybe most distinctive about China's economic reforms, which is how meek and gradual those reforms were. To think about what's distinctive about China's reforms, it's maybe useful to think about what they didn't do, especially as compared to Russia, [which] we discussed in an earlier lecture.

The Communist economy of the Soviet Union was stagnant, but it was stagnant at a much higher level of industrialization and human capital than China had back in the late 1970s. Russia also experienced the political overthrow of the Communist Party. It had fairly free elections soon after, in the 1990s, in the breakup of the old Soviet Union. Russia's move away from Communism led to mass privatization of existing large firms, freeing up of prices, and sort of a mass movement toward a free market.

China didn't have the same kind of large industrial operations as already existed in Russia. China didn't really privatize, and it continued to have a large number of state-owned enterprises. It didn't immediately eliminate the system of central planning. Some prices were freed up, but a lot of prices continued to be set by government, and China's Communist Party stayed well in control. In the lingo that economists sometimes use, Russia's move to the market, Russia's transition, was "big bang"; that is, lots of stuff happened in a relatively small period of time in the 1990s. China's move to the market talked a big game in the late 1970s—they would talk about the "four modernizations," agriculture, industry, science and technology, and defense—but when push came to shove, the actual changes that really mattered, the changes that happened right away, were much smaller and were gradualist.

In fact, you can really say there were just three changes at first. One was freeing up agriculture; one is shifting workers to township and village enterprises; and one was opening up to foreign trade. Let me talk about these in turn.

First of all, turning the farmers loose: Until the late 1970s, China's farmers worked in collectives, and if you produced more than your share in the collective, you got the great honor and privilege of delivering the extra to the government; that was your incentive. Perhaps not as a big surprise, per capita grain output in China was basically the same in the late 1970s as it had been in the 1950s, and frankly, it hadn't been so great in the 1950s either.

But during the 1970s, farmers began to bribe their way out of the system. Some of them promised to grow their share of the quota for the collective privately, and then they went out and looked for other sources of income. In fact, it turned out that you could fulfill your quota with the collective farm by buying your share of the production from someone else. By 1978, China's central government

©2008 The Teaching Company.

accepted this pattern by endorsing what was called the "household responsibility system," and what that basically meant was that collectively owned land was assigned to individuals for periods of up to 15 years. In 1978, less than 10% of the agricultural commodities in China were sold in markets. By 1990, just 12 years later, 80% of agricultural commodities were sold in markets. The main exceptions were some grains where China was really trying to be 95% self-sufficient in grain.

Agriculture had been 30% of China's GDP in 1980. By 1995, it was down to 21% of GDP. What had happened was that agriculture grew a lot in size as people had access to their own plots and they could grow a lot more, but the rest of China's economy was growing even faster, so as a share of the economy, agriculture was shrinking. There really was explosive growth in agriculture, though, under the household responsibility system. Agricultural output had been growing in the 1970s at less than 3% a year. When they put that system in place in the late '70s, the growth of output zoomed up to 6% a year almost immediately. I don't want to sort of overstate what happened in here. There is a huge jump in the late '70s and into the 1980s, but then that jump kind of levels off in the mid-1980s. For a time, though, perhaps a decade, agricultural productivity really did help to drive overall economic growth forward in China.

A lot of farmers were freed up from farming as agricultural output went up and there was private land. Where are those farmers going to go? Some went to the cities. The cities' share of population in China was 18% of population in 1978; it was up to 29% of population by the mid-1990s, a substantial shift from rural areas to cities. But many of those farmers went to what are called township and village enterprises. These were owned mainly by local governments or sometimes even by citizens of a township or village. They produced mainly consumer goods, simple things, like pots and pans, and plates, and simple appliances. There was a huge potential market for these kinds of things, because the earlier state planning in China hadn't focused very much on consumer goods or on light manufacturing, so there was a big pent-up demand for these goods, and as rising incomes came, a lot of people could afford them.

Township and village enterprises were about 13% of gross domestic product in 1985. By the mid '90s, they were more than a third of gross domestic product. They were making something like 40% of all of China's industrial output and growing at something like 25% a year. These township and village enterprises worked in a very competitive market. They were essentially exempt from central planning, and they really worked by getting foreign investment to come in and put in the money and help build the factory. There was intense competition among them to get that foreign investment and, thus, intense competition to be well run and to attract that foreign investment. They needed to be self-supporting or they got shut down. Local governments didn't have either the desire or the resources to tax their own people in the township for working in their own factory. But by about the mid-1990s, the growth of these collectively owned township and village enterprises seems to have slacked off, and companies became more and more owned by private shareholders or foreign owners or sometimes by individuals.

Overall, state firms made 78% of China's output in 1978. By the mid-1990s, state-owned firms were making only 33% of output. The township and village enterprises are not government-owned firms in the sense of the old-line companies, and they seem to be sort of a transitional form that led the way from centralized state production and transformed the economies of rural areas by helping lead toward greater production and openness to foreign trade.

That openness to foreign trade was another big change. In the old Communist system, all trade was handled by government corporations, and each government corporation had a monopoly on certain areas. If you wanted to export to China, you had to sell to the government corporation. If you wanted to import from China, you had to sell to the corporation, and then you would buy from the corporation. You didn't even really know who your eventual customers were. Everything was handled through these government corporations, and all foreign currency was handled through the Bank of China. There was, early on, a fair amount of hostility to foreign trade, and foreign investment in China barely existed. This system, as it existed before the reforms up through the 1970s, was sometimes referred to as an "airlock": an airlock that separated China's economy from foreign influence.

The reform in the late 1970s was to set up foreign trade zones, set up in different regions and areas, and this allowed thousands of companies to export and import, often these same township and village enterprises just mentioned. Often these companies really wanted to buy new machinery and equipment. After all, they'd been largely shut away from new plant and equipment since 1960 or so, except maybe for some old stuff from the Soviet Union and Eastern Europe that was probably already outdated when they got it. Gradually, the airlock was opened up in the 1970s and into the 1980s. Exports from China were something like 6 or 7% of China's GDP back in 1980. By 1995, [this number] was more than 20% of GDP.

How did this work so well? How could you open up and have these township and village enterprises be so involved in foreign trade so quickly? Foreign investors are really behind only about 2% of China's total manufactured goods for its economy as a whole, but they were behind about 30% of its manufactured exported goods, and that number seems to be growing. The foreign investors were helping provide a link to what the ultimate market would be. In particular, China, of course, has connections with the Chinese diaspora across Asia, particularly through Hong Kong and to some extent through Taiwan, and that group certainly helped expand trade and investment very rapidly. It helped figure out what to make, and where to market it, and where to get the finance.

It's worth emphasizing here—this is not your typical Japanese approach; it is not your typical East Asian approach. To see what's so distinctive about China's gradualist approach, let's contrast it with those others. Remember, China's early surge of growth from its reforms was not the result of some increase in education. Education in China had been pretty well torched during most of the 1960s and 1970s. Nor was it a result of higher levels of investment. Investment levels were already high in China since the 1950s. In fact, investment levels may have dropped a little in the early 1980s, although being able to buy modern machinery and equipment made a huge difference in China's growth. Moreover, China really didn't do a lot of targeting particular industries, as it was sometimes argued that Japan and East Asia did.

These early Chinese economic reforms were more about just stepping aside, shifting some of the inherited organizational forms in the economy, moving away from the state-owned enterprises, allowing freedom for the farmers, allowing freedom for the township and village enterprises, and slowly opening up to trade. Those who said that after decades of Communism, China's people just weren't entrepreneurial—they wouldn't respond to market incentives—those people were clearly wrong. Given some freedom in markets, the people of China responded just astonishingly well.

But by the late 1980s and into the 1990s, this set of gradualist reforms had begun to sort of run into some natural limits. Agriculture had this big one-time surge over a decade or so; the township and village enterprises were shifting to become sort of real companies, publicly owned; and there were still other steps that needed to be taken. It was time for China to go through a second wave of economic reforms that would happen in the later part of the 1980s and into the 1990s. And this wave [had] two really big changes: getting rid of price controls in China's economy and diminishing the relative importance of the state-owned companies. Again, let's talk about these two in turn.

Price controls were gradually phased out in China's economy. This sort of started early in the reforms but picked up considerable speed in the late 1980s and into the first half of the 1990s. For example, for retail goods, only 3% of all the prices were set by the market in 1978; 34% of those prices were set by the market by 1985. By 1995, 89% of the prices of retail goods were set in the market. The remaining group might be fixed by the state, or sometimes they say, "guided by the state," which is sometimes kind of like being fixed. There was a similar pattern of freeing up prices for producer goods and for agriculture. By 2003, most prices for producers, for retail sales, and in agriculture were being set by markets rather than by China's government. I should say, these numbers are actually from the Chinese government, and maybe they're a little optimistic on how much prices have been freed up. There are certain pretty important prices, like the exchange rate of China's currency, that are still administered by the government, but there's really just no question at all: China's economy is vastly more determined by market prices than before.

From an economic perspective, I just can't emphasize how big a deal this is. Prices are messengers in the economy. They reveal what people want to pay for; they reveal what it costs to provide it; they provide incentives to use less of what's expensive and more of what's cheap; they give incentives to firms to provide what people want. Letting markets set prices is just an enormous step toward providing incentives for efficiency and innovation in an economy.

The other big change at this time is dealing with the state-owned enterprises. At the end of the day, China just couldn't bear to sell them or privatize them, and when you think about it, you can understand why. Remember all the difficulties Russia had in trying to sell off its enterprises. Ending up with a bunch of oligarchs in China was certainly not appealing. Moreover, if they were going to sell them off, would they sell off to foreign buyers? Can you imagine, say, Taiwanese businessmen buying government firms in China or Japanese firms or U.S. firms? I don't think so.

There was a feeling [that] they couldn't sell off the firms; instead, they started a process where state-owned firms operated in essentially two markets. They operated partly in the planned market and partly in a more free market. What happened was the state-owned enterprises were required to buy a certain amount of inputs at the government price and were required to sell a certain amount of output at the government price, but they were also allowed to buy additional inputs, if they wanted, at the market price and to sell additional output, if they wanted, at the market price. And if they did this, they could keep an increasing share of any profits they earned.

If you think about how this worked, it sort of gave the state-owned firms a safety net. They had some inputs and outputs that would sort of guarantee them some level of profit, but they were also oriented toward the external market in shifting in that direction. Some of them were making large losses, but they could get loans from the state-owned banks to cover those. It's really a very interesting strategy. It avoids the outright collapse of these firms, which would have happened pretty quickly without subsidies of some sort, and it avoids the disruption and unemployment that would have resulted from these firms collapsing, at least for a time. They also took away, at about this time, a lot of government monopolies. So, if the state-owned firms wanted to sell in the market, they needed to compete with other market-driven firms.

In the early 2000s, there were still some industries with a lot of government ownership in China. Energy industries, like oil and gas, coal; infrastructure industries, like tap water, electrical power; transportation-like industries, like cars; a few oddball industries, like tobacco, were still state monopolies. But by the early 2000s, private-sector firms accounted for about 60% of China's economy, and that share was steadily rising. Some state-owned firms had issued shares that were being bought and sold in stock markets, although often with state-owned firms, the shares only represented maybe one-third of the ownership of the firm, so no one could actually take the firm over.

The difficulty was that in the early 2000s, the state-owned firms were still sucking up a huge amount of financial capital. Something like two-thirds of all the investment in plant and equipment in China through the mid-'90s was happening in the state-owned sector. As late as 2003, probably half of all investment—plant and equipment—was happening in the state-owned sector. And a lot of this was state-owned banks funneling loans to state-owned companies which were losing money.

Some state-owned firms remain a disaster. They're sucking up loans from the state-owned banks, and they really have no chance of repaying. China has essentially tried to deal with the state-owned firms by letting the rest of the economy outgrow them, rather than by reforming them in a direct way. But when you're sort of feeding a stream of subsidies to the state-owned firms, this strategy of trying to let the rest of the economy grow faster is clearly a mixed message.

Does China's set of reforms, its gradualist approach, offer a general lesson for economic reform? Many countries wonder if China's economic approach might work for them. In particular, many autocratic leaders around the world would love to keep political control while having really rapid economic growth, so they look to China as an example. But China has always had a distinctive background in various ways that is really hard for other countries to copy. Let me talk about a few of those.

One, for example, is it has neighbors who are really very hard to copy. In particular, I'm thinking of Taiwan and Hong Kong. Taiwan and Hong Kong offer trade, in a way, and trade ties that are just impossible to duplicate in really any other way, and thus, they've really eased China's integration into the rest of the world economy.

A second advantage that China has in thinking about the rest of the world: It has relatively limited control by the government. China's government before the economic reforms was repressive in many ways, but it didn't interfere in the economy nearly as much as the old Soviet leaders. The 1960s and 1970s in China were chaotic; it wasn't like careful central planners were doing everything. In the USSR, for example, they say that people were allocating about 60,000 commodities through central planning in the late 1970s. In China, the central planners were only allocating about 600 commodities. Moreover, the state-owned firms in China, because the country was so poor, really didn't have a big welfare state. They didn't offer a lot of health care and pensions and all those things. When you started trying to get rid of those state-owned firms, the change had a lot less resistance, involved a lot less disruption, than it had in the old Soviet Union. A fair amount of China's production was already out of the control of the central government in a lot of industries even back in the 1970s. In 1979, for example, two-thirds of cement production was already outside government control.

Another advantage for China was that it had a very entrenched political class. China's Communist Party has never had to seriously fear losing power, so it was perfectly willing to reform. And, finally, there was really ardent political support for the reforms. China's economy had been so strangled for so long and the people were so poor that they were desperate to have some kind of economic reform. There's one economic study that said in a rare moment of poetic license: "China's economy could be described as a dry prairie, parched by years of planning, awaiting the first sprinklings of market reform."

In fact, when I hear people from other countries, low-income countries, say they want to take the Chinese approach, I suspect that at some level, they don't really mean it. I mean, do they mean, for example, they'll let farmers own land, and produce what they want, and free up prices? Do they mean that they're willing to let small enterprises flourish, and welcome them buying foreign equipment, and taking foreign ownership, and selling stuff on world markets? Do they mean when they say we want to copy China that they'll let large enterprises keep the profits and buy and sell at world market prices? Do they mean they'll start phasing out all their price controls over the next 15 to 20 years and they'll move state-owned companies into the stock market?

The truth is many low-income countries with nondemocratic or authoritarian governments, they claim to really like China's approach, but what they're really saying is they like the continued authoritarian power of China's government, and they wouldn't actually dare to try those kinds of reforms themselves.

Lecture Fourteen
China's Challenges for Continued Growth

Scope:

China's economy in the 2000s seems to have moved into a new stage. The already high levels of saving and investment have climbed even higher. The emphasis in China's economy has shifted to heavy industry, using increased amounts of energy and natural resources. This approach leads to continued high economic growth but also creates high levels of pollution. Moreover, on strictly economic grounds, this strategy can't go on indefinitely. China needs to shift toward an economy driven more by domestic consumption. China's low birthrate in recent decades will soon lead to declines in the nation's overall workforce. China needs to start its transition away from being a low-wage producer and move toward higher wage levels.

Outline

I. China's growth in the 2000s has been driven by a combination of investment in physical capital and in exports, with a high level of national savings underpinning both factors.

   A. China's gross national saving rate—which combines all saving by households, firms, and government—was already at about 30% of GDP at the start of the reform period in the early 1980s. The saving rate climbed above 40% of GDP in the 1990s and touched an astonishing 50% of GDP in 2005.

   B. An economy with an extremely high saving rate is swimming in investment capital. A good portion of the savings ends up in state-owned or state-controlled banks, which in turn, lend it to industry. In the 2000s, China has seen a surge in growth of heavy industries, which are highly capital-intensive and often use large amounts of raw materials and energy.

II. A high-investment economy has certain consequences.

   A. One way of measuring GDP, or economic output, is to divide it into five parts: consumption, investment, government spending, exports, and imports. In China, with investment and exports so high, consumption has tended to be quite low as a share of the economy.

B. The rapid growth of heavy manufacturing in China has led to much higher demand for energy and for other commodities, such as metals and food. In fact, China's demand for commodities has spurred a global rise in prices for these commodities in the late 2000s.

C. As China expands its heavy industry at a rapid pace, it creates considerable air and water pollution. China's laws to moderate pollution have tightened and the available technologies to reduce pollution have expanded, but the sheer growth of industry continues to create environmental problems.

D. When consumers don't buy a high proportion of a country's output, then a large share of that output ends up being sold in other countries. China didn't have especially large trade surpluses in most of the 1980s and 1990s, but growth in exports and China's trade surplus have been important factors in its economy in the first decade of the 2000s.

E. With the Chinese economy running huge trade surpluses, much of the incoming foreign currency has gone into building up enormous foreign exchange reserves—totaling over $1 trillion in the late 2000s.

III. China needs a broad shift in its economy, away from the heavy-investment, heavy-industry, export orientation and toward a greater emphasis on domestic consumption and provision of services. In academic writing about China, this shift is called "rebalancing."

A. China can't sustain its current pattern forever: that is, extremely high rates of national saving, much of which ends up being held by the government as part of an extraordinarily large stash of dollar-denominated foreign exchange reserves.

B. One likely approach is for China to increase spending on consumption-type items, such as education, health care, and social security for the elderly. Given the low budget deficits and the high level of national saving, it would make economic sense to use moderate deficit spending for this purpose. This kind of social spending increases consumption in two ways.

    1. The government is spending money directly.

    2. People feel less need to save because some level of government support is available.

C. If the Chinese central bank stops accumulating high reserves and allows the value of the yuan to rise, exports will tend to decrease and imports will be encouraged. Overall, this change would foster the necessary rebalancing.

D. China has had a pattern of depositing its huge savings in state-owned banks, then loaning money to large state-owned companies. In the 1990s, it was a common fear that many of these loans would never be repaid and that the state-owned banks were facing huge losses. China has made progress in reducing these problems over time, but further steps are needed.

IV. Much of China's economic growth has been based on cheap and plentiful labor, combined with high levels of investment in physical capital. But is China's era of cheap labor coming to an end?

A. The general pattern of labor movement in China since the economic reforms has been from the western and northern areas of the country (more rural and less developed) toward the coastal and southern parts of the country (urban areas). But some areas are now reporting unfilled jobs and rising wages.

B. The migration from rural to urban areas will continue for a few more years, but the size of China's workforce will be reduced over time by demographic trends and increased levels of higher education.

    1. In 2005, 45% of total Chinese employment was still in agriculture. Given past and future trends in agricultural output, perhaps 150 million or more workers can still be expected to migrate from rural areas to cities. China's great migration from the farms isn't over yet but is slowly drawing to a close.

    2. Education in upper-secondary and college-level institutions has been low in China. But as it rises, fewer people in the 15- to 24-year-old age group will be available as low-skilled workers.

3. China's birthrates dropped significantly in the 1970s, partially as a result of the one-child policy adopted by the government at that time. The lower birthrates mean that China's working-age population will start to shrink around 2010.

C. In the long-run, maintaining perpetually low wages is not the path to economic success. China has not reached the end of its low-wage era yet, but as education levels increase and the size of the labor force levels off (perhaps even declines), China's wages should start to rise.

V. In early 2008, the U.S. economy is the largest in the world, and China's economy is the second largest. If the U.S. economy grows at 3% per year and China's economy grows at 9% per year, then China will have the world's largest economy in roughly 15 years. This growth may take slightly longer—sustaining 9% annual growth rates for several decades is not a sure thing—but it seems likely that China's economy will displace that of the United States some time in the next two to three decades.

Suggested Readings:

Lardy, "China: Rebalancing Economic Growth."

OECD, *OECD Economic Surveys: China.*

Questions to Consider:

1. What are some of the problems with China's pattern of economic growth in the 21st century?

2. Is China likely to suffer a labor shortage that will hurt its economic growth?

Lecture Fourteen—Transcript
China's Challenges for Continued Growth

The pace of China's economic growth from about 1980 up through the first decade of the 21st century already makes it a historic episode in the history of the world economy. Can China conceivably keep growing at a similar annual rate into the future? It is easy to compile a list of possible worries: improving education and health, raising the skill levels of workers, better governance for corporations, reform of state-owned enterprises, rising pollution, labor shortages, possible shortages of energy, maybe a backlash of Protectionism from other countries against China's exports. I could go on and on, but you get the idea here.

What I want to do in this lecture is focus on one key pattern in China's economy that links many of these facts together and that I think will absolutely have to change over time if China is to continue to have healthy, strong economic growth. This key pattern may not at first seem obvious or central, and I certainly wouldn't claim it is the only big problem for China's economy, but I do think it is at the center of many of the issues that are going on right now. And, oddly enough, this factor is China's amazingly high rate of national saving and investment.

We discussed briefly in previous lectures that maybe the one positive economic aspect of the Communist period for China was that the rate of saving rose sharply. In China, gross saving was already about 30% of GDP in the early 1980s, when the market-oriented reforms began. Saving then edged up, and by the 1990s, saving in China was running at 40% of GDP and a little higher than that. Now, this is just an astonishingly high level. For comparison, those 30% rates of saving, or a little higher than that, had been seen before a few times in countries like Japan and [places in] East Asia as part of their economic miracles. But 40% is well beyond the experience of other countries.

For the world as a whole, typical gross saving for an economy runs about 20 or 22% of world GDP in the last couple of decades. In a low-saving country, like the United States, it typically runs in maybe the 14 to 17% range, at least during the first decade of the 2000s. China's saving rate in the 1990s was already astonishing, and in the mid-2000s, it went up even higher. Gross savings rates in China went into the mid-40s as a percent of GDP, and in 2005, gross saving in

China hit a completely astounding (I'm running out of superlatives here) 50% of GDP. Just to be clear, when I am talking about gross saving, this measure of saving is a very broad measure of national saving. It includes personal savings, savings by companies that are reinvesting in plant and equipment, and it also includes saving by government, if the government is running budget surpluses.

For Americans, we maybe need to say a little about what it would look like to be in an economy with a very high savings rate. It is not really something we are used to seeing in the U.S. economy. In an economy with a really high savings rate, firms are swimming in investment capital. The supply of capital is very large, and so the interest rates tend to be quite low, and so do the returns on investment. In the only sort of partially reformed Chinese savings system, much of the saving goes into banks, and then it ends up in state-owned or state-controlled industries.

In the 2000s, China has seen a surge of what is called "heavy industry." Heavy industries are very capital-intensive, and they often involve using large amounts of raw materials and energy. Examples would include something like steel, paper, iron, cement, aluminum, glass, and manufacturing things like cars. For example, steel production in China tripled from 2000 to about 2007. China now makes more than one-third of all the steel in the world. Similarly, the number of cars made in China went up by a multiple of 6 from 2000 to 2006.

You might be asking: What is the problem here, Tim? This sort of sounds like basically what you were talking about before: high savings and high investment being poured into industry [and] industry expanding rapidly. The difficulty is that even a good thing can be pushed to extremes, and I need to talk about some of the consequences of a super-high investment economy.

Let's start off by talking about low consumption. One way of measuring GDP, or economic output, is to divide it into five parts: consumption, investment, government spending, exports, and imports. In China, investment and exports have been quite high. Government spending has been rising as a share of the economy, but it is still relatively small. It is probably about a quarter of GDP in the mid-2000s, and that compares with government spending as maybe a third of GDP in the United States. It is much higher in many countries of the European Union.

In China, consumption has tended to be pretty low as a share of the economy, and that has been falling as investment goes up. Consumption was about half of China's economy in the 1980s. It was a little below half in the 1990s, and in 2005, when savings and investment were so remarkably high, consumption in China was just 38% of GDP. This is really peculiar, because in comparison, in the high-consumption U.S. economy, consumption is typically 65 or 70% of GDP. Even in Japan, which is well known for its very high savings rates, consumption is typically about 60% of GDP, and that's a common level for lots of countries around the world.

Because of the extremely rapid growth in the standard of living, standard of living is rising. There is more consumption for the average person. But when you look at the output of China's economy, there are lots of factories and lots of stuff being produced for use in other countries. There is relatively little being produced in terms of housing, and education, and health care, and food and entertainment, travel, all that stuff we think of as household consumption. Up until now, China's economy has been growing so fast that many people in China haven't really noticed that this huge and rising share of the economy is going to investment. But at some point, I suspect the people of China will start wanting more and more consumption, and that will be a point of stress for the super-high investment economy.

Next issue: The super-high investment economy all going into heavy industry leads to much higher demand for energy and for other commodities, including metals and food. There had been a pattern in China's economy in the 1980s and 1990s. That pattern was that every time gross domestic product went up by 1%, energy consumption in China went up by about half of 1%. And that pattern was the basic way that people forecast China's future energy use. They would forecast growth, and they would say half of that growth will represent the growth in energy demand.

But starting in the early 2000s, as China moved to heavy industry, this pattern changed. Then it became true that every time China's GDP went up by 1%, energy consumption rose by about 1.5%—not half a percent but 1.5%. In other words, for a given rise of GDP growth, energy consumption was rising three times faster than would have been expected based on earlier experience. Now, energy use has gone way up in China; China's use of oil tripled from 1990 to 2005.

China used to be an oil exporter back in 1990. By the late 2000s, China was importing half of the oil it used. China used to export coal back in the 1990s but no more. In 2005 and 2006, China actually added more electrical-generating capacity than the entire electrical-generating capacity of France. These energy demands are going up and up and leading Chinese firms to strike deals all across Africa, and Latin America, and Asia for access to more energy resources and to mineral resources.

Of course, the later part of the 2000s has seen an enormous surge in prices for many commodities around the world. Oil prices, for example, went well above $100 a barrel in 2008. One reason that oil prices went so high so unexpectedly was China's sharp increase in energy usage. It takes years to make really large adjustments in the supply of energy. You have to find sources of energy and work out the whole process of transportation, and refining, and distribution. [Thus,] if you don't see a big demand increase coming, it's going to be very difficult for the market to adjust in the short term. No one really predicted, based on China's experience of the '80s and '90s, that it was going to have this enormous boost in its energy demand in the 2000s, and that has altered world energy markets in a profound way.

In addition and similarly, it has led to very high prices for metals, from iron to copper and gold. In a later lecture on world agriculture and hunger, I will emphasize that a similar lesson applies to food—that is, rapid growth in incomes in China has increased demand for food. And I don't just mean more food in raw terms but more demand for meat, which is very grain-intensive to produce, and this has driven up the price of grain all around the world.

The third issue of moving to this high-investment, heavy-industry economy is high pollution. As China keeps expanding its heavy industry at a very rapid pace, it's creating considerable air and water pollution. It's pollution of a sort that happened in U.S. cities some decades back. I'm talking about air pollution so thick that you cannot see the Sun on some days. This, of course, has a high cost in respiratory sickness. I'm talking about acid rain that eats away at crops and buildings, river basins where the water is no longer fit for human consumption, and lots of contamination going into the ocean off the coasts. World Bank studies of this pollution put its costs in China at about 6% of China's GDP. In fact, rumor was that some early drafts of the World Bank study said [that] pollution was killing 750,000 people per year in China and that the Chinese government got them to take that part of the estimates out.

This sort of number is not a crazy one. Regulators at China's own state environmental protection agency have been quoted as estimating that environmental costs in China are something like 8 to 13% of GDP, and that upper end is about double the World Bank estimates. The Chinese environmental regulators themselves have also been quoted as saying that, with current trends, levels of air and water pollution in China will double in the next 15 years. These are enormous issues in China. There are reports of tens of thousands of protests each year on environmental issues. It's sort of a nonpolitical outlet for concern, but you really have to watch and see whether it might at some point turn political. In fact, as we talked about earlier, environmental protests were probably part of what diminished political support for the old Soviet regime back in the 1980s. It should be a real worry to China's regime now.

Of course, China's government has plans—more rules for energy efficiency, more rules for fuel efficiency, better antipollution technology, switching to natural gas instead of oil, all the things you would sort of expect—but enforcement of the new rules really has not been very aggressive, and there has just been so very much growth in heavy industry over the last decade or so that it has overwhelmed any efforts toward cleaning up.

The high-investment economy is also leading to some macroeconomic imbalances. When consumers in an economy are not buying much output, then a lot of that output ends up being sold to other countries. In the first decade of the 2000s, we are thinking of China as an export superpower, but actually, this is a fairly recent development. China actually did not have especially large trade surpluses during most of the 1980s and 1990s. For example, in the 11 years from 1985 through 1995, China had trade deficits in five of those years, a trade balance that was almost zero (neither a trade surplus nor a deficit) in two years, and a trade surplus in the other four years.

It has only been in the mid-2000s, as China's savings rate has skyrocketed, that production was way, way up and consumption wasn't, and China's trade surplus has gotten very large indeed. In 2005, that year when the gross savings rate hit 50% of GDP, China's trade surplus that year was 7% of GDP, which is an extraordinarily high trade surplus. Of course, China does a lot of importing of energy and minerals, as we talked about a little bit ago, but a lot of that energy and minerals just go into products which then have value added in China and are then re-exported somewhere else.

The related macroeconomic imbalance here is that China is building up extremely high foreign exchange reserves. China earns foreign currency with its exports. You sell in the United States, you earn U.S. dollars. In fact, most world trade is denominated in dollars. China has been saving up those U.S. dollars that it earns in its central bank, and this is called "foreign exchange reserves." Total foreign exchange reserves in China have crossed over $1 trillion toward the tail end of the first decade of the 21st century. To get some return on this money, a lot of these reserves are invested in fairly safe U.S. assets, like U.S. treasury debt.

In short, China is earning a lot of dollars; it's lending the money back to the U.S. economy and also to some corporations who borrow. Should we Americans be worried that the U.S. economy has well over $1 trillion in debt to China? It reminds me a little bit of an old joke. The old joke is that if you owe a bank $1 million, then you have a problem, but if you owe a bank $100 million, the bank has a problem. China has over $1 trillion in U.S.-dollar assets, and China really doesn't want the U.S. economy to go down the tubes. Think of it: If you own $1 trillion in U.S.-dollar assets and the value of the dollar declines 10%, you have just lost $100 billion dollars in buying power.

How much should China be worried? There are reasons why it makes good sense to hold some foreign exchange reserves. The main commonsensical one we talked about in the East Asia lectures was that if global financial markets start panicky selling of your currency, then the central bank can buy back that currency using its foreign exchange reserves, which helps stabilize the market.

The other reason, though, is that these foreign exchange reserves help keep the value of the Chinese yuan low. How does this work? There are two steps to understand here. The value of a currency is really just like any other value. If there is lots of demand for it, it tends to push the price up. If there is not so much demand, it tends to keep the price down. Basically, right now, whenever anyone wants to trade dollars for [China's] currency, the yuan, China's central bank says, sure, we will take those dollars; we will add them to our reserves; and here is the currency you want. So China keeps supplying its own currency, enough to absorb any extra demand.

What does a low exchange rate value of the yuan do for China's imports or China's exports? Remember, when you are an exporting firm, your costs are incurred in the currency of your home country, and your sales revenue comes from the currency of other countries. If a currency is relatively weak, your costs in your home country are relatively low, and your revenues from the other country are relatively high, so you do lots of exports. Conversely, if a currency goes up in value, then your exports are not going to be as attractive.

By holding large dollar reserves, China's central bank helps keep the value of its currency low, and this helps stimulate its exports. But this, in the long run, is not going to be a sustainable strategy. You cannot just keep building up foreign exchange reserves forever. China has already passed $1 trillion in the later part of the first decade of the 2000s. It is adding a few hundred billion more dollars to foreign exchange reserves every year. That won't go on forever.

What needs to happen with China's economy? China's pattern of having extremely high rates of national saving, much of which ends up being held by the government as part of this large stash of dollar foreign exchange reserves, can't go on forever. At some point, people in China are going to want to consume things, like housing, and health care, and education, and a clean environment, just like other people all over the world. They are not going to go with saving half of GDP and massive investment forever. Some of this will happen through the gradual nature of politics. Of course, I am not talking about democratic politics as Americans understand it, but the regime in China clearly knows that the one reason it can keep going is that economic growth is so popular and it's delivering the goods on economic growth. Growth is a lot of what gives China's regime whatever legitimacy it has. [Thus,] making sure people's consumption keeps rising is something the regime wants to do.

In academic writing about China, the shift that needs to happen is called "rebalancing," that is, rebalancing from less investment to more consumption. How is that shift going to take place? One likely approach is for China's government to increase its spending on consumption-type items, like education, health care, and social security or pensions for the elderly. There is a great irony here. The

Socialist people's economy, like China (where everything is for the people, right?), it has a government that spends [very] little on education and health care, and it has little income security for the elderly and the poor.

Think about education, for example. In 2005, China's public spending on education was about 3.1% of GDP. That compares with more like 5.9% of GDP for high-income countries and 4.6% of GDP for upper-middle–income countries around the world. As a share of its economy, China is spending maybe one-third less on education than the kinds of countries to which China could easily be compared.

There are similar issues that arise for health care spending. In 2005, China's public spending on health was 1.8% of GDP. In high-income countries, we spent 6.7% of GDP on health care. In upper-middle–income countries around the world, the average was 3.8%. The same is true for other kinds of social insurance, like welfare for the poor or pensions for the elderly.

I mentioned in the previous lecture that one reason China has such low social benefits was that it was low income in the past. Those low benefits actually made economic reform easier in China. People didn't have to fear losing their government benefits because they weren't getting any in the first place. But as China becomes a higher-income country, there will be a push for it to rebalance its priorities toward its citizens.

How should they finance this extra spending? You don't want to use higher taxes, because then the higher government spending would be offset by lower private spending. It may sound a little strange to those of us in the low-saving United States, but China should probably use deficit spending in order to stimulate its spending.

China's government has typically run really small budget deficits, maybe 1% of GDP. Given the humongous savings rates in China's economy, you could easily bump this up to, say, 3% of GDP, which would still be really modest for an economy which is saving almost half of its economic output.

It's important to note that this kind of government spending increase would actually increase consumption in two ways. One is a direct effect: There is just more spending. But the other, indirect effect is also important. If China provided more in terms of education, health care, pensions, protection of the poor and unemployed, then people would feel less need to save so much against the fear that these problems would happen within their own families.

Another change in the process of rebalancing is that China should allow the value of its currency to strengthen. I explained above that one reason for China's central bank to build up these huge foreign exchange reserves was to keep its currency weak, and that is to help China's export industries. But that process can work in reverse, too.

As China's exchange reserves have climbed up passed $1 trillion and have continued to climb in recent years—that process may go on a few years more, but it's not sustainable, over the long run, to keep building up those sorts of magnitudes. If China's central bank at some point just stops accumulating so many foreign exchange reserves, that means they are less willing to supply Chinese yuan and to trade them for U.S. dollars. With less supply of China's currency, market pressures would gradually push down the value. That would tend to damp down China's exports and encourage consumption and imports. And that would, again, be part of the process of rebalancing.

Another step is the reform of state-owned banks and firms. China has had a pattern in the 1980s and 1990s that its huge level of savings went into four major state-owned banks. There really wasn't anywhere else to put your savings other those big four state-owned banks. In turn, the state-owned banks tended to make loans based on political considerations, which often meant funneling the money to state-owned firms so that those firms wouldn't go bankrupt. Now, of course, as a result, many of these loans are never going to be repaid.

In the 1990s, it was a common fear that because these loans wouldn't be repaid, the state-owned banks would somehow just go broke and have to be totally reorganized. China has made progress in its gradualist reform style in reducing this problem over time. Back in the Communist period, China just had one bank, and then at the start of the reforms, they broke this up into four banks. And while the four big banks still have more than half of all banking deposits, now other banks are being allowed in. China has actually started having regulatory and accounting standards for banks, saying they have to have enough money for the loans that they are making.

They've also recognized that some of these loans are not going to be repaid and [have] raised money by issuing bonds to make up some of the money that has been lost. In banking, they have opened up

China's market to some competition and actually even to part ownership from foreign banks. This means savers throughout China's economy have new options, and as these foreign banks come in, they bring in sort of the financial practices and the regulations from other countries. It gives some sort of a standard for making judgments about what loans make sense.

For state-owned enterprises, the number of them is way down. There were several hundred thousand state-owned enterprises in China in the late 1990s. About 40% of them were in industry, but by 2004, they were down to only 32,000 state-owned enterprises, and less than 10% of them were industrial. From 1998 to 2004, total employment in these state-owned industries fell from 37 million down to 20 million. The difficulty is that a lot of this gain was achieved by getting rid of the very smallest state-owned enterprises; a lot of the big ones are still out there, and they include big industrial firms that account for something like maybe half of all the assets of China's enterprises and maybe for half of all the losses that China's enterprises experience.

There's no question, however, looking at the whole picture, that considerable progress has been made, and the problem of state-owned banks handing over savings to loss-making state-owned companies isn't nearly as big as it was back in the 1990s. The problem hasn't been cured, but progress has been made. There is still a lot of worry that China's banks are under political pressure to loan in certain ways. There is still a lot of worry that they don't yet understand the risks that are being taken, but the numbers of state-owned firms have been reduced. Many of them have even sold stock on the stock markets. There is still a worry that perhaps there could be a collapse of certain banks, and we need further progress on cutting loose those banks, but overall, there does seem to be genuine progress made in aiming money in China toward where it can actually get returns, not just toward where political considerations would push it.

I should emphasize that none of the kinds of changes I'm discussing here, none of this rebalancing, either requires or assumes that China's economic growth will slow down. Indeed, more effective use of financial capital would tend to increase economic growth, not decrease it. Driving growth with domestic demand from China's consumption, instead of from export sales, would be less vulnerable to foreign economic pressure or whether people in other countries want to buy Chinese goods. None of this is about slowing down China's economy. I am just arguing that the current path of China's growth is very high saving, very high investment. Pushing exports through heavy industry is not a sustainable approach, and rebalancing, one way or another, is going to start occurring.

Let me talk, though, about one possibility that could be an actual threat to China's economic growth, and that's the risk of a labor shortage. A lot of China's economic growth has been based on cheap and plentiful labor, combined with the high levels of investment we were talking about. Is China's era of cheap labor eventually on the way out?

The general pattern of labor movement in China since the economic reforms has been that labor has moved from the western and northern areas of the country, more rural and less developed, and toward the coastal and southern parts of the country, where the big cities are. But some areas in those cities are now reporting unfilled jobs and rising wages. In 2007, for example, Guangdong province said it had 2.5 million unfilled jobs, and wages were rising in that province at 10 to 15% a year. Is this just a local, one-time thing, maybe just in a few industries? After all, employers are always complaining that they would like labor to be cheaper, and maybe when an economy is growing 10% a year, wage increases up 10% in a year are not all that crazy. Or is it some signal that China's era of cheap labor may be running out?

The migration from rural to urban areas does have a little while longer to go, but over time, it sounds like the size of China's workforce will be reduced. Let's think about farm migration first. In 2005, 45% of total Chinese employment was still in agriculture, maybe 300 million people in round numbers, like the entire population of the United States. You can roughly estimate how many of these people are needed for farming in the future, given the levels and trends in agricultural productivity. When you do that, you tend to get estimates out of these studies that there is still room for another 150 million or so people to migrate to the cities. That estimate may be a little low if agricultural productivity rises quickly over time, or it may be a little high, because a lot of the people in rural areas are older people who probably aren't going to move to the cities. But broadly speaking, China's great migration from the farms isn't over yet. The end is maybe not all that far over the horizon, though.

The next big change is that there is going to be, over time, more education in China. In the past, education in upper-secondary and college-level [institutions] has been low in China. If you look at the 2000 census data for China, among 15- to 24-year-olds, only 20% of that age group had completed secondary school or was enrolled in secondary school. They're way behind Malaysia, and Thailand, and Indonesia, other countries in East Asia.

But as education rises, there will be a smaller number of those low-skilled workers which have been driving growth in China. The nature of jobs in China will shift, and the pay of those workers is going to start to rise. China's birthrates also have dropped a lot in the 1970s. Part of that is the one-child policy the government adopted in the late 1970s. There are various issues with the one-child policy, issues about global population, issues about the effects on gender balance. I'll take those up in later lectures. Here, I want to talk about the workforce, and China's lower birthrates means that the working-age population in China is going to start to shrink by around 2010.

Of course, if you have a larger share of working-age adults actually working or they are retiring later in life, then the number of workers could continue to rise in China for a time. But overall, the low birthrates mean there won't be any huge expansion of China's workforce over the next few decades—not a lot more migration coming in from the farms, not a high birthrate, and education reducing the supply of low-skilled labor. In the long run, China's low-skilled labor economic model probably can't continue. But that's not a bad thing. Perpetually low wages are not a path to economic success. China hasn't quite reached the end of this low-wage era yet, but as education levels rise and the size of the labor force levels off, China's wages will probably start to rise over time. Economic growth is, broadly speaking, all about making people better off. And from that point of view, of course, perpetually low wages are not a path to economic success. Sure, they help businesses produce cheaply and export, but the point of economic growth is to help people get more income. So, over time, we expect that change to continue.

How long until China is the biggest economy in the world? In 2007, according to World Bank estimates, the U.S. economy is still the largest in the world by far. It's about 2.3 times as large as China's economy, which is number two. You can do simple projections here. If the U.S. economy grows, say, 3% a year into the future, and China's economy grows 9% a year, then China will have the world's largest economy in roughly 15 years.

That actually isn't my exact prediction as to what is going to happen. The reason is that China has already had 9% economic growth rate since about 1980. The idea that you can just sustain that, not just for three decades but for a fourth decade and a fifth decade, is not at all a sure thing. It is especially unlikely if China's economy is not rebalanced along the lines we discussed earlier. China is going to need to alter the roots of its growth in various ways. The economic changes that raise China up from very low income to sort of middle income are not the same set of changes that will help China keep growing. Just as Japan and East Asia had growth miracles for a time, which were then followed by a time of slower or stagnant growth, I expect China will eventually go through such a period, too. But even so, impossible as it would have seemed in, say, 1975, it does look likely that China will displace the United States some time in the next two to three decades. Indeed, China could end up spending the majority of the 21st century as the world's single largest economy.

Lecture Fifteen
India and the License Raj

Scope:

The economy of India after independence was heavily influenced by a belief in Socialism, filtered to some extent through Gandhi's beliefs about self-sufficient village communities. The result was an economy smothered to an almost unbelievable degree by government licensing requirements. The heavy government control of firms, combined with heavy labor market regulation, became known as the "license raj." This system led to a persistently slow rate of economic growth over time that was sardonically called the "Hindu rate of growth." But by the 1970s and 1980s, watching the rapid economic growth in East Asia and China and perceiving the country's ongoing and enormous problem with poverty, India began to be willing to experiment with more market-oriented policies.

Outline

I. Our story begins with India's independence from Britain in 1947 and Mahatma Gandhi.

   A. Gandhi's economic beliefs were an extension of his moral beliefs about nonviolence, broadly understood. He emphasized self-sufficient village communities in which people would contribute to the common good out of a sense of duty, working primarily with their hands. He tended to view the realities of using machinery or engaging in large-scale production as acts of violence.

   B. India's first prime minister, Jawaharlal Nehru, was a great admirer of the Soviet economy and Socialism. He believed that state ownership was fundamentally fairer than private ownership and that centralized economic planning would work far better than private markets. He thus set up a large public sector and many restraints on private business.

   C. Chakravarthi Rajagopalachari, another prominent Indian leader at the time of independence, coined the term the "license raj" in the early 1960s. "Raj" (meaning "reign") was the name given to British colonial rule over India from 1858 to 1947. The license raj conveyed the idea that India had thrown off British rule but was now under the rule of copious intrusive rules and regulations.

II. Following independence, India adopted a "mixed economy" with strict regulations.

    A. After 150 years of feeling exploited by trade with Britain, India reacted with an inward-looking philosophy of self-sufficiency that discouraged foreign trade. Policies included imposing high tariffs on imports and maintaining a strong currency to discourage exports. India largely withdrew from foreign markets.

    B. The result was sometimes called a "mixed economy" or a "Socialist economy." Whatever the name, it was heavily planned, with a combination of government monopolies and strict licensing for all key decisions of private firms. The overall justification for this system was that as a poor country, India needed to focus its resources on what was important.

        1. In the 1950s, India decided that 17 key industries would be reserved for the public sector. In the 1960s, another batch of industries was nationalized. By the 1980s, state-run industries produced about one-quarter of India's GDP and consumed much more of its investment capital.

        2. Starting in the 1950s, the government created a number of licensing rules for private firms, including requirements that a government license be obtained for setting up or expanding a unit of production or changing what was produced. These licenses were typically reviewed for months or years before decisions were made.

    C. India's distrust of market forces was evident in the passage of 50 major laws concerning labor markets. These laws were so stringent, requiring extensive benefits and preventing firing for almost any reason, that they deeply inhibited the growth of industry in India.

    D. Keep in mind that India is a diverse country, with a huge population and a number of linguistic and religious divisions. To some extent, the many interventions in the economy were aimed at maintaining democracy across India, avoiding feelings of grievance, and knitting the country together.

III. India's economy grew moderately from the 1950s up into the 1980s, averaging about 3.5% per year. But changing domestic and international conditions, combined with the persistence of widespread poverty and an impending fiscal crisis, all led to pressures for change.

    A. Well into the 1970s and even the early 1980s, the West viewed India as a poor but basically admirable economy, not slavishly devoted to the market, forging its own way. With the "green revolution" and various technological accomplishments, the sense was that India's growth rate should be counted as a genuine success.

    B. When Indira Gandhi was reelected in 1980, she almost completely changed her economic orientation. In the 1970s, she had been an avowed Socialist. In the early 1980s, she aligned herself with the private sector and allowed many licenses to be issued for expanding and altering production. India's economy grew more quickly as a result, for a time.

    C. With the collapse of the Soviet Union and the rise of Capitalist East Asian economies, the Socialist model of India began to look dated.

        1. By the 1980s, the Soviet economic model was clearly not working well and had become less attractive.

        2. Compared with the vivid economic success stories of Japan, China, and East Asia, India's 3.5% growth rates began to look tepid.

    D. The fundamental justification for India's economic policies had long been that they were necessary to help the poor. But by 1990, although some progress had been made, poverty remained a significant problem in India.

    E. India's government ran large budget deficits through the 1980s, typically about 9% of GDP each year. Inflation rose, and it became clear that India was in danger of defaulting on its debts. In 1991, when Narasimha Rao became prime minister, he took the government financial crisis as justification for starting to dismantle the license raj.

Suggested Readings:

Crook, "India's Economy."

Das, *India Unbound: A Personal Account of a Social and Economic Revolution from Independence to the Global Information Age.*

Questions to Consider:

1. In what ways did India's legacy of British colonialism lead to economic policies that hindered growth?

2. What is the "license raj," and why did it restrain economic growth?

3. What developments in the world economy made India's economic model begin to look less politically acceptable in the 1970s and 1980s?

Lecture Fifteen—Transcript
India and the License Raj

It seems to me that, as a country, the United States is somewhat blind to India. American foreign policy often focuses on Iraq, or Israel, or Mexico, and there are real issues and problems, but those are relatively small countries compared to India. Among the bigger countries, the United States probably tends to focus more on China. In fact, one of the reasons that India exploded a nuclear bomb in 1998 was the sense in India that it was a way to be taken seriously, to get attention, to be treated as equally important with China and Russia, who have their own nuclear bombs.

Even before the bomb exploded, I had been thinking to myself that India has more than a billion people. One-sixth of the global population lives in India. It's a huge country in land mass, about one-third the size the United States. It's also an interesting combination of a low-income country with many ethnic and religious divisions, but nonetheless, it has a proud and even a fierce attachment to democracy. Moreover, India, since at least the 1980s and certainly since the early 1990s, has been carrying out far-reaching changes in national economic policy, a genuine and deep reorientation of economic policy toward market forces. And this change has had sweeping effects on economic growth and on the poor in India. In fact, it's on the verge of making India a real player in the global economy. To the extent that we've been ignoring India in the past, we really can't do that anymore.

The economic philosophy of India's independence can be traced back to India's declaration of independence from Britain in 1947, more than 60 years ago. And of course, the leader at the time was Mahatma Gandhi. What did Gandhian economics look like? His economic beliefs weren't always all that well spelled out, but roughly, they were an extension of Gandhi's moral beliefs about nonviolence, broadly understood. I'm not just talking about nonviolence in the specific sense of not whacking people up side the head but about a certain harmony of human interaction and community. Gandhi emphasized, when he spoke about economics, a tradition of small-scale production at the craft level, at the village level. Let me give you an example of one of his comments. Gandhi said once:

Now I have no historical proof, but I believe there was a time in India when village economies were organized on the basis of non-violent occupations, not on the basis of rights of man, but on the duties of man. ... [Those who engaged themselves in such occupations did earn their living, but their labor contributed to the good of the community. And Gandhi continues.] Body labor was at the core of these occupations and industries, and there was no large-scale machinery. For when a man is content to own only so much land as he can till with his own labor, he cannot exploit others. Handicrafts exclude exploitation and slavery.

In this comment, you can hear various echoes of Gandhi's overall philosophy. There's this concept of a nonviolent occupation, and that means working out some sort of sense of your duties about contributing toward the community, not some individualistic sense of rights and what you should get or what you are owed. There is a focus on what he called "body labor," not large-scale machinery, no farms larger than what one person can work with their own physical body labor. He refers to handicrafts and says they avoid exploitation and slavery. The handicrafts are okay—"handicrafts" refers to small-scale things made by individuals—but he seems to say that any large-scale production relationship—where people don't own all of the means of production but are instead employed by someone else—is a form of exploitation or, perhaps, even, at least metaphorically, a form of slavery. His concern over exploitation is understandable given India's colonial history but also leads to some peculiar places.

If you start saying that all jobs and all employment in large organizations are exploitation, it's not sure where that takes your economy. I can't resist adding here a comment that was attributed to a prominent Socialist economist named Michael Kalecki, who was visiting India many years ago, and after seeing the tremendous poverty that India had at that time, Kalecki said, "The trouble with India is there are too many exploited and too few exploiters."

Right from the start, India's politicians took a somewhat more pragmatic view of economics than Gandhi's approach. But nevertheless, Gandhi's feelings capture a real sense in India, a sense that is perhaps now fading in the 21st century, about how living with personal self-reliance, even if it looks like poverty to the rest of the world, has great dignity and value. And there's a lot of concern about going outside of that framework. This set of values, I think, has had a real effect on India's economic policies.

However, the first prime minister of India after independence was Jawaharlal Nehru. Nehru had visited the Soviet Union in the 1920s, and he was a big fan of Socialism and Communism. When discussing the Soviet economy in earlier lectures, I talked about some of the enormous appeal of that model during the middle decades of the 20th century, after the experience of World War I, and the Depression, and World War II. And these positive attitudes toward Socialism are still alive and kicking in various circles, at least, certainly in the academic circles where I hang out. The general mindset is something like, sure, maybe the Soviet Union had practical problems, maybe it wasn't perfect in a lot of ways, but fundamentally, Nehru thought government ownership was more fair and more socially just than private ownership. In his mind, in fact, that was pretty much an indisputable point, and once you had made that point, you had settled the classic argument between Capitalism and Socialism in favor of Socialism. Nehru once told an industrialist who was talking with him: "Never speak to me of profit. It is a dirty word." Nehru also thought it was obvious that state planning would work much better than some sort of competitive, chaotic private markets that lacked any central organizing.

The kind of economy he encouraged in post-independence India had a very large government sector. It included large government monopoly producers. There were lots of government controls and rules limiting anyone else who wanted to enter and start their own kind of company. But even at this point, from early on, India's politics also included yet another strand of thought. It was a strand of thought that didn't have quite such a benign view of the state.

There is a guy with the great name of Chakravarthi Rajagopalachari, another prominent Indian leader at the time of independence. In the early 1960s, he coined the term the "license raj." Now, "raj" comes from the Hindi word for "reign," as in the British reigning over India. The raj was British colonial rule from 1858 up to 1947. His term, the "license raj," conveys the idea that maybe India has thrown off British rule, but now it is under the rule of copious intrusive licenses, and rules, and regulations.

Chakravarthi Rajagopalachari was much more oriented toward market economics. In fact, he started a political party in the 1960s to oppose this web of government rules and regulations. To give you a sense of his point of view, let me quote him directly. He said once:

> I want the corruptions of the permit/licence raj to go. … I want the officials appointed to administer laws and policies to be free from pressures of the bosses of the ruling party, and gradually restored back to the standards of fearless honesty which they once maintained. … I want real equal opportunities for all and no private monopolies created by the permit/licence raj.

Let's think about that for a moment, because his complaint has several sort of interlocking parts. One is that the intrusive system of licenses and permits was blocking opportunity and creating monopolies. By creating monopolies and the chance for high monopoly profits, it was feeding corruption, because people would pay bribes or other things in order to get that monopoly power. But it took some decades before he was finally on the winning side of that particular argument.

Let's talk about India's economy and practice during the first four decades or so after independence. After 150 years of feeling exploited by trade with Britain, India reacted with a very inward-looking philosophy, a philosophy of self-sufficiency that discouraged foreign trade. India essentially became a closed economy. It is sometimes called a policy of "import substitution." That is, if we're importing it, we don't view that as useful trade with the rest of the world. Instead of importing it, we should try to make it domestically.

This kind of policy involved very high tariffs, and anyone who wants to import anything needs a special license to make sure that it is being imported for the right reasons. And it becomes very hard to trade the currency in foreign exchange markets and, thus, very hard for foreign firms to invest in India.

As a result of this general policy, if you looked at, say, cars on the road in India in about 1990, before its reform started, you saw basically one kind of car. It was called a Hindustan Ambassador, based on an old 1950s model, the Morris Oxford, that was made in England. They were pretty much all cream colored; they were all made in India; and nobody else anywhere in the world wanted to buy one.

There is sort of a side note here that I find really interesting. Imagine that there is one country which is (and we will use the word here) exploiting another country through trade. What's your guess? Would the exploiting country have a trade surplus or a trade deficit? I mean, in modern times, it's common to say Japan or China is exploiting the U.S. economy because they have trade surpluses and the United States has a trade deficit. Just for the record, India, under the British raj, ran trade surpluses with Britain for most of that time, usually about 1.5% of GDP every year. If you think a trade surplus proves exploitation, then India was exploiting the United Kingdom during the license raj, which seems kind of unlikely. In fact, it should make you strongly reconsider whether a trade surplus is a measure of unfairness or exploitation at all. Economists certainly don't see it that way.

In less emotive terms (not using that word "exploitation"), a trade surplus meant India was sending Britain more goods, and it was sending capital abroad to invest in Britain. If there was exploitation happening here (if that's a useful word), that was what was happening. But whatever the historical patterns, trade with that history—with Britain in colonialism—was regarded in India as a ploy to stifle India's manufacturing and keep it dependent on commodities instead.

Given that point of view, it shouldn't be a big shock that India had about maybe 2.5% of global trade in 1948, right after independence. But by the 1980s, India had about 0.5% of global trade. This shutdown of international trade was accompanied by heavy government control over production. The justification for this was that because India was a low-income country, it was argued, they needed to focus their resources on what was truly important. The philosophy was sometimes called a "mixed economy" or a "Socialist economy," but whatever the name, it was heavily planned, with a combination of government monopolies and strict licensing for all key decisions of private firms. For example, in the 1950s, India decided that 17 key industries would be reserved for the public sector. They included iron and steel, mining, machine-tool manufacturing, and heavy electrical plants.

In the 1960s, another batch of industries was taken over and nationalized by India's government. There were additional public monopolies then in cement, textiles, plastics, electronics, drugs, steel, copper, aluminum, motor scooters, refrigerators, fertilizer, batteries, bread, soda, paper, telecommunications, rail, air, banking, insurance—you're getting the idea. Practically everything was nationalized. By the 1980s, these nationalized firms had half or more of all of India's investment capital each year. They had half or more of the investment capital, and they are producing about one-quarter of the country's gross domestic product.

Starting in the 1950s, to keep these monopolies in place and avoid competition, India's government created a number of licensing rules for private firms. It is a little hard to convey just how intrusive these licenses were in business planning, but for example, companies needed approval of the Indian government to invest or make a new product. They had to do this because [the government] wanted to avoid any company from getting too large a share of the economy.

These licenses controlled prices; they controlled quantities produced; they controlled wages paid; they controlled the size of the labor force; they controlled sources of supply, as well as not allowing new varieties of existing products to be produced. Anything you did there, you needed a license. The administration of these licenses started off with low-level engineers reviewing thousands and thousands of applications every year. It took months to do this. Then, they would send it up a stage to the ministry or the cabinet level, where the same information was reviewed again for months and months; and then, up to an interministerial council, where it was reviewed for more months; and then, up to a cabinet member for final approval. For example, if you wanted to import foreign equipment at that point, you had to start with a new set of requests for licenses, and you had to go through that whole process. If you had a foreign partner, you had to start a set of requests for licenses for foreign partners. If you wanted a loan from the state bank, you started a new set of requests for that loan.

There were no particularly clear rules for these licenses. Everything was pretty ad hoc. The big worries were issues like: In the view of the bureaucrats, does my attempt to get a license fit with the national plan for investment? Can I argue that it fits? That national plan focused on stuff that was thought to be important, like steel, not on stuff that was thought to be unimportant, like consumer goods. Also, in the view of the bureaucrats, would my request for a license preserve regional balance and where industries were located across the country? In the view of the bureaucrats, would my request compete too much with existing small business or, perhaps, end up forming too large a business? These were all things going into the license process. To someone out of an economics background like me, this set of licenses sounds so extreme that it's almost not serious. It's like something out of the imagination of Franz Kafka. It's like some sort of bad dream, but it was very, very serious.

One result of the license process was that for consumers, since their interests were not put very highly in these licenses, it took literally years on a waiting list in the 1980s to get a phone or a motor scooter, because these were consumer goods that just weren't a big part of the plan. And then, surprisingly, huge lobbying bureaucracies grew up around the firms and around government cities, with enormous possibilities for working the system and a fair amount of graft and corruption in how licenses would be granted and how people would get them.

I will give you an example of another favorite trick: Imagine you are an existing firm, and what you want to do is put lots of applications in the pipeline saying you want to expand output. You put in lots and lots of applications over time. As that happens, the government bureaucrats would turn down any applications from other new competitors. And the reason, of course, is [that] they would think since the existing firms were going to expand (after all, they'd applied for all these licenses), there was no need for any other competition. You never actually needed to expand your business. All you needed to do was apply for a lot of licenses and make it look as if you might expand in the future, and that would be sufficient.

These rules blocking what firms could produce and how they could produce it are really just the beginning, because that is one set of rules, and there is another whole set of rules which affects labor. In the late 1980s and into the 1990s, only 3% of India's economy is officially in private firms that have more than 10 employees, and the reason is [that] the regulations about labor are just crazy. Even in the late 1990s, there were 45 or 50 major separate labor laws. There were laws about providing pensions, and health insurance, and subsidized lunchrooms, and health clinics. You had to notify the government, if you were a large-size company, of any change in job content, what the job involved, or employee status.

In some places, employees had to agree before any such change occurred. If you had more than 25 workers, you had to fill all vacancies at your company from a state list. If you had more than 100 workers, you needed government permission before you could fire anyone. In the public sector, there wasn't just lifetime employment, but there was employment literally beyond the grave, in the sense that after your death, your job could be inherited by a son or a relative.

When you've got all these restrictive laws, you get laws and more laws about the exceptions, and the counter-exceptions, and the rules. You begin to get categories in India's laws like "working nonemployees," who are not employees for certain purposes, even though they're working for you. In fact, it was even true in the labor laws that declaring bankruptcy because of all of this was forbidden. You were forbidden to go broke. What happened, of course, is that lots and lots of businesses were trying to hide their employees or somehow not have them go on the books and also, in some ways, to hide their output, as well.

It got to the point where in the public sector, workers began to believe that their salary was just sort of an entitlement to a paycheck, and if they showed up and worked at all, they deserved overtime. It got to a point where, even when a government agency shut down for a time and was not open, the workers in that government agency argued they shouldn't just keep getting their salary—because it wasn't their fault the agency shut down—but they should also keep getting overtime, as well, even though the agency hadn't been functional.

At this point, you should be getting a sense for what's meant by the license raj. It has been said sometimes that India's greatest misfortune was to have brilliant but prideful economists who believed they could plan everything, and they kept coming up with new plans and new justifications. South Korea and Taiwan, places like that, didn't have so many economists to explain why they needed to plan everything and have licenses for everything, so their economies just grew.

While all these licenses were happening, I have sort of hinted that one of the goals was to maintain democracy across India. And while this goal isn't specifically economic, it really should be remembered that India is a very diverse country. It has a huge population and a number of linguistic and religious divisions. There is a real need to unify the country. At the time of independence, in the late '40s, Britain really controlled only about two-thirds of India. The rest was hundreds of independent princes with people speaking literally dozens of different languages.

Winston Churchill once said about the time that India was just a geographical expression, like the equator or the Western Hemisphere; it wasn't actually a nation. Even today, there's something like 1,600 languages spoken across India, and 400 of them are spoken by more than 200,000 people. There are 24 languages spoken by more than a million people. Most of the languages are mutually unintelligible. English is sort of the consistent language of business, but there's enormous diversity across the population. It helps explain why India has 25 separate states and lots of issues of local control. To some extent, all these interventions in the economy were aimed at avoiding feelings of grievance and knitting the country together. In economic policy, all the licenses gave government a lot of freedom to support local projects and to direct local spending and not always much sense of what an overall policy might be that would make sense for a healthy economy across the entire country.

India's economy grew moderately from the 1950s up until the 1980s. It averaged about 3.5% per year. But a set of changing economic conditions, along with widespread poverty, all led to pressures for change at about that time. Well into the 1970s and even the early 1980s, I would say India was often viewed very optimistically and hopefully by a lot of people in the United States. I mean, true, sometimes people were a little irritated with India, because politically, it led what was called the "nonaligned movement." That is, it officially claimed not to be aligned with either the United States or the Soviet Union, although the United States always suspected that a country like India, which claimed to be Socialist and emulated the Soviet Union, might not actually be all that neutral. But there was this hope: The hope was that India would show a democratic model of development and how this worked.

There was a lot of doubt sometimes. There was a belief that only Communist countries, like China, could be able to force savings and force mobilization of capital and that low-income democracies might not be able to move toward higher economic development. There was also sort of this happy picture of the "green revolution"—that is, new technology for crops that allowed growing a lot more food. After all, India had technological centers; there were explorations by India to Antarctica and the ocean depths; Indian scientists won Nobel Prizes in science. They even had nuclear bombs in the 1990s. In raw numbers, with its very, very large population, India may have among the highest total of scientific and skilled workers of any nation in the world. Sure, there were some bad moments, like when Indira Gandhi declared martial law in 1975, but then she was out of office in 1977, which sort of showed the system worked, and then she was voted back into office in the 1980s, which sort of showed again that there were no hard feelings.

As I mentioned, the good news: The GDP is growing about 3.5% a year, and this looked okay if not exactly munificent. A lot of people said it's faster than the growth India had in the first half of the century, which was only about 1.3% a year. Indeed, India's 3.5% growth over that time was faster than Britain was growing over that time.

India also had high and rising savings rates, rising from maybe 10% of GDP in 1950 up to more like 20 or 25% of GDP by the mid-1980s, higher than the U.S. rate of saving. They stayed a democracy, and in general, there is a real image we have, in the United States certainly, that Indian folks include a lot of hard-working entrepreneurs. Nonetheless, this 3 to 3.5% a year growth rate was often referred to in a somewhat dismissive way. In the economics and political literature, it was sometimes called the "Hindu rate of growth," which of course, has a sort of a dismissive, patronizing, "how nice for them; aren't they doing the best they can given the troubles they have" kind of sound to it. But the domestic political context for thinking about this rate of growth and whether it was acceptable or not began to sort of shift in the 1980s.

I mentioned Indira Gandhi a moment ago—first elected in 1966, voted out in 1977 after declaring martial law, reelected in 1980, and eventually she was assassinated in 1984. For our purposes, the interesting fact about Gandhi is that she almost completely changed her political stripes from the 1970s into the 1980s. In the 1970s, Indira Gandhi was a big-time Socialist. For example, she actually added the word "Socialist" to the preface of India's constitution, and her public image was that she was a very secular, nonreligious political leader. But when she was reelected in 1980, Indira Gandhi ran as a friend of big business and as a Hindu leader appealing on religious grounds to voters.

I don't want to talk about the secular-to-religious part of her political makeover, but on the economic side, she made a total rhetorical shift toward supporting business, and she looked for ways to get business support in a lot of different ways. She began to reduce taxes. She made it easier to get licenses for access to imported capital inputs and easier to get licenses for firms to expand production. After she was assassinated in 1984, her son Rajiv Gandhi became prime minister, and he largely continued these kinds of policies. Releasing some of the constraints on India's economy helped economic growth speed up a little at about this time, although the looming prospect of licenses was still out there.

The international context for India is also changing in the 1980s. With the collapse of the Soviet Union and the rise of Capitalist East Asia, that Socialist model of India began to look kind of dated. I mean, after all, by the 1980s, it's clear that the Soviet economic model is just not working all that well and had become ever less attractive as a model for any economy. The negatives of central planning and state planning were becoming all too apparent. Pressure was building inside India's society for reform. The collapse of the Soviet Union, the breakup of the Soviet Union, meant the Socialist model was really in disrepute.

The growth of Japan, China, and East Asia also made India's growth rate look awfully meek. I mean, the good news for India had been growth with 3.5% a year. It began to look, based on these other countries, like the bad news for India was growth of only 3.5% a year. Instead of sort of seeing the glass as maybe three-quarters full, it began to look three-quarters empty instead. It was clear that India was really having terrible productivity performance given its quite high level of national savings and investment. In a way, the growth rate and the fact that it existed at all was testimony to the incredible entrepreneurial efforts of Indian managers and workers in the face of a smothering bureaucracy.

Moreover, the fundamental justification for India's economic policies had long been that they were necessary to help the poor. But by 1990, although some progress had been made, India's poor continued to be in just terrible condition. In 1990, something like 40% of India's population was malnourished and below the poverty line, which was about $1 a day. More than half of all the adults and two-thirds of all the women were illiterate.

The average level of schooling for an adult worker in about 1990 was 2.4 years. In terms of maternal mortality, a measure of how many women die in childbirth, about 427 out of 100,000 live births resulted in the death of the mother. That is like roughly 1 out of every 200. In China, it's a much lower level; it's about 115 out of every 100,000 live births result in the death of the mother. And in the United States, it would be less than 20. Infant mortality levels are also extremely high in India, very close to the levels in sub-Saharan Africa. Half of all the children in India were malnourished, and there was serious discrimination against women.

Essentially, India had tried to abolish poverty by nationalizing industries and banks, squeezing foreign investment, and having lots of price and trade controls. They had been doing this for decades. You can take all the nice rhetoric about good intentions, and by about 1990, you toss it in the garbage. The hard bottom line is that it hadn't worked very well, and people in India had noticed.

I mentioned before that part of the reason for India's growth in the 1980s was giving the government monopolies and private firms more freedom to expand production. Another part of the reason for India's economy growing faster in the 1980s was a huge and really unsustainable boost from government budget deficits. The average total budget deficits through the 1980s ran almost 9% of GDP on average per year. For comparison, if the U.S economy in the late 2000s ran deficits of this size, it would be something like $1.1 or $1.2 trillion in deficits a year.

India's government budget deficits had soared; inflation was rising. It seemed clear that India might not be able to repay these debts, which were measured in U.S. dollars and other foreign currencies. India was facing a possible financial crash, and this helped to force a change: It was time to do something different. All these factors come together. There was a sense that even former Socialists, like Indira Gandhi, believed it was time to loosen up. There were a growing number of people in India who were willing to vote that the license raj had become too restrictive. Russia's model of Socialism was increasingly unattractive. Compared to neighbors in East Asia, China, and Japan, it seemed clear that India's economy is badly lagging. Poverty in India had stayed disturbingly, grindingly high. The government was running on borrowed money and couldn't pay its bills. Rajiv Gandhi resigned after losing an election in 1989, and after two very short-term prime ministers, Narasimha Rao became prime minister in 1991. He took the government financial crisis as his justification for starting to dismantle the license raj.

Lecture Sixteen
India's Turn toward Market Economics

Scope:

India began a series of economic reforms in 1991, taking large steps toward reducing the license raj and allowing more competition. The economy performed somewhat better in the 1990s and quite well in the first decade of the 2000s. The challenge for India is to continue with its economic reforms, particularly by reducing labor laws and business regulation and avoiding huge budget deficits. India's economy needs substantial investment in the basics, such as education and infrastructure. If the current economic reforms and faster growth are to be sustainable, India must provide perceptible and widespread benefits across the country, not just create a few high-technology enclaves.

Outline

I. When Narasimha Rao became prime minister of India in 1991, he launched a profound change in economic policy that caused growth in India first to rise, then to take off.

   A. Rao was expected to be a safe, stopgap choice at a time when India's economy was under severe strain.

   B. Rao's reforms, however, involved reversing many elements of India's earlier economic philosophy and heading toward fewer restrictions on trade, less licensing, increased foreign investment, and greater domestic competition in many industries.

   C. The economic reforms of 1991 were followed by a modest rise in growth rates compared to the 1980s, but by the mid-2000s, growth was considerably faster.

      1. The economic reforms of 1991 were followed by economic growth that was higher than that in the 1950s to the 1970s but only a little higher than the 1980s. In addition, the East Asian financial crises of 1997–1998 slowed down economies all around the region. A decade after the reforms, it was clear that they hadn't brought on disaster, but some questioned whether they had done much good either.

2. India's economic growth surged faster, hitting 8 to 9% per year in the mid- to late 2000s. Poverty rates plummeted. Although no one argued for a return to the license raj, controversy continued over whether the benefits of growth were distributed equally.

II. India has made great strides in freeing up its economy and realizing benefits of faster growth, but a number of steps remain if growth is to be continuing and widespread.

A. India's labor laws, for example, remain restrictive. These laws protect a limited number of workers who have formal employment contracts with large companies, but they sharply limit job creation and create inefficiency in the rest of the labor force.

B. Although the license raj is mostly dead, India continues to have a large number of rules and regulations that can make it a difficult place to start a business.

C. India also continues to have relatively low rates of education, especially for the poor. The government spends relatively little on education, and many parents—even low-income parents—have responded by paying to have their children attend private schools. An educated workforce is an essential building block to sustaining rapid growth in the future.

D. India's infrastructure has failed to keep up with its growth. This is true in a number of areas, including electricity, transportation, and water. If the government cannot improve the infrastructure, it may need to coordinate private efforts to do so.

E. India has been running chronic budget deficits, incurring debt but not building infrastructure or helping the poor. On the spending side, it needs to curtail widespread subsidies and, instead, target spending to build long-term capital and assist the poor. On the tax side, India must take steps to institute a more broad-based set of taxes.

III. If India's growth is to be economically and politically sustainable, it will need to demonstrate that its effects are reaching most citizens, not just a few.

A. In the United States, we hear a lot about high-tech enclaves in India, which are certainly growing and flourishing. But India's population is still mostly rural, and it continues to include several hundred million people in deepest poverty. Nobel laureate economist Amartya Sen once remarked that India would not flourish if it was "half California, half sub-Saharan Africa."

B. Economic growth is often unbalanced—that is, it happens predominantly in certain industries or regions rather than everywhere at once. But a range of government policies concerning education, health, infrastructure, and internal markets can help to spread the benefits of economic growth to some degree. Without such policies, India's growth may not be either politically or economically sustainable.

Suggested Readings:

Das, *India Unbound: A Personal Account of a Social and Economic Revolution from Independence to the Global Information Age.*

Meredith, "The Elephant and the Dragon."

Varma, "Profit's No Longer a Dirty Word: The Transformation of India."

World Bank, "India: Inclusive Growth and Service Delivery: Building on India's Success—Development Policy Review."

Questions to Consider:

1. What is the substance of the economic reforms that India carried out in the early 1990s?

2. How persuasive is the argument that India's reforms have led to additional economic growth?

3. What are some of the main economic challenges India faces in the early decades of the 21st century?

Lecture Sixteen—Transcript
India's Turn toward Market Economics

In 1991, India's economy seemed to be in sad shape. It was staggering through a debt crisis because of the huge budget deficits incurred through the 1980s. It was still true in 1991 that 60 to 80% of all industry in India was subject to licensing and controls, and this was even after the reductions in licensing that had happened in the 1980s. India still had sweeping, difficult labor laws. It still had immense poverty. It still looked at nearby [regions], like China, and East Asia, and Japan, and felt as if it were falling further behind every year.

All of these factors set the stage for India's situation in 1991 and its big economic changes. Rajiv Gandhi, Indira's son and the prime minister for most of the second half of the 1980s, was assassinated in 1991. The wave of sympathy for the victim and revulsion against the crime helped propel his party, the Congress Party, to victory in the elections. At that point, the Congress Party chose a nonthreatening, even boring candidate to be prime minister. His name was Narasimha Rao. Rao was about 70 years old; he was just getting ready to retire. He had been a top minister in the government for a long time in many different areas, although not actually in economics. He was an intellectual guy who, by reputation, spoke nine languages, but he was really viewed as a short-term stopgap. The government at that time was a coalition of different parties. It wasn't expected to last for very long, so he was the figurehead to be in the front of the coalition.

But India at this moment was also in the middle of a debt crisis, and if it wanted to avoid defaulting on its debt, it needed to make some show that it was serious about making economic reforms. Rao appointed free-market types to key positions, and he gave them the green light to do some substantial economic reforms. Sometimes, he even pushed them beyond their original proposals to go further still.

These reforms involved reversing many elements of India's earlier economic philosophy. Let me give you a few examples: There was an opening up of international trade. In 1991, the average tariff (tax) on imports was 90%. It ranged up as high as 400% for some products. By 1998, seven years later, the average tariff on imported products was only 27%, and the top level was only 50%. Even in Latin America and East Asia, which haven't always been very friendly to imports, their tariffs were only half as high as those in India, so India felt like it had to keep cutting. And by the mid-2000s, they had cut their tariffs down by another half or so, into the range of about 15%. These tariffs aren't particularly low by the standards of developed economies, where average tariffs are something like less than 5%, but it's just an enormous change in opening up India's economy.

These reforms also dramatically cut back on the need for import licenses. That made it much easier to buy and sell India's currency, the rupee, which encouraged trade and investment across India's borders. With all of the business licenses, they essentially got rid of most of them. There was no more licensing for industry. India's industries could invest, or diversify, or do new products without a license. There were some limited rules about pollution management and urban zoning, but that's really about all. This is a truly enormous change that essentially wiped out 40 years of the license raj almost overnight.

The plan was to limit the public-sector monopolies to just a few areas, like defense and atomic energy, maybe coal, petroleum, railways, and some mining. And then, in other areas, even if there were public firms, you could compete with those firms. For example, there were some areas that used to be public monopolies but then had competition allowed. These would include airlines, telecommunications, electricity, iron and steel, heavy electrical equipment, and some others. With foreign investment, it used to be that every foreign investment in India needed to be justified on the grounds that it was the only way for India to get some particular new kind of technology. For the bureaucrats, that pretty much meant they just never allowed it. But after 1991, foreign firms were allowed to invest in India and even to own a controlling interest in firms. It's a little hard to convey how briskly this all happened.

How in the world did a little-known, stopgap prime minister do all this? Remember, this is a political system where the prime minister is chosen by a leading political party, if necessary in a coalition with others. When the prime minister proposes something, either that prime minister has the votes to get it through, or else the ruling political coalition fractures and has to boot out the prime minister and form a new government. The presumption in this kind of a system is that a lot of what the prime minister wants is going to be enacted. [The year] 1991 is a time of crisis in India. No one else really has a better idea. The opposition was overrun, and 40 years of India's economic policies were erased much more quickly than anyone had realistically expected.

What were the effects of these economic reforms? India's economy had a year of recession in the 1990s as it got through the financial crisis, and then it was adjusting to the economic reforms. But then growth jumped almost immediately to 6 or 7% per year. In the first decade or so after 1991, growth really went up, but exactly how you interpreted this fact was sort of like one of those inkblot tests that reveals your own personal frame of mind.

The optimists and supporters of reform tended to say something like this: "Wow, compared to that 'Hindu rate of growth' nonsense about how India had 3.5% growth, look how quickly we've nearly doubled the rate of growth. See how right we were to do all these reforms?" The pessimists and the opponents of reform tended to say something like this: "Well, growth had already started picking up in the 1980s. Those reforms in 1991 were kind of unnecessary overkill. Besides, it kind of looks like growth is slowing down in the second half of the 1990s, so those reforms aren't such great stuff after all." And then the optimists would say something like: "Well, the growth of the 1980s was based on those unsustainably large budget deficits, so that's not a fair comparison, and the reason growth slowed down a little in the second half of the 1990s was spillover from the East Asian financial crisis of 1997 and 1998."

This dispute went back and forth and back and forth. It is clear the reforms hadn't led to disaster, but there were still a fair number of skeptics who said they might not be doing a whole lot of good either. My own reaction to this dispute as it went on was that when you have a system going along for four decades like the license raj, and then you change it abruptly, unless the new system is an outright disaster, it probably deserves a couple of decades to prove itself one way or the other. But by the mid- to late 2000s, the reforms sort of faced a test of time, and they were passing that test of time. Economic growth in India in the 2000s accelerated to 8 or 9% per year, and it began to seem clear that the economic reforms really deserved much of the credit.

Exports from India were way up; they quadrupled from 1995 up to 2005. There were huge gains in reducing poverty. For example, back in 1980, about two-thirds of India's population lived on less than $1 a day, that standard measure of poverty used by the World Bank. But by the early 2000s, [the number] had fallen from two-thirds of India's population to only about one-third of India's population at less than $1 a day. Of course, many people in India are still deeply poor by the standards of any high-income country, but lifting several hundred million people out of the worst kind of subsistence poverty is a genuine gain.

There have also been declines in infant mortality. You see higher literacy, more people with clean water—all that good stuff that goes along with higher per capita incomes. Of course, if economic growth can keep going, there is room for a lot of additional progress, as well. But while no one is arguing quite for going back to the license raj, there is a lot of controversy in India over how equally the benefits of growth are being distributed. Was this new growth creating too much inequality; was it dividing the country? These controversies continue even today.

What's India's agenda for continued reform at this point? Although India has made great strides in freeing up the economy and recognizing a lot of benefits of faster growth, a number of steps remain if growth is going to be continuing and widespread. A first step, for example, is further reform of the restrictive labor laws. Although there doesn't seem to be a political consensus in India that yearns for the return of the business licensing laws, India's labor laws continue, and they remain very restrictive. We talked a lot about those in the previous lecture, how they protect the rights of workers, as they would say. But that statement about protecting the rights of workers is really a little bit disingenuous. What really happens with the labor laws is that they offer extremely high levels of protection to those in what's called the "formal" sector of India's economy. That basically means employers who have more than 10 workers or that have more than 100 workers. There are rules for those particular companies on conditions of work, wages, benefits, insurance, hiring, firing, social security, and there are still, I think, 28 different major labor laws across India in the first decade of the 21st century. These disputes all get settled by state governments and courts, and the outcomes are sometimes capricious.

But how many workers are in this protected group? It depends a little bit on just who you include, but reasonable estimates are that something like 7 to 15% of current workers are in the organized formal sector of the economy protected by all these rules. To put it another way, there might be two or three times as many unemployed people in India as there are specially protected workers. Many studies have shown that these strict labor market rules discourage hiring. It is extremely difficult to fire anyone in a firm with more than 100 workers, so a lot of India's firms would avoid hiring people in the first place. In fact, under the current labor laws, you can't fire workers because they steal from a company. You can't even fire workers who are convicted in court of assaulting other employees. Nothing overrides employment protection. A standard result is that India's firms stay small rather than expand, because at a larger size, a lot of these stricter labor laws will kick in.

One estimate in the 21st century is that only about 4% of workers in India are in companies that have more than 10 employees. There was a study done by the consulting firm McKinsey, and they found that in the textile industry, India's companies are only about 10 or 20% the size of textile firms in China. And India's textile firms have much lower efficiency because they can't take advantage of economies of scale. One reason India has focused so much on the service sector, rather than on manufacturing, is that the labor laws are much more restrictive in manufacturing.

Just to be clear here, I'm not saying countries shouldn't have labor laws or that these laws don't serve some functions. I am saying that most laws can be pushed too far to be useful. I mean, couldn't you just have maybe three to five major labor laws in India, instead of, say, 28 of them? India's labor market laws are a sweet deal for a small minority of workers. They sort of depend on the myth that someday, everyone will have a similar sweet deal, but for now, they're contributing to unemployment and slower growth in India.

Another step is to continue loosening business regulation. The license raj is mostly dead. Only a handful of industries remain reserved to the public sector or require the old-style licenses, but India does continue to have a large number of rules and regulations that can make it hard to start a business there. The World Bank does a ranking in what they call "ease of doing business," how easy is it to do business in a country. Out of 178 economies where the World Bank does this ranking, India ranks 132nd.

There are lots and lots of procedures to go through, and in particular, it's really hard to close a business. Some examples: In Mumbai, it takes about three months to start a business. Two months are just to get a personal account number and a tax deduction account number from the government. To enforce a claim that a contract isn't fulfilled in India, it takes about 40 steps to get a legal judgment. This typically takes more than a year, and the cost of doing this whole process averages something like 40% of the value of the contract you're trying to enforce.

It remains true that many products in India are still reserved for manufacture by the "small-scale sector," as they call it. In a modern sort of echo of Gandhi's argument that small-scale production would not exploit, India continues to have a large number of rules and regulations that make it hard to push past a certain size. The number of goods reserved for manufacture by small-scale enterprises was about 799 in 2002. It was down to 326 by 2007, and that's fine, but it's still hundreds of products where the scale is limited. India also needs to do more to encourage education. It continues to have relatively low rates of education, especially for the poor. The government spends relatively little on education, and many parents— even those with very low incomes—have responded by paying to have their children attend private schools. As we've learned over and over from other examples of development around the world, an educated workforce is really an essential building block to sustaining rapid growth in the future.

India's government sometimes argues that almost all children are enrolled in school, but this doesn't actually appear to be true when you look at the statistics. There have been gains in India to be sure, but there's a long way to go. Toward the end of the first decade of the 21st century, adult literacy in India is still under 70%. The current average level of schooling in India is about 10 years, which is on the low side compared to countries with rapid growth, like the East Asian tigers. But this 10-year average is, like so many things in India, an average of extremes. It includes those who dropped out of primary school and those who have master's degrees in engineering. The really big concern for India is at the bottom end. For example, among those with low incomes, only about 75% complete primary school, which in India are the first five years of schooling. There seems to be a real breakdown of the public sector here. India spends about 3.8% of its GDP on education. Even nations in sub-Saharan

Africa, which are very poor, often spend 6% or more of GDP on education.

Families in India are often enthusiastic about education, but the teachers are still in that great chain of labor laws. They often can collect payment without even showing up at schools. Meanwhile, huge numbers of children in India, even the very poor, are going off to private schools. It is common in urban areas to have 40 or 60% of the children attending private schools. In fact, that estimate is probably on the low side, because it focuses on recognized private schools, not on all the tutoring programs and all the other unrecognized programs. For the long run, an educated workforce is just tremendously important, and right now, India probably just doesn't have the skill level in its workforce to sustain 8 or 9% growth over the next decade or two. It needs to train the next generations of workers in real time, as we are moving ahead.

Another step for India is to invest in infrastructure because its infrastructure has really failed to keep up with its rapid growth. Looking back, in 1980, for example, India had more electrical power, more roads, more communications, more telecommunications facilities than China. Now, it's far behind in all areas. One estimate is that if India could raise its infrastructure spending from the current 3 or 4% of GDP to maybe 12.5% of GDP (which is unrealistically high) and keep it there maybe for the next decade or 5 or 10 years, up to 2015, it could have the level of infrastructure China had back in 2005. For example, in electricity, across India, it's very common to have power outages. They say the average business in India has a power outage every other day. For comparison, say, in Brazil, you might have a power outage once a week or, in China, once every two weeks. Many companies in India need to buy their own electrical generators, which is not an efficient way to provide power, so India's cost of electricity is 40% above China, maybe 75% above Malaysia. Electrical power across India is run by state electrical boards, which often are not allowed to cut anyone off for nonpayment, and there are all kinds of pirate hookups to the electrical lines.

Transportation is another important form of infrastructure. It always seems better politically to launch a new road or rail project than to complete one or to maintain one. India has lots of miles of paved roads, but they're not in good condition. A World Bank study said that maintenance on national highways is about one-quarter of the needed level. Maybe 20% of the roads in India are in good condition. If you do a similar measure for Thailand or Korea, something like 50 or 70% of the roads would be in good condition. Even the lousy roads in India are often better than the rail system, even though they have been trying to adjust that and rebuild it in various ways.

When it comes to water infrastructure, statistics from India's government suggest that only about 78% of the population has access to safe drinking water, and that's lower in rural areas. And, like a lot of government statistics, those estimates may be somewhat high. India's rivers, like the Ganges, are extremely polluted by sewage and by agricultural runoff. Twenty-two% of the rural population and 60% of the urban population have access to good sewage facilities; the rest don't. In rural areas, Mahatma Gandhi was talking about the health virtues of clean latrines back in the 1940s, and it's still an issue today.

Government infrastructure investment in India has historically been about 3 or 4% of GDP, and the current government goal is to raise that up to 9% of GDP. This would be just an enormous shift, and it's not clear that it's altogether possible. Just to give a sense of this, 4 or 5% of GDP is the size of the U.S. defense budget. Imagine you wanted to shift an amount of tax money and other spending roughly equal in proportion to the U.S. defense budget into some other area. There are huge problems involved in doing this. For example, India probably has lots of engineers, but they aren't civil engineers to work on these kinds of infrastructure projects.

However, India needs to spend much, much more on infrastructure, and if government can't do all of it, then it needs to help coordinate private efforts to do so, perhaps private electrical supply; private water supplies; private partnership for roads, seaports, airports, and so on. The model in mind here is the telecommunications industry. This used to be a heavily regulated monopoly, but when it was opened up to competition, mobile phones were able to spread very quickly. The question is whether competition could work in other areas, as well. The lack of infrastructure is probably slowing economic growth in India by 1 or 2 percentage points a year. You might notice a common theme in all of this. India's government is failing to provide the sorts of basic public goods that governments are really well suited to provide, like electricity, roads, education. It could also add health, although that isn't my main focus here.

India has been running chronic budget deficits over time, incurring more and more debt while managing not to help with infrastructure and the poor as much as it could. Remember that the string of huge budget deficits in the 1980s caused the debt crisis in 1991. And India doesn't seem to be quite able to kick this habit. In 2002, for example, India's budget deficit was 10% of GDP. By 2006, it had come down to 6% or so. But remember that India's economy is growing very, very fast. Tax revenues are also growing very fast, but apparently, spending is growing just as fast or even faster.

India's economy has been accumulating a lot of debt. Another near-default like 1991 seems unlikely, but high government borrowing can be a problem even if it doesn't actually default. For example, it locks more and more government spending into making high-interest payments on all that debt. And when India's government borrows, less investment capital is available for the private sector. Economists call this a "crowding-out effect." If you want to invest more in education and infrastructure, you need to find ways to do that.

On the tax side for India's government, the traditional problem has been that India really didn't have any political ability to tax agriculture or services, so it ended up with a tax code where a lot of things were not taxed, and then high rates on whatever was taxed. Most taxes were raised from industry, which is only about 25% of India's economy. And then there were lots of indirect taxes on international trade, or on trade between states of India, or on transfers of property. Just in the last few years, since 2006, India has been moving to a value-added tax for goods. It has been planning to combine this with a general goods and services tax, sort of like a national sales tax. If it can avoid having too many exemptions in this tax, it should be a vast improvement to India's tax code. But even if the tax code can raise the same amount, you probably need to go after the expenditure side in India's government, too.

Wages and pensions for employees of the government are something like 25% of all spending in India, and high because, of course, government spending is high in India, because the government provides health and education benefits. But still, there is just a lot of money going to wages for government employees. Public-sector employees have protected jobs, and they are paid just much, much more than equivalent workers in the private sector. It's also true that India's government continues to give large subsidies for things like food and fertilizer, propane and kerosene, and in general, those subsidies tend to benefit the middle class the most rather than the poor.

If India's growth is to be economically and politically sustainable, it's going to need to demonstrate that the effects of that growth are reaching most citizens, not just a few of them. In the United States, we hear a lot about high-tech enclaves in India, places like Bangalore, with lots and lots of software engineers. We hear about outsourcing and the way in which workers in the United States can e-mail projects to India at the end of a workday in the United States, [then] Indian workers will work on it while it's daytime in India and nighttime in the United States. The U.S. workers come back the next morning and have completed work waiting for them. You hear about lower-tech jobs, like call centers run out of India. And, of course, the software engineers, the call-center workers, are all paid far less per hour than U.S. workers. But in India, those lower wages can still translate into a really nice standard of living.

These service industries are certainly growing and flourishing in India. One of the really remarkable facts about India's growth is how it hasn't focused on low-wage manufacturing, as was common in Japan, and East Asia, and China, but how it has focused on services instead. Sure, this is partly true because of how the laws on licensing, and taxes, and labor put India's manufacturing at a disadvantage. But still, it's remarkable for a low-income country that over half of India's GDP is in service industries.

But this mental image a lot of Americans have, where India is sort of a suburb of Silicon Valley in California, is just dreadfully incomplete. Americans tend to see high-tech enclaves like Bangalore and to hear about the outsourcing, and they kind of conclude that India's whole economy is like that. India is an enormous place with more than a billion people. It has room for all kinds of very disparate parts. Overall, in India, it's worth remembering that even in the first decade of the 21st century, 70% of the people are still living on farms. There are still several hundred million people in deepest poverty, below those basic standards of living like $1 a day or $2 a day. Those people lack basics, like safe drinking water. India's extremes of economic inequality are simply enormous. The Nobel laureate economist Amartya Sen once summed all this up with a pithy phrase.

He said India was not going to flourish if it was "half California, half sub-Saharan Africa."

Is it possible to have balanced growth that benefits all parts of India? Economic growth is often unbalanced by its nature. A UCLA economist named Al Harberger once said that economic growth is more like mushrooms than yeast. Economic growth pops up in a few places; it's not a general expansion that happens everywhere at once. And when these mushrooms of growth pop up, it will create some inequality for a time. A range of government policies can help spread the benefits of growth. For example, better education policies prepare more workers to participate in growth. Better infrastructure policies prepare more areas to be possible hosts for growth. Flexible internal markets (buying and selling across the country), people moving to where there are jobs, businesses starting up where there are willing workers—all of these things can help spread the benefits of growth, and none of them has been all that common in India.

People often don't move because of language and other cultural issues. Firms didn't used to start up in new locations because it was so hard to deal with the bureaucracy, and licenses, and tax rules. But without policies to help spread the benefits of economic growth, India's growth may not be, ultimately, economically or politically sustainable. It won't be economically sustainable because when you talk about growth of 8 or 9% a year, you don't mean just a few industries growing at that rate; you mean that this entire country of a billion people has economic growth of 8 or 9% a year. And a small number of well-functioning industries aren't going to create that kind of national growth on a sustained basis. You need broad participation, more skilled workers, firms expanding to more locations, all those kinds of forces.

It's probably also not politically sustainable to have limited growth. There was a national election in India in 2004, and the pro-reform party lost badly in that election. A lot of the votes against them were from people who didn't feel as if they were sharing in the gains of economic growth. After that election, the process of privatizing the monopolies, which had just been sort of getting under way, really halted. The idea of trimming back a lot of subsidies halted, as well.

There are a lot of fears that a large share of the 70% of India's population still on the farm will start moving to urban areas, creating the possibility for extraordinarily huge urban slums. In many countries, those kinds of slums are a recipe for political unrest. The difficulty here is to find the right balance and to think about what the bar should be for inclusiveness. For example, if we think about growth reaching most citizens, that's a bar for inclusiveness that can be crossed with appropriate policy. But there is a danger that in thinking about inclusiveness, they set a higher bar. The higher bar would mean not just that growth benefits most citizens, but that it benefits most citizens in equal amounts. In other words, one person only gets a higher income if everyone else also gets a higher income, and this just isn't economically plausible. Across India, there are vast differences in the qualities of workers, from illiterate farmers to highly qualified engineers. This is a huge country with a great range of laws and background, lots of different industries, and growth is just not going to affect all of them equally.

The danger, which has sometimes happened in India in the past, is that being a successful firm or a successful entrepreneur makes you a target for the government to step in with a whole new group of requirements. India continues to have substantial Socialist sentiment, continues to have substantial anti-market sentiment. There is a sense, still, that the market is fundamentally about poverty and about exploitation, not about raising the standard of living for average people. I'm not expecting any outright return to the license raj here, but there is still a huge temptation to try and micromanage every producer in the economy, rather than having the government focus on education, health, infrastructure, better tax and spending policies, the sort of stuff that government really can do well. India has all sorts of difficulties, but it also has all sorts of momentum.

By about 2040, given the projected population growth rates into the future, it seems possible that India will overtake China and become the most populous country in the world. Depending on growth rates in the two countries at that time, if China hits a bad patch and India manages to keep growing at 8 or 9%, it's also conceivable that India could end up overtaking China and becoming the largest economy in the world at some point later in the 21st century. Back in the late 1980s, just a few decades ago, no one would have believed that was even remotely possible. It may be true that India's economic reform starting in the 1980s and early 1990s will, over the next few decades, prove to be almost as momentous as India's independence itself.

Lecture Seventeen
Inherited Institutions in the Middle East

Scope:

About eight centuries ago, the Middle East was probably the most scientifically advanced and economically powerful region in the world. A few centuries later, it has been outstripped by other regions and has remained a relatively lower-income part of the world economy ever since. Drawing links from cultural and religious backgrounds must be done with considerable care, but economists have pointed out that certain economic traditions common across these Islamic countries may hinder adaptation and development.

Outline

I. The total population of the Middle East is similar in size to that of the United States, but Middle Eastern economies are much smaller than the U.S. economy.

   A. International organizations, such as the World Bank and the International Monetary Fund, usually define the Middle East as stretching from North Africa and across the Red Sea to the Arabian Peninsula.

   B. The total population of the Middle East region is somewhat greater than that of the United States at roughly 315 million. The GDP of the United States is about $12 trillion, but in the Middle East, it is only about $2 trillion. Thus, the per capita GDP for the region is about one-sixth of the U.S. level.

   C. Economies of the countries of the Middle East are small relative to the U.S. economy—comparable in size to the economies of medium or small U.S cities.

      1. The biggest economy in the Middle East—that of Saudi Arabia—is roughly equal in size to the economy of the Boston metropolitan area.

      2. The economy of Egypt, the most populous country in the Middle East, is similar in size to the metropolitan area of San Diego, California.

II. Connections from culture to economics have often been made too casually, but it seems true that Islamic countries have lower per capita incomes after adjusting for other potentially relevant factors.

    A. From the standpoint of an economist, cultural or religious traditions often seem to change when economic incentives change. For example, Eastern religions were once thought to be antithetical to Capitalism because in these religions, the emphasis is on the community rather than the individual. The experience of economic growth in Japan, China, and India, however, has shown that financial incentives may have more influence on behavior than cultural traditions.

    B. Most countries across the Middle East have populations that are at least 90% Muslim. However, only about 20% of the Muslims in the world live in the Middle East. Further, modern Islam has many varieties.

    C. Using data from countries around the world, every 10 percentage-point increase in a country's share of Islamic population means, on average, a 4% fall in per capita GDP. When adjusting for other factors, the specific numbers change, but the general pattern continues to hold.

III. The rules or customs in the Middle Eastern versions of Islam may have made the people less well suited to compete in the modern economy.

    A. A claim is often made that Islam prohibits the payment of interest. This claim is doctrinally and historically weak, but it suggests some hostility to the financial sector more broadly.

    B. Traditional Islamic law limited the size of partnerships and the ability to pass wealth and businesses through time by inheritance. These factors probably limited the development of large-scale economic organizations in the Middle East.

    C. In traditional Islam, public assets were often provided by a *waqf*, or "Islamic trust." This organizational system offered a way around inheritance laws and enabled the construction of hospitals, mosques, orphanages, and other public works, but it was also inflexible over time.

D. Women in the Middle East have relatively low levels of education and health care. They often lack political equality, as well. These patterns affect economic growth in a number of ways, including reduced output from women workers and lower levels of education for children.

E. The Middle East was the world leader in science and technology around the 12th and 13th centuries, but it has lost that leadership position. A hesitant attitude toward science and technology persisted well into the 20th century.

IV. Part of the reason for the slow evolution of Islamic financial institutions may be the greater emphasis on Communalism in the Middle East compared with a greater emphasis on Individualism in Western Europe.

Suggested Readings:

Kuran, *Islam and Mammon: The Economic Predicaments of Islamism*.

———, "Why the Middle East Is Economically Underdeveloped: Historical Mechanisms of Institutional Stagnation."

United Nations Development Programme, *Arab Human Development Report 2002: Creating Opportunities for Future Generations*.

Questions to Consider:

1. What are some of the potential difficulties in attempting to link culture or religion and economic outcomes? In what situations might these problems be more or less severe?

2. What are some of the deep-rooted Middle Eastern economic institutions that may have hindered the economic development of the region over the last half millennium?

Lecture Seventeen—Transcript
Inherited Institutions in the Middle East

The Middle East is clearly of great importance to the U.S. economy and to the world economy, as well. One big reason, of course, is that it's a primary source of oil, one of the main fuel sources that drives the world economy. In addition, the Middle East has been a sort of tinderbox of military confrontations. You can think about the confrontations between Israel and Arab states, and the history of the region also includes any number of wars between and within countries. Think of the Iran-Iraq war of the 1980s, for example. There is also a widespread fear that this area is creating conflict elsewhere in the world, both as a matter of radical ideologies and by providing monetary or logistical support.

At the most basic economic level, the Middle East region is roughly 300 million people, about the same number as in the United States. As you've surely noticed in this tour around the world, I'm generally spending one lecture talking about an earlier time period that sets the stage for what's happening in each region and then using the second lecture to talk about the last decade or two. In talking about the Middle East, I want to start off with basic facts about the countries and economies of this region, just to get us all sort of located at the same place on the map. Then, I want to give some historical perspective on this region, reaching way, way, way back before the 1980s, and the 1970s, and the 1900s, really, all the way back to about 800 or 900 years ago. That's the time when the Middle East was probably the most technologically advanced and the most high-income part of the entire world. And one of the great world historical questions for economists is: What happened? How or why did the Middle East lose this economic lead?

I'll argue that it has something to do with the relationship between certain aspects of the Islamic religion and the institutions that make economies work. In fact, I'll argue that these aspects echo into the economy of the Middle East today. Then, in the next lecture, we'll tackle the modern economies in the Middle East, and in particular, we'll ask this question: With all that oil, why isn't that region more rich? I mean, it sure seems that if you're paying $3, $4, or more for a gallon of gasoline, the average person in the Middle East ought to be really rich. Why aren't they? We'll need to investigate that question.

Let's start with some basic background information, some facts about the Middle East. What do we mean when we say the "Middle East region"? The World Bank and the International Monetary Fund divide up all the countries of the world into regions, and I'm essentially adopting their grouping here. What they talk about is what they call the Middle East and North Africa region, so visualize a mental map here. Start in North Africa, work your way across the top of the continent. That would be Morocco, Algeria, Tunisia, Libya, and then Egypt. Egypt is at the upper-right of a map of Africa. It has the Mediterranean Sea up to the north and the Red Sea reaching along the east. On the other side of the Red Sea, then, is the Arabian Peninsula. Saudi Arabia sits smack in the middle of the Arabian Peninsula. To the north of Saudi Arabia, we have the area where that news reports often refer to when talking about the Middle East, so we're really talking about Israel, the West Bank and Gaza Strip, Lebanon, Syria, Iraq, Iran, Kuwait. To the south and east of Saudi Arabia are the countries like Yemen, Oman, and the very small, rich countries, like Bahrain, Qatar, and the United Arab Emirates.

Do we include Israel in the Middle East? Geographically, of course, it's in the Middle East, but for purposes of these lectures, no. I'm going to leave it out for both a bad reason and a good reason. A bad reason that Israel is often left out in these discussions is that because of politics in the Middle East, Arab countries often don't want to treat Israel as a part of the region. In many cases, when you look up international data on the Middle East region, you find that Israel has been left out. That's a bad reason to leave it out. But here is what I think is the good reason: Politically and economically, Israel is just very different from other countries of the Middle East. Israel is high income; it's democratic; it's market-oriented; it has no oil to export. It has a very different cultural and religious orientation. Israel just has a different set of issues, and it's best dealt with in a different speech or a different context.

Overall, the Middle East and North Africa region had 315 million [people] in 2006—again, this is roughly comparable to the population of the United States. However, the GDP of the United States is about $12 trillion, while the combined GDP for all the countries of the Middle East region is only about $2 trillion. Thus, per capita GDP for the Middle East and North Africa region is about one-sixth of the U.S. level. Sure, some of the small oil-exporting countries look pretty good on per capita GDP. If you look up the numbers for Kuwait, or Bahrain, or Qatar, or United Arab Emirates, their per capita GDP looks very comparable to high-income economies, like Western Europe and the United States. But each of these countries has a population of only a few million people or even less. The big population countries of the Middle East–North Africa region are actually fairly poor.

To think about where the population really is in this region, you might consider that eight countries in this region have almost 90% of the total population. Those eight countries would be Algeria, Egypt, Iran, Iraq, Morocco, Saudi Arabia, Syria, and Yemen. You take U.S. GDP, divide it by population in the late 2000s, it's about $42,000 as a per capita GDP for the United States. If you look at Egypt, the biggest population in this Middle Eastern region, with a population of 75 million people, its per capita GDP is $4,800.

Among the big population countries, Egypt is about average. Iraq, Morocco, Syria, Yemen are all below Egypt's level of per capita GDP. Of course, oil-rich Saudi Arabia has a higher average per capita GDP, at about $21,600 in 2006, but income in Saudi Arabia is very unequally distributed between members of the royal family and everyone else. As a result, income for the people right in the middle of the income distribution in Saudi Arabia might not be all that different for people in the middle of the income distribution for, say, a country that appears much poorer, like Iran. Just for comparison (although I don't want to focus on Israel here), Israel in 2006 had a population of about 7 million people and GDP of $123 billion. You divide it out, and that works out to a per capita GDP of about $24,000.

The economies of these countries in the Middle East are very, very small. The biggest economy in the Middle East, the economy of Saudi Arabia, is roughly equal in size to the economy of the Boston metropolitan area. The economy of Iraq is basically the same size as the economy of the metro area of Tampa, Florida. The economy of Egypt, the most populous country in the Middle East, is similar in size to the economy of the metro area of San Diego, California. And a small country like Tunisia, with a small economy, has an economy equal to the metro area of Madison, Wisconsin.

My broader point here is that when we think about the Middle East, I think that we Americans have a certain tendency to think about a certain kind of stereotype. We're thinking about really rich people. We're thinking about people who are living off of oil money. We're thinking about people who own lots of fancy cars. You think about the tourist palaces that get built in some small countries, like Dubai or the United Arab Emirates. But remember that these little countries have tiny populations, and they are almost floating on oil. They are really not at all representative of the Middle East as a whole.

These images of some people in the Middle East being rich are, of course, true, but they aren't representative. It's a little bit like saying that Donald Trump is an average American wage earner or something like that. The overwhelming numbers of people across the Middle East and North Africa region are quite poor. It's not quite African levels of poverty, of course, but remember that the average is something like one-sixth of the U.S. level, and for poor people, it might be something like one-tenth of the U.S. level.

The focus of this lecture is talking about why this area has failed to build the kind of economic institutions which would help it develop further, and in particular, I'm going to draw on connections from Islam to economic institutions. Let's start off by talking more broadly about making connections from culture to economics. In our diversity-conscious and politically correct world, talking about links from religion or culture to any actual behavior can really be a set of landmines, but as you may have noticed in these lectures, I often intend to plunge ahead where more sensible people might fear to tread. I want to start off by talking about the relationships between culture and economics, and then we will get to specifically how Islamic law might have hindered economic growth in the Middle East.

Economists have a long tradition of being really very hesitant about drawing connections between religious or cultural statements and economic behavior. The reason is that what appears to be culture or religion often seems to transform itself when economic incentives change. For example, back in 1848, the famous economist John Stuart Mill wrote about the Irish in the 19th century. Basically, Mill wrote something like: Why are the Irish so lazy, and drunk, and useless in Ireland, and then, these same Irish folks go to the United States, and all of a sudden, they become hard working and industrious? Maybe, Mill hypothesized, it's because of economic institutions. These people had no real hope of material advancement in Ireland, so they acted in one way. When they came to the United States, they had real chances for economic progress, and so they acted in a completely different way.

The issue wasn't culture; the issue was economic incentives. There was also a time—not that long ago—when people used Eastern religions, like Shinto, or Confucianism, or Hindu religions, to explain why Capitalism would just never really work in places like, say, Japan, or China, or India, because after all, these religions and cultures meant that people described their place in the world as part of the community. They didn't think of themselves as workers and consumers; they just weren't very interested in Capitalism. Or sometimes it was claimed they weren't very interested in democracy either.

Clearly, when there were incentives for economic gains, all of a sudden, Japan, and China, and India moved ahead pretty briskly. Again, it wasn't culture; it was whether there were incentives in the economic institutions. If someone from a certain culture is placed into a situation where their financial incentives for success are different, you actually can see what really matters. Is it culture here, or is it incentives? And over and over in these kinds of situations, it often seems that financial incentives are more important than culture.

Drawing connections from culture to economic behavior needs to be done with great care. More broadly, you need to have caution about identifying the Middle East and Islam too closely. And I think about this in terms of several statements. First of all, most of the Middle East and North Africa region really is Islamic. I mean, if you look country by country, typically 90% or more of the population is Islamic. However, it is also true that most Islamic people in the world do not live in the Middle East. For example, Indonesia and Malaysia have more than 200 million Muslims each. India, Pakistan, and Bangladesh all have more than 100 million Muslims each. Turkey and Nigeria both have more than 60 million Muslims. Lots of other countries, from Russia to Ethiopia, have millions or tens of millions of Muslims in their population. Altogether, maybe 20% of the world's Muslims actually live in the Middle East. Islam also comes in many different varieties. It's not a particularly centralized religion. There isn't a pope who hands down doctrine. Clearly, there is a range of Islamic belief, from traditionalists, to fundamentalists, to modernists, and so, again, generalizations about Islam can be somewhat hazardous.

Having said all that, though, I do think there are long-term connections that you can draw between Islamic institutions and economic institutions. And in drawing those connections, one begins to see some of the issues which have been difficult for economies in the Middle East and North Africa region right on up to the present. Statistically speaking, Islam is linked to lower income levels, and I should say that in the rest of the lecture, I'm relying heavily, but not at all exclusively, on the work of Timur Kuran, who is an economist at Duke University and who has studied these questions pretty extensively.

Here is a calculation from Kuran. He said: Let's plot all the countries of the world on a graph. On the horizontal access, plot the percentage of people in the country who are Islamic. On the vertical access, plot per capita gross domestic product, and draw a line to see if there is any connection between the two. If you draw that line, you'll find that every 10 percentage-point increase in the share of the population which is Islamic means about a 4% fall in per capita GDP. That is just a statistical fact; there is not any explanation there.

You can, of course, do a more complex statistical analysis, where you adjust for factors like is a nation a member of OPEC, or is it in sub-Saharan Africa. But when you adjust for those kinds of factors, you still find that when a nation has a greater share Islamic [population], it tends to be somewhat poorer in terms of per capita GDP. This fact is really strange for a number of reasons, but one is that from about 900 to 1300 A.D., the Middle East was the highest income part of the world.

Again, there is a huge question here: Why did the Middle East fall behind after its early advantage, and what sort of legacy built up in terms of its economic institutions which kept it poor and low income for centuries and centuries, coming up into the 20th century? My strategy here is to talk about specific rules or customs within Islam—especially the versions of Islam that are most popular in the Middle East region—that could lead to economic institutions which are perhaps not well suited to compete in the modern economy.

I don't want to try and sell you these as definitive answers but more as a list of the kinds of problems that exist in the Middle East economies of today and what some of the historical roots of those problems might be. For example, there is a claim that a strict interpretation of Islam means that you cannot pay interest, and in fact, Islam does prohibit something called *reba*. The ancient practice of *reba* was where debtors who didn't repay on time saw the following episode unfold: First, their debts doubled; then, if you couldn't repay, your debt redoubled again; and then, if you couldn't repay, you were sold into slavery. The practice of *reba*, way back 1,000 years ago, tended to be a way to push the poor into slavery. It was highly unpopular, as you might imagine, and there's no question that the Qur'an bans *reba*. But does this mean that all payment of interest is also banned? As a practical matter, no country in the Middle East or elsewhere has ever completely dispensed with interest payments. In fact, this prohibition on interest that is sometimes talked about in the modern world wasn't even claimed to be true for most of Islamic history.

In the last 25 years or so, some folks have started what they call Islamic banks, which claim to not have any involvement with interest payments. But in the countries that have Islamic and non-Islamic banks, scattered across the Middle East and elsewhere, the market share of these Islamic banks is maybe 1% of the total banking market. These Islamic banks actually seem to be largely an exercise in semantics. They often get around the prohibition on interest by using a complicated contract. For example, you put your money in the bank, and the bank does not pay you interest. Instead, you become a partial owner of the bank, and you get a return according to what the bank has done, what the payments are that the bank received, what the bank's costs are. Some share of that is what you get paid for putting your money into the bank. It looks a lot like interest, but it's not called interest.

I talked a little while ago to a friend of mine who works for a U.S. home loan finance company. He told me that they have a special form for lending to American Muslims who really care about not paying interest. Apparently, the terminology on this form is completely different from the loan form I sign, but the payments and the legality are all exactly the same. It's not at all obvious to me that interest really is banned by the Islamic religion, but it is clear to me that banks and financial institutions in the Middle East right up to the present time are tremendously underdeveloped.

It's very hard there to get a loan for a house or a business. It doesn't matter if you have collateral; you just can't get a loan. There is almost no bond market, no stock market, no venture capital. If you look at poor households across the Middle East, something like 2% of them have access to financial services. They don't have checks, or debit cards, or bank accounts, or contact with the financial sector. And I think the argument that banking is immoral, that charging interest is immoral, may well be one of the things which, over the centuries, has contributed to the financial inadequacies that exist across the Middle East economies.

Let me give you another example. Say, again, we're now back in the 10th century. Traditionally, in Islam, large businesses were either family enterprises or partnerships. The reasons for this were set out in the Qur'an. Partnership law in the Qur'an specified that partners in any business were only liable as individuals. That is to say, if you were owed a debt, you needed to collect from both partners individually, and you could only sue the partner that you specifically dealt with. Moreover, any partnership ended with the death of any member of the partnership. And this actually was legally true even if the surviving partners hadn't yet learned of the death. The partnership was over when someone died. Heirs did not step into a partnership. Whenever a partnership ended, it was true that everything from the partnership had to immediately be paid out in the form of currency. Imagine some partnership where you buy goods and you ship them somewhere else to sell them, but along the way, one partner dies. All of a sudden, all of your money is tied up in these goods which were in the middle of being shipped, but at that point, you have to settle up in cash right away. That can be chaotic.

Inheritance law was also set by the Qur'an. At the time of death, traditional Islamic law let you bequeath only one-third of your property in the way that you personally wanted it. The other two-thirds was divided up by formula among all your relatives, and this formula, of course, tended to split up wealth. If you owned a shop and you died, it might suddenly end up with a dozen co-owners, all of whom were trying to operate under this partnership law.

You combine these two rules—partnership and inheritance rules— and what's the outcome? The outcome was that partnerships traditionally in the Middle East stayed very small. They were typically just two people, and they were often limited to only be partnerships for a certain deal at a certain time. The problem, of course, was that any partnership had a risk that if someone died, the whole partnership had to end immediately, and you wanted to make clear who was responsible for debts and loans. This Islamic partnership law was the basis for business organization in this region well into the 19th century.

Think of the difference of, say, stock companies in Europe or U.S. firms in the 19th century. There were lots of different kinds of ownership and contracts between firms and individuals. Or think about the rule of prima geniture in Europe, that rule which said that when there was a big inheritance, the first son got all the wealth so the family wealth didn't get all divided up. Think about the idea that hundreds and hundreds of employees might act on behalf of a corporation. The corporation can be sued for the actions of those employees, and eventually, the corporation will outlive any of the employees.

It's possible that these Islamic partnerships could have evolved into modern corporations, but they didn't. And the Middle Eastern area didn't really develop banks or corporations until well into the 20th century. When you think about why this region has had economic difficulties, I suspect the lack of business development, the lack of large-scale enterprises, the lack of large-scale manufacturing, to some extent, comes out of this historical background of how these institutions developed.

Here is another example: In traditional Islam, back around the 10th century again, there was a system called the *waqf* system. This was called an "Islamic trust" or sometimes a "pious foundation." The notion was that you would build a public good, like a lighthouse, and set up a foundation with assets to fund that lighthouse. Once you set up a *waqf*, it was exempt from taxation, and it couldn't be confiscated by the government. You avoided the problem of splitting up the property because of inheritance laws, because you'd put it into this foundation.

The assets behind the *waqf* needed to be physical assets, like land, or residences, or shops, or production facilities. There was one *waqf* back in 1552 that covered 26 villages, along with shops and a bazaar. It had two soap plants, 11 flower mills, two bathhouses, and the assets from this *waqf* were used to operate a mosque, two hostels, and a soup kitchen for travelers. Across the Middle East, lots of huge public buildings—mosques, hospitals, orphanages—were all funded through these *waqfs*. There were even *waqfs* devoted to things like cultivating roses or protecting storks. Maybe a quarter of them were explicitly religious; another quarter were educational.

You could also have what was called a family *waqf*, where the beneficiaries over time were some members of your family. Basically, you could put your heirs in charge of the *waqf* and pay them a salary over time for looking after your wealth, and that would help you get around the inheritance laws, which might otherwise break up your fortune. You had to declare this arrangement publicly in front of a court, and it worked fairly well for centuries—got a lot of things built across the Middle East—but it's not especially suited for modern economic development. I mean, it's good for individual mosques and hospitals, but this system is inflexible. If something changed over time, you couldn't alter the original conditions of the *waqf*. If you said, "I'm going to grow cabbages," you can't switch to some other crop. If you said, "The *waqf* would hire 100 workers," you couldn't hire 120 workers or 80 workers. If you said, "I'm going to build a mosque," but there was no budget for repairing the mosque, you couldn't repair it.

Often, this ended up in long arguments in court, where they would take the original agreement and try and challenge it. The law at the time was: One change was allowed but only one. Also, *waqfs* are harder for setting up systems, like a municipal water system, or road infrastructure, or a seaport, or an airport, or firefight, or sewers. Broad-based things don't work as well with a *waqf* system. The *waqf* system led to a lot of "who you know" kinds of corruption. A lot of rules were being violated in secret, and really up into the 20th century, the *waqf* system persisted.

In recent decades, *waqfs* have turned into basically—they look a lot like Western foundations. It's not so easy to shelter your income there; they get lots of small donations. They're run by trustees who have some flexibility. They're not expected to be society's main way of dealing with public goods, but because of the *waqf* system, it meant the Middle East came relatively late to the notion that you had to develop governance systems and local governments for collecting revenues and figuring out how to provide public goods.

What about the status of women in Middle Eastern countries? They have really had a relatively low level of education and health. Is this

Islam, or is this just the sort of Islam practiced in the Middle East or just some sort of traditionalism that cloaks itself in Islam but isn't really about Islam? I guess this is all too deep for an economist like me, but I just want to say that as Islam is practiced in the Middle East, it does seem to hold women back. For example, let me quote from the 2002 *Arab [Human] Development Report* (which comes from the United Nations), where a group of economists from the Middle East really made this point quite openly. They wrote:

> More than half of Arab women are still illiterate. The region's maternal mortality rate is double that of Latin America and the Caribbean, and four times that of East Asia.
>
> Women also suffer from unequal citizenship and legal entitlements, often evident in voting rights and legal codes. The utilization of women's capabilities through political and economic participation remains lowest in the world in quantitative terms. ... Qualitatively, women suffer from inequality of opportunity, [which is] evident in employment status, wages, and gender-based occupational segregation. Society as a whole suffers when a huge proportion of its productive potential is stifled, resulting in lower family incomes and standards of living.

I would also add this isn't just a problem in terms of the workforce; more educated women have a huge impact on how well children are educated. They also have a huge impact on the behavior of young men in that society.

A final element which I think has come down traditionally is a feeling about science and technology in the Middle East and in North Africa. From about 900 to 1300, again, the Arab Middle East was probably the world leader in science and technology. But it really has lost that leadership position. One Islamic publisher in 1987 put out a book of great Islamic scientists, and in this book of great Islamic scientists, basically two-thirds of the scientists lived before 1250. Another third of the great Islamic scientists lived between 1250 and 1750, and none in the book lived since 1750. What happened around, say, 1250 or 1300 which caused this withdrawal from science? A famous writer named Ibn Khaldun, who is sort of the Arabic Adam Smith, wrote around 1370 that the economies of the Middle East were losing their dynamism. They were losing their advantage in scientific learning.

Traditionally, it was said that about this time, "The gate of *ijtihad* was closed. *Ijtihad* translates loosely as something like "independent interpretation." That means, to say the gates of *ijtihad* have closed is to say that all the answers were now known. Independent judgment wasn't any longer useful. It was more important to have social stability than knowledge. The education system of the region went to rote learning.

There is a big historical argument over exactly how to interpret this change, but something definitely seemed to happen in the Middle East at about that time. Again, this echoes into modern times. Islamic societies over the last couple of centuries have been slow to accept knowledge from the West. For example, the *Arab Human Development Report* said the Arab world translates about 330 books a year into Arabic. That's about one-fifth of the number that Greece translates into Greek. The cumulative total of all the translated books into Arabic since the Caliph Maa-moun's time (this is back in the 9th century) is about 100,000. Now, 100,000 is about the number that Spain translates in every single year. Knowledge is not flowing into the Middle East. A recent UNESCO study on research in the universities in the Middle East said:

> There is little renewal or production of knowledge, but merely transmission of what is already known. This early spirit of Arab researchers, which has greatly contributed to the advancement of human learning, has almost disappeared.

Why is it that Islamic institutions didn't evolve in a way that was more conducive to economic growth? After all, Europe had some similar issues through the Middle Ages, but it was consistently true in Europe that the power of consumers and new competitors broke through time after time. Guilds and existing merchants and rules weren't able to block new competition in new products and new ideas. But that didn't happen in the Middle East. There is no really great answer here. Timur Kuran suggests that one of the differences is a difference in Communalism versus Individualism. In the United States and the West, individuals belong to a lot of different associations—family, work, church, political, volunteer, all sorts of clubs—and there's a lot of movement and discourse across and between these groups. In the Middle East, on the other hand, people tend to belong to fewer groups but to be more closely identified with those groups, like, say, family and church. When you've got

Individualism and lots of separate groups, that sort of encourages depersonalized economics. It encourages anonymous buying and selling, reaching out to new customers, being willing to buy from new producers. In a world of intense Communalism, you tend to have smaller groups and separation between those groups.

As an economist, this kind of explanation is frankly a little bit too facile for me. It feels sort of made up after the fact to fit the situation. I don't quite know how I would prove it or disprove it, but fortunately, my theme for this lecture is simpler than that explanation. I hope to have introduced to you the basic contours of the economy of the Middle East and to have opened your mind to some of the ways in which Islamic law may have shaped the region's current economic development.

Lecture Eighteen
The Curse of Oil Wealth in the Middle East

Scope:

A few tiny oil-rich countries in the Middle East have high average incomes, but most people in the region do not have high incomes and have not experienced substantial economic benefits from living in oil-exporting nations. The economic theory of "Dutch disease" explains why countries that have substantial oil reserves have, over recent decades, grown more slowly than countries that don't. Some countries, such as Norway and Indonesia, have found ways to manage this problem and to spread the benefits of oil wealth throughout the economy, but again, others have not. As the Middle East looks ahead, its major economic problem will be to develop a non-oil private sector that can provide jobs for the large expansion in the workforce that is already taking place.

Outline

I. Despite their position as major oil exporters, many countries across the Middle East have experienced levels of per capita GDP that are generally flat or even declining in recent decades.

A. Large-population countries in the Middle East, such as Algeria, Egypt, Iran, Iraq, and others, have seen either small increases or outright decreases in living standards over the last few decades. On other measures of a healthy economy, including health care and education, these economies have not performed well either.

   1. Life expectancy and infant mortality are two common proxies for the overall level of health in a given country. Especially in infant mortality levels, countries of the Middle East are far behind such high-income countries as the United States.

   2. Illiteracy rates in the Middle East are worse than the average for other developing countries around the world.

B. Other factors underlie this poor economic performance.

   1. Physical infrastructure includes provision of water, phone lines, roads, and so on. Countries of the Middle East have not performed especially well on these measures.

2. Economies of the Middle East have had widespread price controls for many decades.

3. Other than oil, international trade involving the Middle Eastern region is quite low, both within the region and with other regions.

4. Banking systems are underdeveloped; thus, getting loans is difficult for both ordinary people and small businesses.

5. Governments in this region have often run large budget deficits relative to the size of their economies.

6. Countries of this region have a desert climate, which means that they tend to lack arable land.

7. Birthrates have declined in much of the world but have done so more slowly in the Middle East. As a result, many countries in the region have large shares of their populations in relatively young age brackets but low job growth. Widespread unemployment among young men is often a recipe for social turmoil.

II. It may seem obvious that oil resources should increase economic prosperity, but we don't see this outcome in the Middle East. Economists have developed theories to explain why oil resources do not necessarily lead to sustained economic growth.

A. Given the importance of oil in the world economy and the size of oil exports from the Middle East, surely the economic performance of the region is underwhelming. Across the world, oil exports do not seem to result in economic growth, nor do they bring about improvements in social or political indicators.

B. "Dutch disease" is the name that economists give to the situation in which discovery of a natural resource weakens other aspects of the economy. In particular, it can lead to inflation, a strong currency that discourages other exports, diversion of investment capital from other parts of the economy, and lower levels of political responsiveness.

C. Well-run government institutions can inoculate their countries against Dutch disease by avoiding government debt, spreading buying power throughout the economy, starting an oil trust fund, and maintaining an arm's-length relationship with the companies that produce the oil.

D. The countries of the Middle East have taken ownership of the oil; now, they need to take ownership of the responsibility for wise economic management of that oil.

III. The future for sustained growth in economies and jobs in the Middle East will require building businesses outside the oil sector.

A. Oil will not be a sufficient source of future economic growth and jobs.

B. Governments can accomplish some important tasks, such as improving health, education, and infrastructure, but governments alone are highly unlikely to create sustained economic or job growth.

C. Most Middle Eastern countries don't have strong growth coming from an array of private-sector companies across a range of industries. Instead, they have numerous costly rules and regulations that make it hard to start a business. But healthy private-sector firms are the typical formula for sustained growth in jobs and the economy.

D. Something like a million émigrés from Middle Eastern countries are now working in the United States and Western Europe. One step in the right direction might be for this diaspora population to reach back to the countries of the Middle East with financial and investment advice.

Suggested Readings:

Christian Aid, "Fuelling Poverty: Oil, War, and Corruption."

World Bank, "Avoiding the Resource Curse."

———, "Oil and Gas: A Blessing or a Curse?"

Questions to Consider:

1. Why are the economies of the Middle East not especially well off?

2. How can oil wealth make a country's economy less well off?

3. What kinds of government policies can help to ensure that oil or other resource wealth benefits the economy as a whole?

Lecture Eighteen—Transcript
The Curse of Oil Wealth in the Middle East

If there is one economic fact from the late 2000s on which all red-blooded Americans, regardless of their political persuasion, are quite likely to agree, it would be something like: "Golly, gasoline seems really expensive." It seems like it should stand to reason that those who have the crude oil, which is made into gasoline, should be prospering not just now but for decades into the past and the future, as well. The Middle East region clearly [has been] the biggest exporter of crude oil in the world for some decades. How has it been doing? Despite their position as major oil exporters, major economies across the Middle East have experienced generally flat levels of per capita GDP from the 1970s, 1980s, up until the mid-2000s.

For example, Saudi Arabia had a per capita GDP of around $20,000 in 1985, and after adjusting for inflation and all the rest, by 2006, had a per capita GDP of around $21,000. This hardly seems like a sufficient economic gain for a country that's practically swimming in oil. Similar patterns of very modest economic growth have occurred across other countries in the Middle East in recent decades, as well.

I should, of course, throw in a couple of warnings. When I come up to 2006, those numbers are just a little bit old (as international statistics often are). They don't take into account the big run-up in oil that happened later in the 2000s. But even as that price increase has sent more money to the Middle East for their exported oil, the basic question remains: Why weren't countries like Saudi Arabia getting rich for decades and decades through the '70s, '80s, '90s, and into the 2000s? Moreover, after the oil price increases of the late 2000s, will these countries actually get much, much richer this time, or will they stay more or less in the same place?

When you think about the standard of living of any country, it can be measured in several different ways—not just by economic statistics, but it can also be measured by things like health and education. These statistics, when you look at them, also show a low standard of living in the large-population Middle Eastern countries. For example, two standard ways of measuring health are life expectancy and infant mortality, real basic health statistics. If you look at life expectancy, for example, the U.S. life expectancy is about 77 years. If you look at the large-population countries of the Middle East, life expectancy is often around 70 years in, say, Algeria, Egypt, Iran, Iraq, Morocco. If you look at infant mortality, you can see these differences in health even more. Infant mortality is, of course, closely linked to prenatal care for mothers and how the baby is actually delivered. U.S. infant mortality in the late 2000s is about 6 per 1,000 live births. Across the Middle East, infant mortality is often 20, 30, 40 fatalities for every 1,000 live births.

Why is it that the oil money, all the oil money flowing to that region, isn't doing more to help pregnant mothers and newborns? There is also in the Middle East region very high maternal mortality. In high-income countries, about 5 women die for every 100,000 live births. In many of the Middle Eastern countries, it's, say, 200 women who die for every 100,000 live births.

What about measures of well-being, like education? If you look at illiteracy, illiteracy rates in the Middle East are worse than the average for other developing countries around the world. Literacy rates for adults in Middle Eastern countries are often 80% or less than in, say, Algeria, Egypt, Iraq, Saudi Arabia. If you look at Morocco and Yemen, illiteracy rates are only a little bit above 50%. And what's really meant by literacy in these kinds of statistics isn't usually extremely demanding. We're really just talking about basic functional ability with reading and writing.

Again, illiteracy in the Middle East is worse than the average for other developing economies. Secondary-school enrollments are low—often only something like 80% of students go on to get a secondary education. When we think about why these economies have not performed so well on either economic or health statistics, what factors underlie this poor performance? Well, there's a famous opening line in the novel *Anna Karenina*: "All happy families are alike; each unhappy family is unhappy in its own way." In a similar spirit, an economist might say that most high-income economies look very much alike, but that is to say that they look alike because a high-income economy involves well-educated workers using up-to-date equipment and technology. They are working in a market-oriented economic environment with good physical infrastructure, good institutional infrastructure, like legal and financial rules, but low-income economies often look different in their own ways. Low-income economies lack many of these things, but their patterns of lacking them are somewhat different.

The Middle East doesn't look quite like, say, Latin America, or South Asia, or Africa. There are all sorts of tough issues for the economies of the Middle East. Let me sort of list many of them briefly without too much detail. Physical infrastructure across the Middle East (here, I'm including provision of water, phone lines, roads, and so on) has not been very good. In particular, this region has the lowest level of access to the Internet of any region of the world, worse than sub-Saharan Africa, which is saying something. Economies in the Middle East have had widespread price control for many decades, going back at least to the 1950s and to the influence of Gamal Abdul Nasser about how Arab Socialism would rule in Egypt. Other than oil, international trade involving the Middle Eastern region is really extremely low, both within the region and between other regions, as well. For example, Middle Eastern nations trade less with other Middle Eastern nations than, say, Africa trades with other African nations or Latin American nations trade with each other.

The United States imports about $5 billion a year of manufactured goods from the Middle East region (not oil but manufactured goods), and that's about half of what the United States imports from tiny Hong Kong all by itself. Before World War I, trade in the Middle East used to be a lot higher. For example, Egypt's exports were 50% of GDP before World War I. Think of all that cotton being exported. But now, Egypt's exports are only about 8% of GDP, which is actually higher than arises in many other countries.

Most of the large economies in the Middle East–North Africa area aren't part of the World Trade Organization. They don't get much outside investment compared to the rest of the world, and what they do get has been dropping off in recent decades. We've talked about their banking systems being underdeveloped, so getting loans is hard for ordinary people and for small businesses. Governments in this region have often run really large budget deficits relative to the size of their economies. And other than oil, these areas have been short of other natural resources like, say, water or arable land. Countries in this region have a desert climate, so it just doesn't help much if you're trying to turn to agriculture. There is a famous comment from Sheikh Yamani, who was the oil minister of Saudi Arabia. In 1979, after the huge up-and-down swings in the oil market of the 1970s, Yamani apparently said, "All in all, I wish we had discovered water."

This region also has high, high levels of unemployment. Birthrates have declined in much of the world, but they have declined much more slowly in the Middle East than in other parts of the world. As a result, many countries in the Middle East have a relatively large share of their population in relatively young age brackets. The current labor force in the Middle East, across all of these countries, is something like 104 million jobs. But because of all the young people who are now going to be a little older in 20 years, in 20 years, they will need something like 185 million jobs. If you work that out, basically, they need to generate something like 6% more jobs per year for the next 10 or 20 years. Without those jobs, there are going to be lots and lots of unemployed young men, which is often a recipe for social turmoil. Again, these folks are all already born; they are just under the age of 20. They are in the pipeline. They are going to be the workers of the future, and this issue is not going away.

The question about the Middle East is: Shouldn't control over a valuable natural resource like oil solve some of these issues? I mean, can't we get the health care people and reduce infant mortality? Can't we get the teachers to increase education? Can't we build the infrastructure for roads, and bridges, and Internet hookups? Why do you even have government budget deficits in a region of the world that has all this oil money coming in? Why isn't oil solving all of the problems of the Middle East?

There is a peculiar relationship between oil and economic prosperity. It might seem obvious to those of us paying $3 and $4 a gallon for gasoline that they should be rich as a result of our money, but this actually doesn't seem to have happened in the Middle East. In fact, there are well-developed economic theories for why oil resources will not necessarily lead to sustained economic growth. I should say that most Middle Eastern nations really do depend heavily on oil exports, not just obvious oil exporters that you have heard of, like Saudi Arabia, Iraq, Iran, Libya, but even countries you don't think of as major oil exporters, like, say, Algeria, Egypt, Syria, and Yemen. They aren't major in world terms, but in their own economies, oil really does play a substantial role in the economic picture.

Does oil help prosperity in the Middle East? The answer is clearly yes in sort of small Gulf coast countries and probably yes in, say, Saudi Arabia and Libya, which have fairly high per capita GDP. But it isn't really leading to the high-level income you might expect.

Think about it for a moment: Saudi Arabia has about one-quarter of all the world's oil reserves. It has the per capita GDP of, say, Slovenia or Portugal. I mean, all that oil, and you are Slovenia? It just doesn't seem to make sense.

In a number of other Middle Eastern countries, all their oil resources don't seem to be leading to very much at all. In fact, I want to propose a radical thought: As you look around the world—not just at the Middle East—perhaps oil isn't all that good for economic growth. In fact, this insight has been suspected for quite some time. In the early 1970s, when substantial oil reserves were confirmed in Venezuela (and the country joined OPEC at about that time), the oil minister of Venezuela was quoted as saying (this was in the early '70s), "Ten years from now, 20 years from now, you will see, oil will bring us ruin. It is the devil's excrement. We are drowning in the devil's excrement." And sure enough, Venezuela's economy has not performed very well since the early 1970s.

Other examples: Nigeria has the largest oil reserves in Africa. It has been actively pumping oil for decades with really no rise in per capita GDP over the last three decades or so. You could make similar arguments about, say, Sudan, or Angola, or Kazakhstan, all countries with large oil reserves that are pumping a lot of oil but don't seem to see a growing economy as a result. There is an IMF study of the Middle East region over the 30 years from 1970 up to 2000. They looked at oil-producing countries and their per capita income over that time. They found that for oil-producing countries, per capita income fell about 1.3% per year from 1970 to 2000.

The non-oil economies, meanwhile, rose 2% a year over that time. You can sort of think, maybe that is anecdotal. You want more systematic evidence? Two economists, named Jeffrey Sachs, who used to be at Harvard (now at Columbia), and Andrew Warner, of UCLA, published papers over the last decade or two systematically looking at economic growth and oil sales and then trying to adjust for other factors, like: Did the economy started out low income, or middle income, or high income? Was the government inefficient or corrupt? Did the economy have a lot of inequality? Was it open to trade or not? They adjusted for all the factors they could think of, and what they found was that higher oil exports across all of the countries of the world were linked to systematically slower economic growth.

Another economist at UCLA, named Michael Ross, looked at oil dependence versus factors like life expectancy, malnutrition, all that kind of stuff. And in one study, again, after accounting for all the other factors as best he could, what he found was that each rise of 5 percentage points in oil exports as a share of GDP led to one-third of a year less in life expectancy. It also led to a 1% rise in malnutrition of children under age five.

In another study, Ross looked at oil and democracy, and what he tended to find was that more oil leads to less democracy, not just in the Middle East but also in African countries, like Nigeria. There even seems to be some connection between oil and civil war in places like Sudan and Angola. You have probably heard about "conflict diamonds," where arms are financed by selling diamonds. But there is "conflict oil," too. The Middle East region is essentially without democracy, and it is, of course, riven with various conflicts and other abrupt changes of government. A few years ago in the little country of São Tomé, there were some seismic readings that were announced that said maybe there was oil under the country. They did not actually find any oil, but they had an armed coup a week later, sort of just in case there was oil to find.

Why is it that oil is not producing economic growth? The key here is the economics of what economists call "Dutch disease." Dutch disease refers back to the situation when Holland discovered offshore natural gas in the 1950s and 1960s. It discovered this natural gas, and its economy experienced a dramatic slowdown. Similarly, when Norway discovered North Sea oil in the 1960s and 1970s, its economy experienced rapid inflation, contraction in manufacturing, and slow growth. Why did these things happen? The economic argument goes something like this. An oil discovery leads to the following sequence of events: It leads to a boom of buying power in the economy, which can easily lead to inflation. Because you have just found oil, it makes focusing on oil look highly profitable and everything else in the economy look unprofitable. Investment capital, and education, and transportation, and communications—everything gets aimed at the oil resources, and the rest of the economy suffers as a result.

Another issue is that the exchange rate appreciates after you have found oil. When you have found lots of oil, you start selling lots of oil other places, and those high exports mean your country has a big trade surplus. You are earning a lot of foreign currency. Say Saudi Arabia is earning a lot of U.S. dollars; they need to convert that foreign currency back to the home currency of the oil-exporting country. When this happens, it tends to drive up demand for that nation's own currency and leads to a strong exchange rate. A strong exchange rate, of course, means all the other export-based industries of that country will suffer, and imports become expensive, which also feeds inflation.

Politically, a government that has oil resources can rely on oil money and oil taxes. What exactly is the need for, say, democracy, or accountability, or a sensible system of broad-based taxes across the economy? Indeed, a government with a lot of oil will discover it is really, really easy to borrow. Banks are happy to lend you money based on the future revenues from the oil reserves, and the huge amounts of money sort of sloshing around can easily lead to inequality and corruption.

Notice that this story explains many of the patterns noted above. It explains why these countries ran up big budget deficits, because people wanted to lend to them. It explains how there was not very much foreign trade unrelated to oil. It explains why there hasn't been very much development unrelated to oil. This is all Dutch disease. Can government policy inoculate an economy against Dutch disease? I should be clear here that Dutch disease doesn't literally mean that oil discoveries must be bad for an economy. It does mean that oil discoveries lead to a very specific kind of economic development, a very specific kind of development that is not especially broad-based, and it can create a lot of macroeconomic stress for the rest of the economy.

Countries like Holland and Norway, with deep-seated democratic traditions and strong civic institutions, have figured out how to make this work. The problem is doing it in other countries. In fact, countries like Indonesia have had some success, as well. What sort of steps do they take? You want to spread the buying power of the oil all the way throughout the economy, not just have it pile up in the hands of elites. You want to pursue a balanced government spending plan—that is to say, build up education, build up rural areas, build lots of roads. Indonesia did a pretty good job with this. You do not want to let those in the oil industry just have all the money. Norway, with their strong trade unions, the trade unions required a lot of the oil money to be paid out to workers. You do not want to go wildly into debt. After all, if you are a country that just found oil, you don't need to borrow money. Also, when you borrow a lot of money, it just stokes up the inflation fires. Norway, for example, when they found oil, borrowed a lot at first and then sort of figured this out and cut off that borrowing.

You need to keep the government honest, and one way to do that is to try and sustain a normal tax base which is apart from oil, with a normal sort of income tax or sales tax. Again, Norway did this. It keeps the government more representative and honest if it has to deal with the tax code. And it can help to redistribute buying power throughout the economy.

It is important that the oil companies don't run the government, that the government has a lot of power over the oil companies. You want to build up civil servants and bureaucratic expertise along with unions and industry groups, and again, all of this helps to spread the wealth of the oil industry throughout the entire economy. There is a different kind of nation-building in Indonesia. I am not a huge fan of, say, the politics that happened under Suharto or Sukarno in Indonesia. There was a very high level of nationalism there for quite a while, and a lot of this, though, was outright antagonism to Shell Oil and other big oil companies in Indonesia. And, in some ways, that was healthy, because they wanted to be confrontational and not have the oil companies draining away all the wealth.

The hard issue in the Middle East is that now, they own the oil companies, and they have become just as secretive and controlling as Exxon and Standard Oil ever were in the glory days when they controlled those oil supplies. Is it possible somehow to open up the oil companies in these countries? For example, in the country of Chad, they were going to build a giant oil pipeline, and the World Bank said: We'll fund that oil pipeline if you are completely transparent about how much is going in, how much money is coming out, and all the money is isolated in a separate fund where everyone can see it.

Indeed, transparency and being clear on the revenues and how [they are] spent really may be the big issue here as much as anything. A number of successful oil-exporting companies have started up an oil trust fund so all the oil sales go into the trust fund. An advantage there is that it stores up some of the buying power for the future.

There is less buying power and inflationary pressure right away if you spread it out over time. And, again, these oil trust funds can be very visible and very transparent. All of these things can help make an oil boom widely beneficial, as eventually turned out to be true in Norway or Holland, but the economic and political strains of being resource rich are very real, and they can be very tricky.

The Middle East does control at least the oil part of its economic future. Just to be clear on this, if you think companies like Exxon, and Mobil, and Standard Oil own most of the oil in the world, you are about four or five decades out of date. More than 90% of the oil reserves in the world are owned by nationalized companies across the Middle East, as well as Latin America, and Africa, and Asia. How this buying power from oil is managed is a major test for these countries, and frankly, a lot of them haven't handled it all that well. The Middle East has ownership of its own oil. Now, they need to take ownership of the responsibility for wise management of that oil.

I don't want to get into specifics of, say, the Iraq situation too much here, but I will say that when you talk about economic reform in that country, there is lots of discussion of things like better commercial law, an independent central bank, and free trade, and all those kinds of things. But in Iraq in the early 2000s, oil was something like maybe 60% or two-thirds of GDP.

In a lot of these countries, what happens with oil pretty much defines what is going to happen with their economy. What is the future of this region? The real future for sustained growth in economies and jobs in the Middle East is going to require reaching beyond oil—not just cashing easy payments from other countries for oil exports but thinking about building up businesses outside the oil sector. The real issue for those with low incomes is that you need economic growth, and there has been an enormous problem of generating enough jobs in this region.

As I said before, population growth has been very rapid in recent decades. A lot of new workers have been entering the workforce. They aren't going to be subsistence farmers in a desert climate. Something has to happen to all these young men entering the labor force, and as a former young man myself, I can promise you it is really important to have jobs available for young men. Young men who don't have enough to do are probably the cause of a lot of disorder in every part of the world.

Where can these additional jobs come from? Oil is not going to be a source of future economic growth and jobs. I mean, if you are in a standard Middle Eastern country with a per capita GDP that is some fraction of the U.S. levels, oil is not going to ride to the rescue and keep multiplying in price over, and over, and over again. I don't think we are going to get up to $30 a gallon for gasoline anytime soon. It is not a safe bet, even, that oil prices will grow continually over time in a way that will drive revenues ever, ever, ever higher. But even if those revenues do grow, it is not going to create widespread jobs. Oil is a very capital-intensive business. It doesn't need a whole lot of low-skill workers. You need to think a lot about how oil can help the rest of the economy grow and how it can create jobs, but the oil by itself isn't going to do it.

Governments of the Middle East also aren't going to be a sufficient source of economic growth and jobs in the future. Governments in this region have had big budget deficits in the past. They probably aren't going to go there again. Governments are good at redistributing funds. They can provide services in areas like health, and education, and infrastructure, but there is a point where what government is doing is sort of completed and where you need people running private-sector businesses. You are not going to have a situation where everybody works for the government. It is very unlikely that governments alone are going to provide the kinds of job growth that this region needs.

If all these young men growing up aren't working in oil, they aren't going to be working for the government, what are they going to do; where are they going to work? Can this region develop a non-oil private sector? Most countries in the Middle East really don't have a strong tradition of some engine of growth that comes out of the private sector across a range of industries. Instead, they have a set of costly rules and regulations that make it hard to start a business. But healthy private-sector companies are the typical formula for sustained growth in jobs and the economy over time.

When you think about jobs in the U.S. economy—jobs building things, making things, servicing things, dealing with records and accounts—I mean, that's what the private sector is. We discussed in a previous lecture that large business organizations, other than the oil companies, don't have a long history in the Middle East, and tons of rules and regulations have drowned them from happening in the last few decades. Again, the World Bank looks at the bureaucratic and legal hurdles an entrepreneur has to overcome to incorporate and register a new firm. They look at a lot of different measures of the procedures, and time, and cost involved in launching a commercial enterprise. Specifically, they said: What if you are launching a firm with 50 employees and a startup capital of a certain size? And then they compare countries and regions around the world. They found, for example, that if you look at the high-income countries of the world, there are about 6 procedures you need to go through to register a firm. In the Middle Eastern region, there are about 10 procedures you have to go through.

The average time per procedure in high-income countries is about 15 days per procedure. You multiply that times the 6 procedures, and it takes about 90 days to start a business. In the Middle Eastern region, it's about 38 days per procedure; multiply that by the 10 procedures, and it takes more than a year to get a business started. If you look at the official cost of each procedure (and they tried to express this as a share of per capita GDP to adjust across countries), in high-income countries, it costs about 5% of per capita GDP for each of the 6 procedures. Starting a company would cost about 30% of per capita GDP. In the Middle East, it costs 66% of per capita GDP for 10 procedures. Starting a company would cost 660% of per capita GDP. It is just much, much harder to start a business in the Middle East. There is almost no non-oil foreign trade, not even between countries in the region. Even if these countries don't want to trade with the United States or Europe for whatever reason, they should at least each try and trade with each other. And somehow, we need this to develop.

Perhaps the best hope for this region, I think, is there are something like 1 million highly educated and qualified workers who have recently left Middle Eastern countries in the last generation or two, and now they are working in the United States and Western Europe. Maybe a lot of them don't care that much about what is happening in the economies in the Middle East (they have made a new life; I don't know for sure), but my guess is that this million workers could be viewed as half of a bridge reaching out to the economies of the Middle East.

If the economic and political conditions were right, you could do an enormous amount with the economic and oil resources of those countries to help them grow very, very rapidly. But before this diaspora reaches out to the countries of the Middle East with financial advice, with advice about investment, with sources for future markets, the countries in the Middle East need to build the other half of the bridge.

Lecture Nineteen
Africa's Geography and History

Scope:

Sub-Saharan Africa has been the lowest-income and slowest-growing part of the world economy since the Industrial Revolution about 200 years ago. This lecture begins with an overview of Africa's economic and social development in the last few decades, which is a mild paradox of stagnant economic growth but moderate growth in some measures of health and education. But why has Africa's economy been so slow to develop? The conventional reason used to be the "poverty trap," which held that low-income countries had a hard time saving and investing for the future, but East Asia, China, and others have shown that it's possible to break out of this trap. A substantial share of the reason for Africa's sluggish growth over the last several centuries probably lies in the continent's disadvantages of geography and climate, which have created issues of a more scattered population, higher transportation costs, and difficulties in agricultural production.

Outline

I. Since the Industrial Revolution about 200 years ago, sub-Saharan Africa has been both the lowest-income and the slowest-growing part of the world economy.

II. The region of sub-Saharan Africa experienced sluggish and even negative economic growth from the early 1970s through the early 2000s. But the continent did see some progress on health and education indicators, an interesting case in which improvements in human well-being were not tracked by a growing economy.

    A. In this lecture, we will focus on sub-Saharan Africa, which consists of more than 48 countries, excluding the countries across the northern part of the continent, such as Morocco, Libya, and Egypt.

    B. Per capita GDP in sub-Saharan Africa barely moved from the early 1970s to the early 2000s. Poverty rates, measured by the $1-a-day standard, remain very high, at 41% of Africa's population in 2004.

C. When looking at standard of living, it's important to consider more than just economics. The standard of living includes not just income but health, education, and other factors.

   1. Life expectancy and infant mortality are two statistics often used for rough comparisons of health over time. Life expectancy in sub-Saharan Africa has changed relatively little in recent decades, in part because of the negative effect of the AIDS epidemic. At the same time, infant mortality has declined significantly.

   2. Africa's education levels remain low by world standards but have increased substantially in recent decades.

III. The "poverty trap" is one traditional, prominent theory of why Africa's economy has not grown. Other countries and regions seem to have overcome the poverty trap, however, raising the question of whether this explanation is as powerful as it at first seems.

   A. The poverty trap argument holds that in countries with low levels of income, people need to spend their time and income on necessities for subsistence living. Such countries have low savings rates, resulting in little financial capital for investment in education. With no development in human capital, the country becomes trapped in poverty.

   B. The poverty trap explanation sounds quite plausible, but in the last few decades, a number of countries have broken out of this scenario.

   1. Some countries that were very poor in the 1950s through the 1970s, often as poor as the countries of sub-Saharan Africa, have nonetheless found ways to grow.

   2. Countries in East Asia and China have sustained some of the world's highest savings rates when their economies were poor; conversely, some high-income countries, such as the United States, have sometimes had very low savings rates.

   3. A number of low-income countries have managed to start programs of mass education, including the United States early in its history and many African nations in the last decade or so.

   4. Economist Alexander Gerschenkron wrote an essay on the "advantages of backwardness," which noted that low-income economies in a world of richer economies can draw on technology and skills developed elsewhere. Some countries have used this strategy aggressively; African countries by and large have not done so.

IV. The development of Africa's economy has suffered over the decades from its geographic and climatic inheritance, which has hindered growth in a number of ways.

    A. Economies develop from specialization and trade, and in early stages of economic development, water transportation and ports have often played important roles in this development. However, Africa lacks rivers that can easily be navigated to the ocean, along with the port cities that often grow around bays or at the mouths of rivers.

    B. Certain factors hold true in tropical climates that may hinder economic growth.

        1. In the tropics, people tend to live in the mountain highlands, rather than in coastal areas, because of heat and disease near the coasts.

        2. The climate and soil are less conducive to high levels of food production.

        3. Certain pests flourish, such as mosquitoes, and affect both human health and the health of crops.

        4. Technologies that are used elsewhere in the world may not transfer well to tropical climates.

    C. Some critics believe that these geographic and climate arguments are a cover-up for the real problems, often rooted in colonialism. Colonialism was not typically conducive to long-run economic growth, but Africa had slow growth both before and after colonialism and in countries where colonialism was both more and less powerful.

    D. Whatever the underlying causes of Africa's economic sluggishness, the current problem Africa faces is to play the hand it has been dealt by history. Issues of geography and climate (or a colonialist past) shape the directions that can be chosen but do not dictate the outcomes.

Suggested Readings:

Bloom and Sachs, "Geography, Demography, and Economic Growth in Africa."

Ndulu, et al., *Challenges of African Growth: Opportunities, Constraints and Strategic Directions.*

Zachary, "Trends: Africa Overreaches."

Questions to Consider:

1. What is the "poverty trap" explanation for slow economic development? Why is it viewed as a less plausible explanation now than it was a few decades ago?

2. To what extent can the geographic and climatic explanations account for Africa's pattern of slow economic growth?

Lecture Nineteen—Transcript
Africa's Geography and History

Since the Industrial Revolution about 200 years ago, sub-Saharan Africa has been both the lowest-income part of the world economy and the slowest-growing part of the world economy. Back around 1820, sub-Saharan Africa had a level of per capita GDP that was about one-third of that of the highest income region of the world, which was then Western Europe. But in the two centuries since then, in the high-income countries, the Industrial Revolution happened, then lots of other things, like mass education and the rise of science and technology. Their economies evolved from agriculture, to manufacturing, and then to services, and now information. And for a lot of that time, a lot of Africa's economy went almost nowhere.

By the start of the 21st century, per capita GDP in Africa was about one-twentieth that of the high-income countries of the world. It's hard to compare standards of living over time, because technology is so different over time, but measured roughly by per capita GDP, the standard of living in Africa in the early 21st century is similar to what Western Europe had in about 1820. If you look back over time, this enormous divergence didn't happen all at once. The growth rate of Africa's economy was steadily worse over just about every sustained period of time in the last couple of centuries.

Maybe the best sustained period for Africa was the quarter century or so after World War II, but in fact, everywhere in the world economy did pretty well at that time. And in relative terms, Africa's economy continued to fall behind during that period, as well. There were lots of predictions that when Africa threw off the oppression and exploitation of colonial rule in the 1950s and 1960s, we'd really see the economies take off then, but it didn't happen. Measured by per capita GDP, Africa was actually perhaps slightly less well off—certainly no better off—in the early 2000s than it had been 30 years earlier.

There is a bloodless economic way of saying this—"measured by per capita GDP"—but remember that per capita GDP is correlated with a lot of the basic good stuff of life. When the average person in the poorest region is not doing any better, may even be getting poorer in some absolute terms. It means hungry people are even more hungry. In this lecture, I want to give some sense of the region of sub-Saharan Africa with basics, like population, and GDP, and per capita

©2008 The Teaching Company.

GDP. I also want to introduce what seems to me a really interesting fact about this region over the last few decades: Even though the economy has performed badly, some other measures of well-being, like education and some measures of health, have made real gains.

This is an interesting case where improvements in human well-being were not being so well tracked by a growing economy. We will then explore a particular set of reasons why economic growth has been so lacking in this region over such a long period of time. The very long-term pattern of slow growth in Africa is not about government policies [in] this decade or last decade; instead, they are reasons rooted in geography and climate. Then, in the next lecture, we will examine the current economic situation in Africa. We will look at the spurt of growth Africa's economy has had in the mid-2000s and discuss some policy steps for the future.

I want to follow convention here by focusing this lecture on sub-Saharan Africa, not on North Africa, which means leaving out the parts of Africa in the Middle East, like Algeria, and Egypt, and Libya. It is hard enough to do sub-Saharan Africa in any coherent way. The [region] of sub-Saharan Africa consists of 48 countries from Angola, Benin, and Botswana to Zaire [Democratic Republic of the Congo], Zambia, and Zimbabwe. In population, they range from nine countries which have 1 million people or less—that would be Cape Verde, Comoros, Equatorial Guinea, Gabon, Mauritius, Mayotte, São Tomé and Príncipe, Seychelles, and Swaziland—four countries in Africa that have more than 40 million people as of 2008. That includes South Africa, the Democratic Republic of the Congo (which used to be Zaire), Ethiopia, and by far the largest-population country of Africa, Nigeria, which has 145 million people. Clearly, there are extraordinary variations across the continent in the population size of countries and in the physical size of the countries. Nine of Africa's 48 countries are larger geographically than the large-population Nigeria. For example, Mali is 10% larger than Nigeria but has a population only about one-tenth as large.

I'll take sort of an arbitrary list here. Let's take the countries with population over 30 million. In order of size, biggest to smallest in population, that would be Nigeria, Ethiopia, Democratic Republic of the Congo, South Africa, Tanzania, Kenya, Sudan, and Uganda. These eight countries are about 60% of all the people in sub-Saharan Africa. And South Africa in this group stands out as the far, far richer and larger economy than the others. Almost one-third of the GDP of all of sub-Saharan Africa is in South Africa, those 47 million inhabitants of South Africa. The other two-thirds of the GDP of sub-Saharan Africa is the other 740 million people living on the continent.

Other than South Africa, the total size of the remaining economies of the other 47 countries with their 740 million people is roughly equal to the total size of a single middle-income economy like South Korea. If you take the basic measure of economic well-being, GDP divided by population, in the United States, the figure is about $42,000 in 2006. In Africa, it is about $1,700. That's a multiple of about 25. If you leave out relatively rich South Africa and just look at the other 47 nations, then per capita GDP would be about $1,270 per person, and that would be a multiple of 33 compared to the U.S. per capita GDP. Even after adjusting for the fact that economic statistics don't capture everything, because a lot of stuff is very cheap in these countries, the standard of living in sub-Saharan Africa is typically less than, say, 5% of the U.S. average, and that's the average for sub-Saharan Africa. Many people are poorer than the average, of course.

Per capita GDP in sub-Saharan Africa barely moved from the early 1970s up to the early 2000s, over a period of three decades. That is to say that the overall economy just grew barely enough to keep up with population. If you look at annual% change in per capita GDP, what you see is a lot of years, it's negative; a lot of years, it's positive. We've talked in earlier lectures about how East Asia took off, how China took off, and how India is now taking off. But Africa is not seeing anything like that. What we need to think about with Africa's economy is that they are the poorest people in the world, and they've been stuck at the same level for a long, long time.

The standard measure of poverty developed by the World Bank and now very widely used is to say what people are living on less than $1 a day per person. If you think of a family of four, that would be $4 a day. Over a year, that would be about $1,400 in a year. That is not very much income. It's basically determined by what's needed for physical subsistence. For comparison, the official U.S. government poverty line for a family of three in the late 2000s is about $13 per day per person.

In 1990, 47% of Africa's population was below that paltry $1-a-day poverty line. By 2004, it was still 41% of Africa's population below $1 a day. As other parts of the world economy, like China, and India, and East Asia, have grown, it means the problem of poverty is more and more concentrated in Africa. In 1981, for example, Africa had about one-tenth of everyone in the world who was under that $1-a-day poverty line. By 1990, a decade later, Africa had about one-fifth of everyone in the world under the $1-a-day poverty line. And by 2004, Africa had almost one-third of everyone in the world under the $1-a-day poverty line.

Of course, when talking about standard of living, it's important to talk about more than just economics. Standard of living includes not just income but your health, and education, and other factors. Nobel laureate economist Amartya Sen has argued for what he calls the "capabilities approach" to thinking about poverty. That is, don't just think about the income you get, but think about your capabilities are able to be exercised because you have education, and health, and other factors.

To give a sense of the potential importance of a capabilities approach, in the United States, life expectancy rose in the 20th century from about 45 years in 1900 to about 75 years in 2000. Per capita GDP over this time went up by a factor of roughly 5. So here is a question: [What] if you had to choose what's more important to your standard of living—income multiplying by 5 or 30 more years of life? If you are an economist, of course, you're willing to put a value on additional years of human life. It turns out that, roughly speaking, for a lot of people, those are equally valuable. Of course, in the U.S. context, those two went together, so the gain in the true standard of living in the United States was much greater than a focus on income alone would have shown. Across much of Africa, they've had large gains in certain indicators of health and education over time, but they really haven't seen the economic equivalent payoff yet.

Life expectancy and infant mortality are two statistics often used for rough comparisons of health over time. Life expectancy in sub-Saharan Africa was growing for a time in the 1970s and 1980s, but by 2005, life expectancy in Africa is only about 50 years. It has been flat and sinking, largely because of the AIDS epidemic and wars across the continent. Infant mortality remains quite high across

Africa (about 50 or 60 deaths per 1,000 births), even in countries that are doing relatively well, like South Africa, Sudan, Ghana, and Kenya. There are other countries which have 100 deaths or more for every 1,000 births. Nigeria and the Democratic Republic of Congo would be examples. The average for the sub-Saharan Africa region is about 90 infant deaths for every 1,000 births, and infant mortality in a developed economy like the United States is going to be less than one-tenth of that level, maybe 5 to 7 per 1,000 births. The levels in Africa look terribly bad, but it's worth noting that actually, they are vastly better than a few decades ago. In many countries, rates of infant mortality have dropped by one-third or one-half over the last few decades. There have been substantial gains, even if the levels now existing look distressingly large.

Similarly, Africa's education levels remain low by world standards, but there has been a real increase in recent decades. I should say that if you look at school enrollment numbers for countries in Africa, it's always a little hard to interpret them. Here is the problem: They calculate the enrollment number by taking the total number of kids in, say, primary school and then dividing by the total number of kids in that age bracket who should be in primary school. That may sound fairly simple, but in a lot of low-income countries, there might be a lot of teenagers who are still getting through primary school. When you take the total number of students in primary school and you divide by the number of kids in, say, the 5 to 11 age bracket, the enrollment rate you can get for primary school might be above 100%. When you see these numbers, you don't always know quite what you're seeing.

However, across the sub-Saharan Africa region, the enrollment rate in primary school is about 93%, and that, of course, includes these older students, and there is pretty good balance between the genders, among both boys and girls. This is one area where colonialism in Africa left an especially terrible legacy. There's really no tradition of mass education, and only recently has this problem been repaired. There have been enormous increases in education across Africa from the late 1990s and into the 2000s. There are still big issues in the next step—that is, moving kids from primary to secondary school and then on to higher education. But around the world, that has been a common pattern. A country first has to start with mass universal education at the primary level, and then it develops additional education levels as the number of people ready to use those levels increases.

I hope that at this point, you have some basic perspectives in mind—Africa's long-term poverty, a sense of some of the most populous countries in the region, how poor the region is, its economic stagnation over a number of decades up through the early 2000s, and some real gains in certain measures of health and education, even if the levels still look very low by standards of high-income countries. A fundamental question, then: Why has Africa's economy lagged? The standard story for a long time about Africa's economy was sometimes called the "poverty trap," and the poverty trap argument starts off like this: What makes an economy grow? Presumably, it's investment in the future, and I'm including investment in people, like education and health, and investment in physical capital, and investment in new technology. It doesn't need to be brand-new, breakthrough technology, but new ways of doing things, and producing things, and updating things. All of this kind of investment, by its nature, means deferring present income or consumption so that you can produce more in the future.

If you are in a situation where you are very, very poor, and you're just trying to get enough nutrition to live, it might be kind of hard to think about these kinds of investments. People living at subsistence are going to find it hard to have a high savings rate, and so a country with a lot of people at subsistence may not be able to save very much. People at subsistence are going to need their children to work in the field. They won't have much money to support schools or invest in education. The result is that when you are low income, it's hard to save, broadly understood, and your country can end up trapped in poverty as a result.

The policy implication of this poverty trap approach is that these countries need investment capital: They need foreign aid, investment from abroad, and financial assistance, in one way or another, so that they can fund the infrastructure, and equipment, and machinery, and schools and give them kind of a jumpstart out of the poverty trap. And a few decades ago, you would have heard this poverty trap argument a lot. But while the poverty trap argument sounds plausible, over the last few decades, a number of countries have actually broken out of the poverty trap. Some countries that were very, very poor, at the subsistence level in, say, 1960 or so—and I'm thinking here of East Asian nations, like South Korea, or China, or some of these others—have determined that they can get out of the poverty trap over time. They found rapid sources of growth, and now, of course, India has found a way out, as well.

Of course, if you go back further in history, every country that has now developed and found a way to break out of the poverty trap at some point suggests the trap may not be totally inflexible. Moreover, a lot of these very poor countries did manage to have rates of investment that were fairly high. We talked about how countries in East Asia and China have sustained some of the world's highest savings rates even when their economies were fairly low income. Conversely, high-income countries, like the United States, have sometimes had pretty low savings rates.

Many low-income countries have managed to jumpstart programs of mass education, including the United States early in its economic history and, indeed, some African nations in the last decade or so. The problem here, a lot of the time, is not the level of investment, but it is that the investment is producing so little return. You can get capital from domestic savings or foreign or private investors, but it seems in a lot of African countries that capital investment goes down a rat hole. The savings, the skilled people of those economies are often fleeing these economies, rather than flowing into them and helping develop the economies of the future.

A prominent economist named Alexander Gerschenkron wrote, about 50 years ago, an essay on what he called the "advantages of backwardness," and that's a famous phrase to economists. He pointed out that if you are a low-income economy in a world of richer economies, you can draw on technology and skills developed elsewhere. And some countries have done this pretty aggressively; Japan, Korea, and others have aggressively sought out technical knowledge in other countries. China has encouraged outside management in financial skills, and African countries by and large have not done this.

The bottom line here is that there is some truth in the poverty trap. Clearly, it's harder to get going when you're already poor; pulling yourself up by your own bootstraps is uncomfortable and difficult, and you're fighting against what feels like the basic force of gravity. But when it seems like almost every other region of the world has moved past a certain stage of development and that sub-Saharan

Africa has not done so, the problem is to explain what's different about Africa and what has stayed different to keep Africa poor and low income over the last couple of centuries.

The development of Africa's economy has suffered over the decades from its geographic and climatic inheritance, which has hindered growth in a number of ways. When I was talking about the poverty trap, I said something that bears a little more examination. I was saying that growth comes from education, investment, technology, investment in the future, and that is fairly true for high-income countries, but it might not be equally true for some low-income countries.

It's clear that in a lot of places around the world, economic growth has been shaped by patterns of geography and climate, and these patterns have been quite disadvantageous for Africa. Let's think about geography, for example, and how it affects transportation costs. Economies are sort of about specialization and trade, and in early stages of economic development, water transportation has often played a really important role. In fact, if you think about it, economies typically revolve around cities or ports where trade takes place. They're often, say, at the mouth of a river, where there is a bay. This serves as cheap transportation into the country, going up and down the river, and then the bay serves as transportation between different areas. You get a population center around that port. Africa, however, doesn't have this advantage of cheap water transport. This has been known for a long time. In fact, Adam Smith talks about this in his famous book *The Wealth of Nations*, written back in 1776. Smith wrote:

> As by means of water-carriage, a more extensive market is opened to every sort of industry than what land-carriage alone can afford it, so it is upon the sea coast, and along the banks of navigable rivers, that industry of every kind naturally begins to subdivide and improve itself, and it is frequently not till a long time after that those improvements extend themselves to the inland parts of the country. ... There are in Africa none of those great inlets, such as the Baltic and Adriatic seas in Europe, the Mediterranean and Euxine seas [that was the word for the Black Sea] in both Europe and Asia, and the gulfs of Arabia, Persia, India,

Bengal, and Siam, in Asia, to carry maritime commerce into the interior parts of that great continent.

Western Europe has one-eighth the area of Africa in terms of land; it also has a coastline that is 50% longer than the coastline of Africa, because Western Europe's coastline wiggles and wiggles and wiggles through all these little bays and different areas. Africa's coastline is fairly smooth. All the major rivers in Africa—the Nile, the Congo, the Zambezi—have large waterfalls as they approach the coastline. They are very limited in their ability for big ships to travel in and out of the continent. You need to portage the freight around the waterfall in one way or another.

In many, many areas around the world, people have tended to live near the coast and near the rivers, and that's how markets have developed. Africa has the lowest share of population living near water, and it doesn't have these giant port cities. For example, in Africa, 19% of the population lives near a navigable river or coast. In the United States, 67% of the population lives near a navigable river or coast. In Western Europe, it's 89% of the population. When you don't have rivers and ports, you don't have cheap water transportation, you don't have groupings of great trading cities, and it makes it hard for an economy to take off.

For the world as a whole, if you look at temperate areas within 100 kilometers of the ocean, what you find is that region of the world—temperate areas within 100 kilometers of the ocean or a navigable waterway that can reach the ocean—is 8% of the world's land area, but it's 23% of the world's population and 53% of the world's GDP. When you have this lack of port cities, it also contributes to other kinds of fragmentation. Groups aren't trading with each other inside the countries; there isn't trade between countries. Small countries and different ethnic and religious and language groups don't bump into each other in the same ways. It keeps people separate. These separate identities can also be a hindrance to development, especially if they lead to civil strife or war, and of course, war makes it really hard for an economy to function.

Another difficulty is climate and its effect on technological progress. A tropical climate tends to have certain economic consequences. Look around the world; poverty is, in general, pretty close to the equator. Wealthier nations tend to be farther away from the equator, with of course, a few exceptions. Even within Africa, the high-

©2008 The Teaching Company.

income countries are the southern ones, like South Africa. If you look in South America, the higher income countries are Argentina and Chile, far to the south. Because there are high temperatures at the equator in Africa, people tend to live away from the coast, where it would be hot, and up in the mountain highlands, which of course, made transportation costs for products even tougher.

In an equatorial zone, there tends to be less food production. A temperate climate with a winter has various advantages over a tropical climate. Winter kills bugs and pests; it breaks up soil; it helps fertilize the soil. A cycle of freeze, and melt, and water flow makes the soil much more fertile. Plants tend to grow better when it is warm in the day and cool at night, not when it is warm in the day and the night. Areas that are right near the equator tend to have lower overall rainfall, especially in coastal areas, and greater heat. The summer in temperate areas actually has longer days. [Elsewhere,] days get longer and shorter; in the winter, the days are shorter, but around the equator, all the days are roughly the same length, and that doesn't actually help growth very much. Around the equator, there tend to be seasons of very heavy rains and very dry weather, which tends to bleach out the soil. There are a lot of reasons why crops don't grow as well around the equator as they would in more temperate areas.

Right around the equator, there also tends to be more disease. Malaria, for example, probably causes something like a million deaths every year and tens of millions of cases where some people get it over and over. The social and economic costs are extraordinarily high and, of course, discourage outsiders from visiting or investing. It is very difficult to think about how you deal with malaria because mosquitoes evolve very quickly, and they keep developing more virulent strains of the disease. HIV/AIDS is bad in itself, but it also brings other opportunistic infections, like tuberculosis, and yellow fever, and hookworm, and river blindness. All of those things in tropical climates are much worse than they are in temperate zones.

Also, there is less spillover of technological progress into equatorial regions. Technology that works well in temperate zones often doesn't transfer well to tropical areas. The green revolution, for example, did golden rice, a vitamin-subsidized rice. That was really good for Asia, but there haven't been similar improvements in things like cassava, and taro, and groundnuts, and yams, and other crops that are really well-suited to Africa.

I don't think we do the same research on malaria and other diseases that affect Africa compared to what we would do if those affected high-income countries. In fact, if you just do a map of the world and you note each country's latitude, you can actually predict its GDP surprisingly well. Is this argument about geography and growth just a cop-out? When I raise these kinds of arguments about geography and climate in front of audiences that have a large contingent of people from Africa, I sometimes get a really negative answer. In a way, I think sometimes people feel like I'm insulting their country or as if these arguments are sort of a cover-up for real problems.

I don't want to sort of unpack all these arguments in full here, but here are just a few thoughts: In the admittedly academic world where I live, facts and statistical connections, like the cheapness of water transport and problems of malaria, are not insults; they're just facts. It's also true, of course, that there are many difficulties that plague the economies of Africa. For example, the history of colonialism hasn't helped a whole lot.

Colonialism was politically indefensible. It denied people a voice in their government, and it often came with a nasty flavoring of outright racism. In economic terms, it didn't really help countries build the basics of long-term growth, like education, and investment, or an equal rule of law. It didn't develop local banks and business expertise or provide an environment where businesses could grow. I am emphatically not arguing that the only thing wrong with Africa was climate, but I would point out for those enamored of the colonialism explanation, that Africa had slow growth for decades before colonialism, and it has had slow growth for decades since colonialism. Africa had slow growth in countries where colonialism was more powerful and in countries where colonialism was less powerful. The richest country in Africa, South Africa, was a colony; so were many of the poorest countries in Africa. Colonialism existed all around the world in different ways, in India and in South America, in different ways, and it has been pushed aside lots of other places.

Colonialism also came in different levels of destructiveness. For example, Belgium's colonialism in the Congo was really egregious. Britain's version in South Africa or India, while not so great, did at least leave behind a rule of law, and independent judges, and some tradition of free speech, sort of something to build on. I'm not trying to convince anyone here that colonialism is good; I'm only trying to say that, in economic terms, its effects are more varied, and they aren't permanently determining what happens in the future. And, of course, the United States was a colony for a time, too.

Some economic statistical studies, admittedly imprecise ones, suggest that more of Africa's economic sluggishness is due to factors like geography and climate than to any issue of economic policy, regardless of who was running the government at the time. Looking ahead, whatever the underlying causes of Africa's economic sluggishness, the current problem Africa faces is that it has to play the hand it has been dealt by history. Colonialism has been gone for a half century or more in most African countries. In many of those countries, the experience with self-government has not been one of enlightened support for civil liberties, and economic liberties, and building a decent economy.

As we will talk about in a later lecture, foreign aid hasn't fixed the problem in the last 50 years. It isn't likely to fix it in the near future either. The current difficulty for Africa is that it has to ramp up education levels and health levels and connect through the rest of the world. It needs to find an economic environment where firms can exist, where they can hire and innovate. It needs to find technology that works, communications that work; it needs to shift away from relying on a few minerals and cash crops. In the next lecture, we will take a look at all these policy difficulties and policy challenges in more detail.

Lecture Twenty
Time for Optimism on Africa?

Scope:

Predictions that Africa's economy is poised to take off have been fairly common over the last few decades—and consistently wrong. However, Africa's economy has seen a burst of moderate growth in the mid-2000s. Some of the major impediments to growth that existed several decades ago have been greatly reduced: Africa has lower inflation, decreased debt, fewer price controls, more democracy, and greater involvement with the global economy. Nonetheless, a lengthy agenda remains if Africa is to become a place where saving, investment, and economic growth can be sustained. Some of the major challenges include beginning work on continent-wide systems of electrical power and highways, along with reducing the burdensome regulatory requirements that still hamper private-sector businesses.

Outline

I. Optimistic statements about Africa's economic future over the last several decades have often turned out to be wrong. But in the mid-2000s, Africa has seen some positive and potentially enduring economic news.

    A. Government reports about Africa's economic development over time seem to feel obliged to imply or predict that economic success is right around the corner. For several decades now, such predictions have failed to come true.

    B. Since the late 1990s, however, GDP growth for Africa as a whole has been in the range of 5 to 6% per year. By the mid-2000s, growth in per capita GDP was often 3 to 4% per year. And, of course, some countries consistently outperformed these averages. Oil exports explain only a modest part of this economic success.

II. Africa has historically had low rates of saving and investment and low rates of return on investment. These factors reinforce each other; that is, low returns on past investment discourage future investment.

III. The advances in Africa's economy can be partially attributed to improvements along some basic dimensions: less inflation, reduced debt problems, fewer price controls, lower incidence of war, and greater interactions with the global economy.

    A. Sub-Saharan Africa has had considerable success in bringing down rates of inflation in recent decades. In the 1980s and the first half of the 1990s, annual inflation rates of 20% per year and more were common. By the mid-2000s, typical inflation rates were in the high single digits.

    B. Many governments of Africa had accumulated enormous debts by the mid-1990s; at that time, total government debt was roughly equal to the GDP of sub-Saharan Africa. Government interest payments alone were often 20% of government spending or more. But faster economic growth has allowed debt repayment for some countries, and debts have been forgiven in other countries. By the late 2000s, debt was down to 40% of Africa's GDP and falling.

    C. African countries made substantial progress in the 1990s on reducing the number of price controls in their economies. Few governments in Africa have truly let go of the market yet, but the move toward greater market freedom has been real.

    D. Some countries in Africa, such as Sudan and Zimbabwe, have been torn with discord and civil war, which are bad news for economic growth. But looking at broad trends, civil discord in Africa has declined over recent decades, and democracy seems to be on the rise.

    E. Export-to-GDP ratios didn't move much for Africa from the 1960s up through the mid-1990s. But in recent years, Africa has begun to participate to a greater extent in the world economy. In addition, Africa is experiencing substantial inflows of financial capital from both private investors and emigrants now working elsewhere around the world.

IV. Despite recent economic boosts, Africa still faces many challenges.

    A. It's hard to run a developing economy without a consistent supply of electrical power. Africa has copious energy resources, but they are extremely undeveloped. As a result, firms pay much higher costs, and households have to rely on firewood and kerosene. A continent-wide program to increase electrical-generating capacity, conducted over five to eight years, could pay off in substantially higher rates of economic growth.

B. The lack of water transportation routes has contributed to the dispersion of population and economic activity in Africa. Roads are a problem, too, with 40 to 50% of firms in Africa reporting that transportation is a severe constraint on doing business. In landlocked countries of Africa, freight costs can be one-third or more of the cost of delivering a product outside the country.

C. The ability to start and operate a business depends on a number of small components, such as the ease of obtaining licenses, registering property, getting a loan, paying taxes, and so on. In turn, many of these activities depend on the smooth functioning of government. Africa's economy lags well behind other regions in the ease of doing business, suggesting a need for systematic and widespread reform.

D. In general, African countries need to increase taxes (which they have begun to do in the last decade or so) and simplify their tax-collection mechanisms. The higher taxes are needed for infrastructure investments and to keep government debt problems under control.

E. Agriculture is still the primary sector of output in most African economies and the occupation of most people. Raising productivity in this sector is essential. The important steps here include using available technologies that are well-suited to Africa and avoiding government policies that are biased against agriculture.

V. Africa is not as politically or economically important now as it was a few decades ago. Even in humanitarian terms, international assistance is increasingly directed elsewhere in the world, where it seems likely to have the most effect. Growth in Africa's economy will ultimately depend on the efforts of the African people and nations themselves.

Suggested Readings:

International Monetary Fund, *Regional Economic Outlook: Sub-Saharan Africa.*

Ndulu, et al., *Challenges of African Growth: Opportunities, Constraints and Strategic Directions.*

Questions to Consider:

1. Do you think Africa's spurt of growth in the mid-2000s is sustainable?

2. What policies seem most important in creating sustainable and rapid growth for Africa in the future?

Lecture Twenty—Transcript
Time for Optimism on Africa?

Reading economic reports about Africa's economic development over time can feel a little odd, because many of the reports seem to feel obliged to imply or predict that economic success is right around the corner, and such predictions have often failed to come true. One prominent development economist named William Easterly, who for many years worked at the World Bank, a few years ago collected examples of premature optimism from a series of World Bank reports. For example, there was a 1981 World Bank report called "Accelerated Development in Sub-Saharan Africa," and I quote: "Policy action and foreign assistance … will surely work together to build a continent that shows real gains in both development and income in the near future." Or from a 1986 World Bank report, "Financing Growth with Adjustment in Sub-Saharan Africa": "Progress is clearly underway. Especially in the past two years, more countries have started to act, and the changes they're making go deeper than before." A 1989 World Bank report, "Sub-Saharan Africa: From Crisis to Sustainable Growth": "Since the mid-1980s, Africa has seen important changes in policies and in economic performance." From a 1994 World Bank report, "Adjustment in Africa": "African countries have made great strides in improving policies and restoring growth." From a 2000 World Bank report, "Can Africa Claim the 21st Century?": "Since the mid-1990s, there have been signs that better economic management has started to pay off."

I could multiply these kinds of examples, but you get the point. That last statement was actually sort of true, because there were some signs of growth, but remember that, overall, these reports are [written] during a time period when average standard of living measured by per capita GDP is stagnant or diminishing across much of Africa. There doesn't seem to be any need in this kind of writing to figure out: Why did I make those poor predictions before, and what happened to those earlier predictions after all? At least optimism is fundamentally well meant, I think. Maybe it's even a necessary emotional reaction to discussing the situation of people with such low incomes and such grim statistics on health and education. But at some point, it also feels a little bit like the triumph of hope over experience.

But with all those warnings in place, here I go again, kind of like a country-music song where you keep falling for the same old line. I think economic growth is starting in Africa. Since the late 1990s, GDP growth for Africa as a whole has often been in the range of 5 or 6% a year. Population is also growing in Africa, so some of that growth is just keeping up with population. But by the mid-2000s, growth in per capita GDP (that is, taking population into account) was often 3 or 4% a year across the countries of sub-Saharan Africa. Of course, this average lumps together some disastrous economies with some that are doing pretty well. The four-star disaster in the first decade of the 2000s is Zimbabwe, where the economy shrunk by maybe 40% from 2000 to 2007. By December 2007, inflation in Zimbabwe was at 100,000% per year. That is not 100%, not 1,000%, but 100,000%, and the trends seem to be up. Basically, the Reserve Bank of Zimbabwe, the central bank, was just printing money for subsidies to one and all.

On the other side, some countries were consistently outperforming the average. In 1960, there were only two countries in sub-Saharan Africa that would have been classified as middle income for the world as a whole; they were South Africa and Mauritius. Now, 13 of the 48 countries in sub-Saharan Africa are in that category. Those 13 countries have about 13% of the total population of the region, but they produce two-thirds of Africa's GDP. Seventeen other countries out of the 48 countries in the region, although they're still classified as low income, have actually had annual growth rates above 5% for more than a decade, from the mid- or late 1990s into the later part of the 2000s.

Oil exports from some countries in Africa explain only a modest part of this economic success. Growth started going up for many of these countries in the mid- and late 1990s, when oil prices weren't rising. More recently, from 2005 to 2007, the GDP of the oil exporters in Africa was growing faster, at about 7 to 8% a year, but the GDP of non-oil exporters was still growing on average about 5 or 6% a year. This period from the late 1990s to the mid-2000s has been the strongest economic growth Africa has experienced in about 40 years, really going back to the 1960s.

What is fundamentally needed to keep this growth going, and to spread it, and to accelerate it? The route to economic growth has a lot of different steps. Africa has historically had low rates of saving and investment and low rates of return on investment (when it happened). These factors reinforce each other. That is, the low returns on past investment discourage future investment. A standard measure of savings in an economy that we've used over and over in these lectures is gross savings. It includes household saving, business saving, and government saving, if the government runs a surplus.

In Africa, historically, through the 1980s and 1990s, often gross saving was only about 15% of GDP per year. Even the low-saving United States saves more like 15 or 20% of GDP, and of course, East Asia, Japan, and China are 30% of GDP and up. In the last 10 years, this gross saving is up some in Africa, but the savings has been mainly due to the oil-exporting countries saving so much more. Nigeria, Angola, Chad, and a few others that export a lot of oil were saving 40% of GDP from 2005 to 2007. But if you look at the oil-importing countries and if you leave out South Africa (which is always an outlier in these statistics), they're saving kind of 13, 14, 15% of GDP, as usual. Now, these savings statistics may be a little misleading. When you've got people living in poor agricultural settings, they may save in non-monetary forms. Maybe they could save in the form of more cattle or developing certain fields, but nonetheless, however you cut it, the savings rate is low.

One study estimated that if Africa wanted to sustain a 7% annual growth rate in GDP, it needs to be saving and investing more like 25% of GDP. But the key here is not the poverty trap argument we discussed in the previous lecture, that it's impossible for low-income countries to save. Lots of low-income countries, like China and East Asia, have had high rates of saving. The problem in Africa is that it's not worth saving because there has been no return on investment. Low return on investment is maybe the worst economic problem in Africa. In fact, it has been frighteningly close to a zero percent overall return on investment from the 1970s up to about 2000.

One result, a study back in the 1990s, found that Africans at that time held about 40% of their wealth outside the region of Africa. They were looking for safety and better returns elsewhere. For comparison, if you look at Latin America, only about 10% of the wealth of that region is held outside the region. In East Asia, only about 6% of the wealth is held outside that region. This idea of thinking about things in terms of return on investment is, of course, a peculiar economist-oriented way of looking at things. But if businesses can't invest, and earn profits, and expand, economies aren't going to grow over time. I'm not making any big ideological statement here about the power of free markets or anything like that. It's just a fact. A lot of the difficulty has been because what scarce investment capital there was poured into sinkhole state-owned firms across the continent of Africa. Costs of transportation, energy, maintenance, operating costs are really very high in Africa compared to those in other low-income parts of the world. Africa needs to create a climate where investment can at least, on average, reap gains.

This leaves us with two questions: What has gone right in Africa since the mid- or late 1990s that has encouraged the moderate surge of growth we've seen? And the next question is: Given that Africa still has a ton of economic challenges, what are the main challenges that might be a useful focus in the next 5 or 10 years?

Africa's economy has improved in part because it has improved along some basic dimensions: less inflation, reduced debt, fewer price controls, less war, and broader interactions with the global economy. I want to talk about those in turn.

Sub-Saharan Africa has had considerable success in bringing down rates of inflation over recent decades. In the 1980s and first half of the 1990s, annual inflation rates of 20% a year and more were common across sub-Saharan Africa, and there were some examples of hyperinflation. But by the mid-2000s, typical inflation rates across Africa were only in the high single digits, even though the prices of some goods, like food and energy, were rising a lot. From a global point of view, this isn't perfect, but it's really pretty good. Essentially, it means inflation is not the big determining issue ruining the possibilities for economic growth. It seems fair to say, most African nations have come to realize inflation doesn't really help anyone in the long run, and they don't want it to come back.

Many governments of Africa accumulated enormous debts by the mid-1990s. At that time, total government debt was roughly equal to the GDP of sub-Saharan Africa. Government interest payments alone were often 20% of government spending or more; maybe 6% of GDP was just going to interest payments. It was a continual drain on these economies. In effect, every time their economy or their government did something good, a big chunk of the gains from that, the economic benefit, went off to pay the debts from the past. But that situation has changed. For some countries, the more rapid economic growth has allowed debt repayment to proceed. For other countries, various international agreements and World Bank programs have led to debts being forgiven. By the late 2000s, debt in Africa was down to 40% of Africa's GDP and falling. In fact, the International Monetary Fund said in a 2007 report that the challenge was no longer to reduce Africa's debts but just to make sure that the debts didn't rise again.

African countries have also made substantial progress in reducing the number of price controls in their economies. One sample of 29 of the larger African economies in the mid-1980s found 26 of the 29 had extensive price controls, and that was defined in this survey as controls on 26 or more goods. By the mid-1990s, only 9 of those countries had no price controls at all, but another 14 had controls on only a few goods. The level of price controls was dropping quite a bit. Still, there is, across Africa, a fair amount of interference in markets. While controlling only a few goods, they tend to be big, important ones, like petroleum or some countries' major agricultural products. And there are still, of course, licenses, and fees, and restrictions, and so on, but I do think one reason economic growth started doing better in Africa in the mid-1990s (and then stepped up further in the 2000s) is that governments weren't as active in setting restrictive rules over all the different prices.

Some countries in Africa have been torn with discord and civil war, like the Rwanda genocide of the mid-'90s, or the Darfur area of western Sudan, or Zimbabwe under the dictatorship of Robert Mugabe. Looking at broad trends, though, the amount of civil discord in Africa has actually declined in recent decades. If you doubt this, you may need to cast your mind back to remember some of the problems in the past. Do you remember Idi Amin in Uganda? Do you remember Jean-Bédel Bokassa and the Central African Empire? We are talking about places where there wasn't just slaughter of civilians, but there were credible accusations of personal cannibalism going on.

Mozambique's civil war from 1974 up to 1992 was a horrible event, Rwanda's genocide in 1994, and Chad, and Sierra Leone, and Senegal, and others had violent, terrible wars through the '70s, and '80s, and into the '90s. But after a lot of changes happened in the early 1990s, it would now be fair to say that 31 out of the 48 countries in sub-Saharan Africa can be classified as democracies. They may be young democracies, they may be fragile democracies, but they are democracies.

It's true that we read a lot about the countries with conflicts, but even in the first decade of the 2000s, fatalities from political violence are down in Africa. Battle deaths are down, for example. There were 15 countries with armed conflicts in Africa in the year 2000. By 2007, there were only five countries with armed conflicts. This matters a lot for making it worthwhile for people and businesses to save, and invest, and plan for the future. Being in the middle of a war is never good for economic growth.

And the last major change is increased commerce with the world economy. The export-to-GDP ratio in Africa was typically around 25% of GDP from the 1960s up through the early 1990s. This is really a very low level of trade when you are talking about small economies with lots of close neighbors. They weren't trading very much with each other or with the rest of the world. Remember, the rest of the world over this time is seeing a rise in the export-to-GDP ratio. Remember that from 1950 up to the present, the export-to-GDP ratio for the world was tripling or quadrupling over time, but in Africa, it wasn't. Since the mid-1990s, though, trade in Africa has drifted somewhat higher, reaching about 35% of GDP by 2006.

High prices for oil and natural resources in the mid-2000s are driving part of this increasing trade, and some economies in Africa are really pretty dependent on these prices of oil and natural resources. In the long term, this dependence may not be a great thing, as we discussed at some length in the lecture on the Middle East, but it does offer an opportunity, if countries of Africa can try and seize that opportunity. For other countries, the growth in trade has happened in manufacturing and agricultural exports and generally being looked at as a possible part of the global chain of production, where some work could be done in Africa, and then things could be shipped to other places.

There has also been a large increase in financial inflows to Africa. U.S. private capital flows to Africa quadrupled from 2000 to 2007, reaching $50 billion a year at that point. This is not large by world standards, but it's huge by African standards. In fact, private money flowing into Africa has now outstripped total foreign aid going to Africa, although of course, these go to different purposes. It's true that most of the private financial capital has mainly gone to a few countries: South Africa, Nigeria, some to Ghana, Kenya, Uganda, a few more. Still, there is now some talk in financial circles, toward the tail end of the first decade of the 2000s, that Africa, of all places, could be the next big destination for foreign investment. Some people say that the situation isn't all that different from the flow of foreign investment that started going into East Asia in the 1980s. Now, you might have some worry there. You might worry about what if too much comes in, what if you have a sudden stop, like East Asia? And that's a real worry, but it's not a worry Africa has ever had to face before, a worry of too much money coming in too quickly.

There are also big inflows of capital being sent home by migrants who left Africa and went other places. By 2004, remittances from migrants going back to Africa were about $160 billion a year, and that's more than double the official development aid. It's much larger than the private capital flows, as well. Migration has tradeoffs, of course, and we'll talk about them in detail in a later lecture. For example, you might lose skilled workers who go elsewhere to work. In many countries of Africa, as many as 30% of skilled professionals have left for Europe or for the United States. But one of the possible benefits of those skilled workers leaving is that their wages are so much higher after they emigrate that they can really help the economy by sending back these remittances. And these remittances are a lot less likely to dry up suddenly than, say, private financial capital, as well.

All of these factors taken together are giving Africa's economy, at long last, what looks like a genuine boost. Of course, a lot of challenges remain. You could write a long book on the economic problems of Africa. Here, what I want to do is focus on some of the big-picture thinking that's floating around among specialists in this area, sort of big, important ideas that, if implemented over the next 5 to 10 years, might have some potential to really transform Africa's growth.

First challenge might be to have good electrical power. It's really hard to run a developing economy without a consistent supply of electrical power. Africa has really copious energy resources, but they are extremely undeveloped, and affordable, reliable electricity is just a huge necessity for economic growth. The total electricity output of the 48 countries of sub-Saharan Africa is basically equal to the electrical output of the country of Spain by itself. Moreover, about 60% of Africa's total electrical output is one country, South Africa. If you look at the other 47 countries, their total electrical output is basically equal to the electrical output of one country, Argentina. This causes all sorts of problems for businesses. One study found, for example, that it takes 18 days to get connected to a power grid in China, but it takes six months to get connected in Zambia. In Kenya in 2007, the government put out a request that all businesses use electricity from 11:00 at night to 5:00 in the morning, when peak demand was lower. Imagine, you're asking all businesses to work all night.

There are lots of power outages across Africa. They're costly in themselves, and they also require firms to buy their own backup electrical-generating capacity, which is costly, too. There are lots of problems for households, too. Across Africa, only 24% of households have electricity. In the other low-income countries in the world, usually it's more like 40% of the people who have electricity. When you don't have electricity, what do you do instead? You do things like burn firewood, burn kerosene, and in fact, indoor air pollution from those burnings is a huge killer. It's one of the world's largest health problems. Also, burning firewood contributes to deforestation and erosion.

Africa has all kinds of potential for electrical power. There are huge hydropower reserves in some countries. There is an estimate that the continent now uses maybe 8% of the hydropower that it could use. Other parts of the continent, like Nigeria and Angola, have lots of oil and natural gas. South Africa and Botswana have lots of coal. There are parts of the continent that have some potential for geothermal energy. The real difficulty here is that there is no electrical grid. There is no way to get the electrical power from one place to another. There is no way to even send it across national borders. If you can't distribute the electricity, then you can't justify building big, efficient electrical-generating facilities, and you end up with firms using costly little diesel generators instead. There are a lot of plans to try and fix this situation, but the basic notion is that Africa needs an overall vision of how its electrical system will fit together. They will probably need private-sector participation for financial capital, and for management, and for technology, and the whole grouping of electrical output will need to be governed in some open way.

A lot of the current electrical utility companies are state-owned government monopolies. They are wildly inefficient, ranging from wasteful to outright corrupt, and they're not very accountable. But overall, if you could invest about $50 billion a year, maybe 7% of Africa's GDP, for about five to eight years, the study suggests you could maybe get reliable supplies for all the businesses in Africa and about 35% of households connected up, as well. One study said that if all of Africa could have an electrical supply as good as the country of Mauritius—which is not a high-income country—this alone could add 2 percentage points a year to long-term economic growth across Africa. It could just be an extraordinarily important step.

A similar big-picture idea is to focus on roads and transportation. Remember that one of the long-term problems for Africa's economic development has been the lack of water transportation routes, so population is dispersed, and economic activity is dispersed. Something like 40% of the population of Africa lives in landlocked countries. Roads are a real problem across Africa. Something like 40 to 50% of the firms in Africa report in surveys that transportation is a severe constraint on doing business.

Africa has lots of roads, maybe 2 million kilometers of roads, but typically, they're in terrible condition. Less than one-third of them are paved. They get worn out, and they never get fixed. In the landlocked countries of Africa, freight costs can be one-third or more of the cost of delivering some product outside the country, and it's not uncommon that theft and delays lead to a loss of 2 or 3% of any shipment going over land. I heard one story about a firm that occasionally ships cement by airfreight—which is just incredibly expensive because of the weight—because it was cheaper than trying to get it shipped by road across Africa.

A number of studies show that spending $1 on road maintenance in a lot of parts of Africa would save at least $2 or $3 on vehicle maintenance, and that doesn't even count the other economic gains from having good roads. The lack of roads really limits possibilities for trade within Africa, and that limits opportunities for developing larger firms across Africa [to] take advantage of economies of scale and build expertise.

One of the remarkable things about Africa is that there is a real lack of trade across the continent. For example, there is not much trade between South Africa and Nigeria. In fact, there's really not much trade between any two large cities you can name that are in different countries. Ideally, you would have a plan for something like the U.S. interstate highway system, a network of roads connecting Africa. One study estimated that a network of roads to connect the capitals of all 48 countries, together with connecting all cities of more than 500,000 people, would cost something like $20 billion total to build and then maybe $1 billion a year in maintenance after that. Some of that could be financed by governments or aid agencies. The building and construction could be run by private firms, and some sort of a construction effort like that would be a reasonable generator of local jobs and skills, too.

Another major step that could help development: For a few years now, the World Bank has been running a project on the ease of doing business in different countries, and they look at a variety of different [aspects of] how easy it is to start a business, like the cost of starting a business, the need for licenses, rules about employing workers, whether your property is secure, getting a bank loan, how easy it is to pay taxes and enforce contracts, how easy it is to export or import—all those kinds of factors.

In their 2008 report, they ranked 178 countries around the world. For high-income countries, the average rank was 22. For Eastern Europe, East Asia, Latin America, the average rank was around 80. The average rank for the countries of sub-Saharan Africa was 136. In other words, Africa's economy lags way behind other regions in the ease of doing business. A lot of changes in doing business aren't necessarily sexy or fun, but they matter just a huge amount. Kenya and Ghana, for example, have been doing a lot of reforms to make it easier for business to operate lately, and that's one of the reasons they've been getting foreign investment and their economies have been growing. There's a real need for systematic and widespread reform here. Have the government do necessary tasks, like enforcing contracts, registering property, collecting taxes. Do not get all mixed up in doing complicated licenses for everything. Focus on what government can do well, and make the rules function for everyone.

African countries, on average, need to increase their level of taxes. The tax take in the average African economy was about 16% of GDP in the 1990s, which is really a low amount by world standards. For example, if you compare the United States, and you count state, local, [and] federal government, the United States collects about one-third of GDP in taxes. By the later part of the 1990s, this has increased a little bit in Africa; it was collecting about 19% of GDP in taxes.

They need more revenue for two reasons. I just described these huge projects that need to be done, electricity and transportation. We've discussed needs for health and education. Sure, some of this can be financed by private investors or paid for with charges and fees, or maybe you can get some foreign aid money, but that isn't going to be enough to foot the bill. You need some extra tax money to make it work. Moreover, if taxes in Africa are about 19% of GDP on average, spending in Africa is about 24% of GDP. Those countries are still accumulating debt. It's not crazy amounts of debt like the bad old days, but you don't want to go back to the bad old days of heavy indebtedness either.

Some countries that export oil or natural resources should be sitting pretty in the late 2000s. They can use that revenue, and there's really no excuse for them going into debt at all. Many African countries, though, need to develop better tax systems with simpler and more straightforward methods. Instead of a million different fees and licenses, all of them with potential for bribery and confusion; instead of trying to just tax corporate profits at very high rates, it would be much better to have basic taxes, like a sales tax or a value-added tax, fairly low rates [that] everybody pays.

The last big area I wanted to talk about is reform of agriculture. Agriculture is still the primary sector of output in most African economies. At the end of the 20th century, something like three-quarters of Africans earn a living in the agricultural sector, and they produce something like one-third of GDP. In a way, this is sort of the pattern you expect in very low-income countries at a much earlier stage of development. I'm not going to do a lot of detail here on agriculture. There's a whole lecture on agriculture and food later on in this course, but here's a quick preview of a key fact: For most of the last three to four decades, the difficulty was that farmers in Africa didn't earn very much. They didn't earn very much partly because the price of food was low and falling over time and partly because the governments in these countries often put price controls on food to keep the city dwellers who bought food happy. With all those people working in farming not earning much, maybe the fundamental problem of farming in Africa was it didn't generate enough income. Farmers had to make a subsistence living.

Starting in 2005 or 2006 and on for several years after that, the price of food rose really dramatically all over the world. As a result, many farmers in Africa were getting a lot more income than ever before. The new problem is that the urban poor and countries that need to import food are having to pay a lot more in terms of higher food prices. The main problem for African agriculture used to be low prices leading to low incomes for farmers, but now the problem is high prices leading to a lack of affordability for food. Economists are always unhappy about something, aren't we?

From the long-run economic view, the story with agriculture is simple enough. Africa needs to get productivity up in agriculture. That will raise incomes. It will generate more food, and it will start the process of sectoral adjustment, where the country doesn't need as many farmers, and those folks can begin to work in manufacturing or services instead. There are a lot of technologies available to move beyond hoe technologies, or pedal power, or animal fertilizer. However, a lot of research needs to be done on crops for African climates. There need to be more irrigation projects run and maintained by farmers, and we could also use a little more rural infrastructure, like roads and electricity.

Of course I could add to this list of challenges. In the previous lecture, I mentioned that many African nations have made gains in education and health, but there's a lot more to do. There are state-owned companies to be privatized. The financial sector could be built further. Any list of priorities is a little idiosyncratic. This will do for now.

Back in the earlier part of the 20th century, Africa was a battleground for colonialism. After they threw out the colonialists, it was, in some ways, a battleground for geopolitics between the United States and the USSR. These conflicts had a lot of negative effects, but that also meant that Africa mattered in a practical way to the rest of the world. In some ways, the practical importance of Africa is less now than it was a few decades ago. It's not a colonial battleground. It's no longer a battle between superpowers like the United States and Soviet Union. It's a smaller and smaller share of world trade. I mean, who depends on Africa?

Let me be just a hardhearted analyst for a moment. Politically, how much does Africa really matter in the world? And the answer, I think, would be: not much. Economically, how much does it matter? Not much. Even on humanitarian grounds—it's true that a lot of places in the world have terribly poor people, like India, China, rural poverty in Latin America. But in a world of scarce time and energy, there is some attraction to helping those where the help is most likely to really raise people's standard of living. Africa does have some real economic possibilities. You can imagine parts of the continent building on their natural-resource wealth, parts of the continent with decent port connections going into exporting manufactured goods. Landlocked parts of the continent could go into long-distance services, like India. Perhaps there are possibilities for ecotourism, for agriculture in areas like wine and flowers, economic connections from the emigrants who have gone elsewhere. Africa has a lot of hard-working people—they have to be hard-working just to get by. But if Africa's economy is to do better, it will have to be because those Africans have a more favorable economic environment in which to work. If Africa's economies are going to step forward, it will be because of Africans themselves.

Lecture Twenty-One
Latin America and Import Substitution

Scope:

Latin America has had one of the most volatile economies of any region of the world, but in the past, bursts of good news and hope have been followed by disappointment. For example, relatively rapid growth in much of Latin America in the 1960s and 1970s was followed by a disastrous "Lost Decade" of economic regression in the 1980s. This lecture tells the story of how the import substitution policies that were popular in Latin America from the 1950s into the 1970s ran their course and set the stage for the debt crises and hyperinflation of the 1980s. One of the most puzzling elements of Latin America's economy throughout this period is that although political leaders have often used the rhetoric of Populism, their economic policies have resulted in the most unequal income distribution of any region in the world.

Outline

I. By world standards, Latin America has long been a middle-income country but hasn't sustained progress toward joining the high-income countries.

   A. Simon Bolivar was known as the Liberator for his leadership in freeing the northern part of South America from Spanish rule in the early 19th century. But by the end of his life in 1830, even Bolivar was dismayed by the turmoil and lack of progress in Latin America.

   B. If the United States is looking for dynamic trading partners and economic opportunities, there is surely as much potential in Latin America as in other places that seem to be discussed more often, such as Eastern Europe.

   C. For our purposes, Latin America refers to a group of 32 countries in South America, Central America, and the Caribbean. The seven largest economies of the region are: Brazil, Mexico, Argentina, Peru, Chile, Colombia, and Venezuela.

   D. In the 1980s, economies across Latin America imploded under the pressure of hyperinflation and enormous foreign debts. Latin America always seems to have great economic promise, but it has become stuck in the middle of the world income distribution.

II. Two powerful and interrelated forces shaped Latin America's economic policies in the decades after World War II: Populism and import substitution.

    A. "Populism" has been defined as a set of economic policies that are intended to mobilize support from the lower and middle classes and from organized labor, with backing from domestically oriented business, while attacking the ruling oligarchy, foreign enterprises, and large-scale industry that operates in world markets.

    B. From the 1950s up through the 1970s, much of Latin America followed the policy of "import substitution industrialization."

        1. In this policy, developing economies seek to avoid importing industrial or technology products from high-income countries and, instead, attempt to produce those products domestically.

        2. The tools used in pursuit of this policy include shutting out imports, implementing price controls, and paying out government subsidies to favored firms.

III. The economy of Latin America shifted from healthy growth in the 1950s to the 1970s into a debt crisis and hyperinflation in the 1980s.

    A. By the mid-1960s, weaknesses had become apparent in Latin American economies. Firms received government subsidies but did not produce goods that were cheap enough or of high enough quality to be sold in foreign markets.

        1. Latin American firms became good at lobbying the government for more subsidies, which bred corruption.

        2. The government generated the money for these subsidies simply by printing more of it or by running large budget deficits, often using money borrowed from abroad. These actions led to inflation and a debt crisis.

    B. Latin America's high levels of borrowing increased even more in the 1970s, and when economic conditions shifted in the 1980s, Latin American countries found themselves unable to repay.

1. In the 1970s, the oil-exporting nations of OPEC raised the price of oil dramatically and deposited the U.S. dollars they earned in U.S. banks. The banks then faced the problem of where to lend those dollars; Latin America seemed a good recipient. Many Latin American governments agreed to guarantee repayment of the loans. At the time, it appeared that much of the money could be repaid at low or even negative real interest rates.

2. Higher interest rates in the late 1970s and early 1980s made these adjustable-rate loans harder to repay. With hyperinflation, recession, and lower oil prices, repayment became nearly impossible for some Latin American economies.

3. In renegotiating debt, borrowers often claim they can repay almost nothing, while lenders offer to forgive some debt in exchange for economic reforms to ensure repayment of the rest. Ultimately, in Latin America, about one-sixth of the debt was forgiven, though in the meantime, while debt negotiations took place through the 1980s, no new capital flowed into the countries of Latin America; inflows of foreign capital did not resume until the 1990s.

C. Inflation rates in Latin America were so high in the 1980s that if it weren't so harmful to the economies, the situation would almost be comic.

1. For example, inflation in the entire region averaged more than 700% per year from 1986 to 1990.

2. Reaching inflation of this magnitude requires extreme macroeconomic policies. The policies in Latin America included enormous budget deficits and expansive monetary policies, under which the central banks handed out loans at a reckless pace.

D. When an economy is suffering from hyperinflation, businesses, consumers, and governments must focus on the day-to-day task of managing money to try to protect against losses from inflation. There is little time or incentive to focus on long-term investments for the gradual improvement of productivity.

E. Overall economic growth in Latin America averaged about 1% per year in the 1980s. But at the same time, the population was growing; thus, per capita GDP actually declined, on average, about 1% per year through the decade. Economically speaking, the 1980s was truly a Lost Decade for Latin America.

IV. Even after decades of Populist leadership aimed at helping the poor, Latin America has long had among the highest levels of income inequality of any region in the world.

   A. A standard measure of income inequality is derived from splitting up income distribution into fifths, or quintiles, and looking at how much income is received by each fifth. Using this measure, the income distribution in Latin America is the most unequal of any region in the world.

   B. This inequality in income is also manifested in government spending for education and health programs. In most of Latin America, spending on education and health care looks quite reasonable by world standards, but a disproportionate share of this spending goes to subsidizing top-level services for the upper-middle class and wealthy. In recent years, some promising steps have been taken to target more social spending to the poor.

   C. Populist societies are often characterized by the existence of powerful in-groups and out-groups in the production of goods and the labor market. For the poor to benefit in Latin America, the forces of Populism may need to be replaced by more conventional democratic political systems.

Suggested Readings:

Cardoso and Helwege, *Latin America's Economy: Diversity, Trends, and Conflicts.*

Reid, *Forgotten Continent: The Battle for Latin America's Soul.*

Questions to Consider:

1. What is import substitution industrialization, and what problems does it tend to bring?

2. What factors led to the Lost Decade of the 1980s in Latin America?

Lecture Twenty-One—Transcript
Latin America and Import Substitution

Simon Bolivar is a towering figure in Latin American history. He was known as the Liberator. He led a series of small military forces, really not more than a few thousand soldiers at any given time, who were successful in freeing the northern part of South America from Spanish rule early in the 19th century. In particular, Colombia, Venezuela, Ecuador, Bolivia, Panama, and Peru all were really in the territories that he fought for. He's sometimes called the George Washington of Latin America.

His legacy lives on. The currency of Venezuela is called the bolivar. If you travel through Venezuela and Colombia, even today you'll find the main square of many cities and towns is called the Plaza Bolivar, and it'll have a statue or a bust of Simon Bolivar there. However, by 1830, Bolivar was terminally ill and he was soon to die. The nations of South America that he'd had such a large role in freeing were entangled in civil wars that, one way or another, were going to start up and die off for decades to come. He was discouraged; he was impoverished; he was ill. Bolivar wrote a letter to another general about the situation of Latin America. In this letter, written in 1830, he just refers to the Latin American region as "America." This is what Bolivar wrote:

> You know that I ruled for twenty years, and from these I have derived only a few certainties. (1) America is ungovernable, for us; (2) Those who serve a revolution plow the sea; (3) The only thing you can do in America is emigrate; (4) This country will fall inevitably in the hands of the unbridled masses and then pass almost imperceptibly into the hands of petty tyrants, of all colours and races; (5) Once we have been devoured by every crime and extinguished by utter ferocity, the Europeans will not even regard us as worth conquering; (6) If it were possible for any part of the world to revert to primitive chaos, it would be America in her final hour.

I smiled a little when I ran across this quotation, thinking of the ups and downs of Latin America's economic and political history over time.

When looking for trading partners and economic potential, I think we Americans do have some tendency to overlook Latin America. We focus maybe on the East Asian tigers, or China, or India, or Eastern Europe, or Russia, but the economic potential of Latin America is really quite substantial. It deserves to be the subject of as much or more business and government attention as any of these other regions.

Let's start off this lecture with a sketch of the economy of Latin America. When we refer to Latin America, we're talking about a group of 32 countries in South America, Central America, and the Caribbean, as well. For the purposes of giving a sketch of the economy of the region, I'm going to stick to some of the larger countries. I'm afraid you're not going to hear much in this lecture about beautiful Caribbean islands, like Grenada or Barbados.

The seven largest economies of the region are, in order from largest to smallest, Brazil, Mexico, Argentina, Colombia, Chile, Venezuela, and Peru. Together, these seven make up almost 90% of the economy of the entire Latin American region. By far the biggest economy—biggest in population, as well—is Brazil. Brazil's economy is maybe something like one-third or so of the entire economy of Latin America. In fact, sometimes when you see statistics for Latin America, they'll calculate it as "with Brazil" and "without Brazil," because including Brazil can sometimes swamp the overall picture.

In terms of population, Brazil had 189 million people in 2006. Mexico had 104 million. Argentina had 39 million. Venezuela and Peru were under 30 million, and Chile had maybe 16 million. Of course, the size of the total economy tends roughly to track the total number of people in that economy. The total number of people in these Latin American countries is about 550 million. That's roughly double the population of the United States.

Latin America as a whole has a GDP of about $5 trillion. If you work that out, call it roughly $9,000 in per capita GDP. In comparison, the United States had annual GDP in 2006 of roughly $12 trillion and per capita GDP in the range of $42,600. If you use per capita GDP as a rough measure, the U.S. economy is about five times as high as Latin America on a per capita basis. Argentina, Mexico, and Chile are the best off. Brazil, with its vastly larger population, lags somewhat behind.

The standard of living is always rough and ready to estimate, but roughly, looking at the whole thing, it would be fair to say that in Latin America, most countries are between 20 and 40% of U.S. levels. That's obviously a pretty big difference in overall standard of living.

When I think about the economic status of Latin America over time, what I really think about is the volatility of Latin America's economy. In the big historical picture, for example, Argentina was one of the highest countries in the world in per capita income around 1900. But, by a century later, it was nowhere near the top. It was very much in the middle. How does a country go from very much at the top of the world rankings to the middle over a period of 70 or 80 years?

More recently, economies across Latin America looked like they were about to enter a period of sustained rapid growth. I'm talking about the 1960s here. It almost looked like the Latin American tigers. If you'd been betting on what region of the world or what economy would take off in the 1960s, you might well have bet on Brazil, rather than what was then a very, very low-income South Korea. But that wave of growth in the 1960s evaporated in the 1980s under the pressure of enormous foreign debts and hyperinflation. In the circle of economists who study Latin America, the 1980s are known as the "Lost Decade."

Latin America has, for a long time, seemed to have great economic promise, but it always seems ultimately to be stuck in the middle of the world income distribution. It's not falling to the bottom, but it doesn't seem to be gaining toward the top either. In the first decade of the 21st century, you can see this pattern of the best of times and the worst of times continuing to alternate. For example, look at per capita GDP for the region over the last few decades. It was actually negative for 5 of the 10 years in the Lost Decade of the 1980s. It was negative for 3 of the 10 years in the 1990s. There has been a real roller coaster ride of ups and downs.

In the rest of this lecture, what we want to focus on is the broad approach of Latin America's economic policies from the 1950s up through the 1970s and the problems that arose with foreign debt and hyperinflation in the 1980s. Then, in the next lecture, we'll look at the market-oriented economic reforms that were put in place across the continent in the 1990s, and we'll evaluate the arguments about how well or how poorly those reforms seem to be working out.

Two powerful and interrelated forces were shaping Latin America's economic policies in the decades after World War II. They are Populism and what's called "import substitution industrialization." Let me try and lay out what those two terms mean.

Let's start off by talking about economic Populism, Latin American style. "Populism" is a term that gets tossed around a lot, usually with a slightly unsavory air to it. It's not obvious at first why it should be unsavory. After all, in a democracy, shouldn't what's popular be good in some sense? A loose definition of Populism might be something like this: Policies that seek to support the ordinary people in their struggle against the elite. Again, it's not obvious why favoring ordinary people is a bad thing. But in that kind of a definition, you begin to hear echoes here and there about "the people" and "struggle" and "elite," and somehow you kind of pick up some undercurrents that you aren't necessarily headed for a system with a whole lot of respect for what free markets can accomplish or maybe what democracy can accomplish either.

In the Latin American context, one academic study of the region defined Populism in this way:

> [Populism] involves a set of economic policies designed to achieve specific political goals. Those political goals are:
>
> (1) mobilizing support within organized labor and lower middle-class groups;
>
> (2) obtaining complementary backing from domestically oriented business; and
>
> (3) politically isolating the rural oligarchy, foreign enterprises, and large-scale domestic industrial elites.

In that kind of a definition, you can feel a little edge beginning to sharpen up. Mobilizing labor and other groups—does that mean that you're benefiting them, you're raising their standard of living? Maybe, maybe not—as long as they're mobilized and marching. [Note the emphasis on] helping domestically oriented business but not international business and not even large-scale domestic firms or, heaven forbid, foreign firms.

If you're pushing that kind of a policy, what are the specific economic policies implied by that kind of a stance? The policy followed by much of Latin America from the 1950s up to the 1970s was called "import substitution industrialization" or sometimes just "import substitution." The development of this theory is associated with an Argentinean economist named Raul Prebisch. He lived from 1901 to 1986, and he spent much of his career working at the United Nations. He was first at something called the Economic Commission for Latin America and later at UNCTAD, the UN Commission on Trade and Development.

Writing in the 1940s, here's how Prebisch saw the world. Remember, he's from Argentina, and Argentina's economy had been high income and growing toward the end of the 19th century and into the 20th century. Much of Argentina's growth about that time was based on selling grain and cattle on world markets. But then, world war and depression came along, and it devastated world markets and world trade. The U.S. economy became the preeminent exporter of these agricultural products, like grain and cattle, and as Prebisch saw it, this really explained why Argentina's economy had performed so badly over that time.

I'll just sort of note in passing that this is a pretty convenient explanation. It sort of suggests that all of Argentina's problems were external; it had nothing to do with how Argentina's government might have managed or mismanaged the economy, or failed to build up education and infrastructure, or anything like that. My point here is not to critique Prebisch's view of the world but more just to explain it.

Prebisch believed that high-income countries around the world liked to purchase commodity items, like agriculture and minerals, from the developing countries. Then they would sell industrial and technology goods back to those low-income countries. Prebisch argued this pattern created a cycle where the developing countries were stuck with producing low-cost commodities, and they couldn't break out of that cycle. His suggestion for breaking out of the cycle was that countries in Latin America and others needed import substitution. That is, don't rely on importing technological goods from other places. Instead, make everything at home. Limit what could be bought from abroad. Control any currencies, like U.S. dollars, so they would only get spent on important things, as determined by the government, not on frivolous things, like consumer goods.

You can really have some emotional sympathy with these views. Much of Latin America has felt economically exploited and ill-treated by the United States and other foreign governments for some time. Clearly, some U.S. firms and the U.S. government have behaved fairly rottenly in Latin America on various occasions over the 20th century and earlier. But deciding that the answer for this was to limit all contact with outside firms is a severe overreaction; it's throwing out the baby with the bathwater.

Latin America undertakes this policy of import substitution industrialization. As a result, it looks pretty good for a time. The economy of Latin America went into fairly healthy growth from the 1950s up until the 1970s. Then, it ran into all sorts of troubles. For a time, it really looked as if import substitution was working well. The governments of Latin America created high tariffs on imports, which protected the domestic producers. They gave subsidies to a lot of favored firms, and there were a lot of state-owned companies, as well. This was very popular with business, which could earn high profits and reinvest them. It was also really popular with the labor unions who worked for these particular companies. Other workers didn't have much of a chance, but we'll get back to their problems a little bit later.

From 1950 up until about 1980, the economy of the Latin American region grew at a pretty healthy rate, about 5 or 6% a year. In the 1970s, Brazil, which remember is by far the biggest economy in the region, had one of the fastest economic growth rates in the world. But there were underlying weaknesses that were starting to be apparent by the mid-1960s, and the costs of these kinds of policies were beginning to become manifest. All these subsidies to different industries, for example, meant that Latin American firms were not very good at either efficiency or quality. They could really only sell in their domestic markets. The goods they made were not cheap enough or of high enough quality to sell in foreign markets. Latin America was about 13% of world exports in the years right after World War II. By 1975, about 25 years later, they were down to about 4 or 5% of world exports.

What happened in Latin America is that firms became very good at lobbying the government for more support, which tends to breed corruption over time. The government needed to keep on giving subsidies to these money-losing firms, so they could have raises and so they could keep the workers happy and the unions happy. At the end of the day, they were pouring in government subsidies. They got the money for these subsidies in two ways. One was: They just printed it. The other was: They ran large government budget deficits, often using money borrowed from abroad. These policies of printing money and running large budget deficits kept pumping up demand in the economy. As you got more and more demand, the classic situation [developed] of too many dollars—in this case, too many currencies of Latin America—chasing too few goods, and eventually, these policies hit the wall, bringing both inflation and a debt crisis with them.

Let's first talk about the debt crisis. Latin America's high levels of borrowing increased even more in the 1970s. When economic conditions shifted around in the 1980s, many countries found themselves unable to repay. What were the roots of the debt crisis that evolved in the 1970s? It really started when the Middle Eastern nations of OPEC raised the price of oil dramatically. When they did that in about 1973 and 1974, OPEC earned a lot of U.S. dollars, which were deposited then in U.S. banks. U.S. banks then faced the problem of where to lend those "petrodollars," as they were called at the time. It seemed to them, as they thought about it, that Latin America, which had been growing well through the 1950s and '60s and into the early '70s, was a good target for lending that money. Moreover, many governments across Latin America agreed to guarantee repayment of the loans. The banks said it's very unlikely that any sovereign government would be unable to repay the loans. That kind of sentiment is, of course, worth a good horse laugh, given how things turned out.

The interest rates at that time looked very low because inflation in the 1970s is rising rapidly around the world. It looked like much of the money could be repaid at low or even negative real interest rates. For example, if you could borrow money at an interest rate of, say, 7% but inflation was 10%, then you could repay the loan in inflated dollars. In effect, you could actually have a real interest rate of −3%.

By 1982, the four countries that owed the most to foreign lenders in Latin America were Brazil, with debts of $93 billion; Mexico, with a debt of $86 billion; Argentina, with a debt of $42 billion; and

Venezuela, with a debt of $33 billion. Total foreign borrowing by Latin America went up by a factor of 4 or 5 from the late 1970s up until the early 1980s. But then, events turned against the borrowers. As U.S. interest rates went up and up and up in the late 1970s and early 1980s as part of trying to fight inflation at that time, inflation rates then came down and down and down in the early and mid-1980s. All of a sudden, repaying the debt looked a lot harder. You couldn't repay in inflated dollars anymore. Moreover, inflation was starting to wreak havoc across Latin America. The collapse in oil prices in the early 1980s meant further that countries like Mexico and Venezuela, which had been counting on their oil revenues to help repay all these loans, all of a sudden had a lot less in oil revenues to repay.

Mexico was the first to declare they just couldn't repay, in 1982. Of course, when one country can't repay, then banks stop lending to the region. They refuse to roll over loans into the future. Then, no one can repay, and everyone needs to renegotiate. Import substitution policies also make it hard to repay foreign loans because your protected firms are really not very good at exporting and earning foreign currencies, like U.S. dollars. The countries of Latin America couldn't earn the U.S. dollars and the foreign exchange that they needed to repay the foreign debts they had incurred.

Whenever you have a problem where someone can't repay their debt, there's going to be a big negotiation, and there are always two parts to that negotiation. Borrowers, of course, would like all the debt just forgiven and written off, and lenders would like all the debt repaid, with interest, of course. Lenders also say, if we forgive some of the debt, we'd like some guarantee of domestic reforms, so that we're at least likely to get the rest. This turns into a long dance that goes back and forth, one way and the other. At the end of the day, about [one-]sixth of all the borrowing was actually forgiven, which really in some ways is not all that high a proportion. The bigger problem may be that in the meantime, through the 1980s, while they're negotiating over this debt issue, no new capital is flowing into the countries of Latin America. It really takes until the 1990s before inflows of foreign capital resume.

The countries of the region are struggling with being unable to repay their debts and not getting foreign capital from abroad. While they're struggling through this period of the debt crisis, there's a howling storm of inflation that hits Latin America, as well. Inflation rates get so high in the 1980s in Latin America that if it wasn't so harmful to their economies, it would almost be comic. You can see the inflation genie beginning to pop out of the bottle in the 1970s, as the costs of propping up the import substitution policies were leading to dumping ever more buying power into the economy.

For example, Argentina was already having triple-digit inflation in the 1970s, and Brazil and Mexico were often having inflation in the mid-double digits, like 25 or 50% a year. But if you put those kinds of inflation rates on a graph, you can barely even see them when you look at what happens in the late 1980s and early 1990s. In the late 1980s, inflation just takes off. Say, if you look at the first half of the 1980s, 1980 to 1985, inflation for the whole region of Latin America was 137% per year. This included some really astounding rates. Bolivia, for example, had inflation averaging 2,200% per year over those five years, and Argentina was having inflation averaging 335% per year over those five years. But that was all just for starters.

From 1986 to 1990, inflation for the Latin American region as a whole goes over 700% per year. Brazil and Argentina, the two biggest economies in the region, both averaged inflation rates of about 1,100% per year over those five years, and they weren't the ones suffering the most. Peru had inflation of more than 2,300% per year. Nicaragua was above 4,800% per year. Just in case you thought it was safe, from 1991 to 1995, the region as a whole averaged 460% per year inflation. Interestingly, though, when you look at this a little more closely, it turns out that most of that high inflation of the early 1990s is Brazil, which averaged inflation of 1,000% a year over the first half of the 1990s. The rest of Latin America was averaging "only" 31% per year inflation over the first half of the 1990s.

You don't get inflation rates like this by accident. It's a self-inflicted wound. We know that inflation is basically a matter of too much money or too much buying power chasing too few goods. Where does the extra money come from? Again, there are only two big sources. One is running huge budget deficits, and the deficits in Latin America were substantial. The average budget deficit in the average country was about 8% of GDP throughout the 1980s. For comparison, the really pretty large U.S. budget deficits of the mid-1980s at their very worst were maybe 6% of GDP and more typically were 3 or 4% of GDP. In your mind, you can take sort of the worst

U.S. budget deficits in any year since, say, the 1980s up until the mid-2000s and double it. Imagine if you were averaging that level budget deficit for a decade.

In addition, to get those truly astronomical rates of inflation, you need to have a central banking system that is almost completely undisciplined, a central bank that just pours out money to every agency that says it needs to borrow, not just to the government but to state-owned banks, to state-owned firms, and to every local government. It just sends out an absolute overload of cash, and it swamps the system.

It's hard to describe how poisonous these extraordinarily high rates of inflation are for an economy. An inflation rate of 400% means that if you buy something at the beginning of the year that costs $100, at the end of the year, the same item will cost $500. That is, the price increase is the original price by a factor of 4. Or, to put it a little differently, if you have $100 at the beginning of the year and you just sit on it, you will find its buying power at the end of the year is only one-fifth of what it was before. You've done nothing, and you've lost 80% of your money.

In this setting, everyone has to focus first and foremost on protecting their capital. Don't get stuck holding money without earning a huge rate of interest on it. What does this mean for various people in the economy? Say you're a consumer. You've got to get your paycheck into an account that earns a high rate of interest immediately, or you have to spend it as soon as possible. Don't carry it around in your wallet for a while. Imagine you're running a company, and some engineer comes in with a great invention that might cut costs by 10% if you work at it, and invest, and retrain. Heck, if you don't handle the funds in your company right, you could lose 10% the next month to inflation.

Say someone owes you a fixed amount of money, and you collect it 30 days late. It might be worth 15, 20% less already. In that situation, who cares about innovation? Who cares about long-term investment? You don't try and save. Saving just loses the value of your money. You don't think about long-term investment in plant and equipment. Long-term investment might give you some productivity gain of 5 or maybe 10% a year, but if you don't manage your cash right with inflation, you'll lose vastly more than that right away.

Given that economic setting, there's no surprise that overall economic growth in Latin America averaged about 1% per year in the 1980s. However, population was growing during that time, so per capita gross domestic product actually, on average, declined about 1% a year throughout the decade. That's why the 1980s are called the Lost Decade for Latin America.

One of the considerable mysteries of Latin America's politics is that even after decades of Populist leadership ostensibly aimed at helping the poor, the Latin American region has long had among the highest levels of income inequality of any region in the world. A standard measure of income inequality is to split up the income distribution into fifths, or quintiles, and look at how much income is received by each fifth. The poorest in Latin America get a smaller share of overall income, and the richest fifth gets a higher share of income than in any other region, except for the poverty-ridden nations of sub-Saharan Africa. If you look at the big economies of Brazil, Argentina, or Mexico, for example, the top fifth typically gets something like 55 to 60% of all income in a year. For comparison, in the United States, we've had a big run-up in inequality over the last 25 years; the top fifth now, in the mid-2000s, gets about 48% of all income. In fact, Latin America is even a little less equal than sub-Saharan Africa.

This inequality in income is also manifested in government spending on social programs, like education and health. Most economies in Latin America spend an overall amount on education and health as a share of GDP that looks perfectly reasonable by world standards. But a disproportionate share of this spending goes to subsidizing top-level services for the upper-middle class and the wealthy, rather than providing services to the poor.

For example, let me talk about education. The average Latin American government spends 4.2% of GDP on education. By world standards for countries at roughly this level of per capita GDP, that's a roughly average share. However, Latin America has only about 60% enrollment in secondary school, while most countries at about this level of development have about a 70% level of enrollment in secondary school. There are also a lot of reasons to question the quality of schooling. For example, more people in Latin American schools end up repeating grades, and they don't have great performance on the international exams that compare school performance across countries.

Of course, Latin America has some really fine private schools and universities—maybe not the equivalent of a Harvard or a Stanford in the United States but really very good by world standards. The difficulty is that to get into those schools, to make use of those institutions, you need money and support throughout your whole life, or else you're unlikely to be in a position to get admitted. A typical pattern is that the public subsidies are highest for the high-profile, top universities, where the children of those with high incomes get a subsidized education. There is too much support for really high, high education and too little support for primary and secondary education.

This was a real problem for Latin America in the 1970s and 1980s. It started changing, to some extent, through the 1990s. But there's still a need, in the first decade of the 21st century, to keep improving the balance. For example, if you look more broadly at all social spending in Latin America in the first decade of the 21st century, about 15% of it goes to the bottom 20% of the population. About 30% of all social spending goes to the top 20% of the population. Of course, the top 20% gets vastly more benefit from higher education. It also gets vastly more benefit from government retirement programs.

This is all, again, changing to some extent. Chile, Costa Rica, Brazil, and Argentina in particular have been doing a much better job at targeting government social spending toward those with lower incomes. There has been lots of experimenting with programs that link cash payments to the poor with school attendance by children, or health visits to doctors, and things like that. This solves an administrative problem of how to target aid. It gives an incentive for investment [in] human capital for those who otherwise might feel shut out of the system.

But at the end of the day, there is just enormous irony in all of this. Populism, after all, was supposed to be about helping the poor against the elites. But throughout the heyday of Populism in Latin America, there was extraordinarily high inequality. How can countries where Populism is so strong generate and perpetuate such a high level of inequality? The answer seems to be that Populism and import substitution often create powerful in-groups and out-groups in the production of goods and in the labor market. When the government is doing lots of import substitution, the government decides who will get the subsidies and who doesn't, who's protected from competition and who isn't. The answer tends to be: who's politically well-connected and who's not.

Indeed, it appears that the force of Populism needed to wane and to be replaced by more conventional democratic political systems before the economies of Latin America could grow and the poor could benefit.

Lecture Twenty-Two
Markets or Populism in Latin America?

Scope:

In the early 1990s, after the disastrous economic performance of the 1980s, some leaders in Latin America were willing to try a package of market-oriented reforms that went under the name of the "Washington consensus." This group of policies included reducing Protectionism, privatizing state-owned industries, and getting budget deficits and inflation under control, among other steps. The reforms at first appeared to have promising effects, but in the aftermath of the international financial crisis of 1997–1998, Latin America's economic growth stagnated again. Thus, Latin America remains entangled in a debate over whether to move ahead with additional market-oriented economic reforms or to scale back these reforms in favor of greater government control over substantial sectors of the economy.

Outline

I. As the Lost Decade of the 1980s came to a close, Latin America faced a choice between continuing Populism and import substitution or implementing the steps of the so-called "Washington consensus."

  A. In 1989, a U.S. economist named John Williamson enunciated what he called the Washington consensus, a list of 10 recommendations for what Latin America should do to reform its economy. The steps were as follows:
   1. Exercise fiscal discipline;
   2. Reorder public expenditure priorities;
   3. Undertake tax reform;
   4. Liberalize interest rates;
   5. Maintain competitive exchange rates;
   6. Liberalize trade;
   7. Liberalize opportunities for inward foreign direct investment;
   8. Privatize state-owned industries;
   9. Institute deregulation;
   10. Define and enforce property rights.

B. The phrase "Washington consensus" often generates a wildly negative reaction that seems out of proportion to its actual contents. To some, it seems like a synonym for policies dictated to Latin American countries by American politicians, and to others, a synonym for extreme market-oriented policies that would ignore any concerns of workers and the poor.

II. In the 1990s, despite the controversy surrounding it, a number of elements of the Washington consensus were undertaken in various countries of Latin America.

A. From the mid-1980s to the early 1990s, many major economies of Latin America took a long step back from Protectionism. Both tariff barriers and nontariff barriers—that is, required licenses and regulations on imports—declined substantially. Also, a variety of free-trade agreements have been signed among various combinations of Latin American nations.

B. Foreign investment used to be somewhat unwelcome in Latin America because it was thought to imply dependence and external control, rather than the preferred strategy of growth from within. But capital flows into Latin America were substantial in the late 1990s, often reaching $50 billion to $60 billion a year.

C. From the late 1980s to the late 1990s, more than half the privatizations in the world (by value) occurred in Latin America. Many state-owned firms had become huge money-losers, gobbling up public subsidies, but under new management, their efficiency often improved dramatically.

D. To an economist, the term "financial development" conveys how well a country's financial sector is able to collect capital from savers (how common it is for savers to have their money in financial institutions) and how often banks use that money to extend loans to the private sector. One measure of financial development is the amount of credit extended from banks as a share of GDP. Latin America has increased this ratio from 15% in the 1960s to 30% in the 1990s.

E. Many Latin American countries have had a problem with borrowing large sums of money and later defaulting on the debt. The ratio of public debt to GDP in the region is around

50% in the mid-2000s, which is not much changed from a decade earlier.

F. In the mid-1990s, Brazil was the last large economy in Latin America to bring its inflation rate under control. For the region as a whole, sensible fiscal and monetary policies brought inflation down to the low double digits by the 1990s and often to the high single digits by the 2000s.

III. A debate has raged since the 1990s about whether the market-oriented reforms across Latin America were working fairly well, were hardly working, or were actually counterproductive.

A. Economic growth in Latin America since the implementation of the market-oriented reforms has been spotty: modest but positive growth from 1991 to 1997, stagnant growth from 1998 to 2002, and more positive growth in the mid-2000s. There is widespread disappointment that the economic reforms have not accelerated the growth rate further.

B. One possible reaction to the slow growth is to decide that more time and further reform are needed. A second reaction is that the reforms themselves are causing the problems. A third reaction is that the reforms that have been carried out are missing the main problems.

    1. The case for additional reform points out that more than a few years may be needed to change the fundamental direction of an economy.

        a. Further, the worst period since the reforms, from 1998–2002, may be attributable to the international financial crises that affected many countries at that time. This crisis period is unlikely to be repeated.

        b. Those in favor of further reform also point to evidence that existing reforms have had positive effects, although much work remains to be done in such areas as openness to trade, reform of labor markets, tax reform, and financial development.

    2. The case for slowing or reversing the reforms suggests that the reforms have been highly disruptive to industry in Latin America and that as governments have sought to control their spending, they have tended to back away from important, long-term infrastructure projects.

    3. Those who view the reforms as somewhat irrelevant argue that even in economies that have numerous issues to address to improve economic growth, it is usually a relatively small number of those issues that form the key constraints to growth at any given time. Economists in this camp tend to emphasize the need for broad institutional reforms.

C. Latin America has made enormous strides in the last few decades (with a few exceptions, of course) in improving its democratic institutions and moving toward a greater market orientation. However, changing long-term growth rates can be a slow-moving experience. No one has a magic key to unlock rapid growth for Latin America.

Suggested Readings:

Oppenheimer, *Saving the Americas: The Dangerous Decline of Latin America and What the U.S. Must Do.*

Williamson, "Did the Washington Consensus Fail?"

Zettlemeyer, "Growth and Reforms in Latin America: A Survey of Facts and Arguments."

Questions to Consider:

1. When talking about Latin American development, what is the "Washington consensus"?

2. What is the case for extending Latin America's economic reforms or the case for taking an alternative path?

Lecture Twenty-Two—Transcript
Markets or Populism in Latin America?

By the end of the Lost Decade of the 1980s in Latin America, one can imagine that Simon Bolivar would have had a weary, rueful smile as he contemplated both all the progress that had been made in building the nations and economies of Latin America and all the economic chaos and hyperinflation that had just occurred. As the Lost Decade came to an end, an academic conference was held in Washington, DC, in the late 1980s. It seemed clear that the choice of Populism and import substitution hadn't worked out very well. An academic economist named John Williamson began to enunciate a new way of thinking. At this conference, many people had policy suggestions, and Williamson tried to enunciate what he called the "Washington consensus," a list of 10 recommendations for what Latin America should do. These are, of course, based on his idea of what the consensus was for economists around the Washington, DC, area.

The 10 items he listed were the following:

1. Fiscal discipline—basically, smaller budget deficits.

2. Reordering public expenditure priorities, that is, switching expenditure toward the poor, especially in areas like health and education.

3. Tax reform; tax everything at a low rate, not a few things at very high rates.

4. Liberalizing interest rates; more broadly, allowing more competition in the banking and financial sector.

5. A competitive exchange rate; that is, don't keep the exchange rate artificially low in an attempt to encourage exports.

6. Trade liberalization; reduce the import tariffs.

7. Liberalize inward foreign direct investment. Williamson was specific here that he was really talking about foreign direct investment, that is, a direct management interest in companies. He wasn't necessarily calling for more openness to portfolio investment or totally free movement of capital going back and forth across the borders.

8. Privatization.

9. Deregulation, that is, reducing barriers to new businesses. We're not really talking about deregulating safety or environmental things but reducing barriers to starting businesses.

10. Better enforcement of property rights, that is, helping the informal sector of the economy to gain better definition of property rights.

You could sum all this up as macroeconomic discipline, free markets, and some openness to trade. When you list out the items like this, as I have, it seems almost too boring and worthy to be really interesting. It's the economic equivalent of "Eat your vitamins and finish your oatmeal, too." It seems more likely to make someone snooze off than to generate a lot of consensus. But the phrase "Washington consensus" often generates a wildly negative reaction in a way that seems to me all out of proportion to its actual contents. It's often said in a really knowing and dismissive way: "the—ha, ha—Washington consensus." It's better if you chuckle a little after saying it. It's sometimes used by critics as a synonym for policies that would be dictated to Latin American countries by American politicians. Sometimes it's used by critics as a synonym for extreme market-oriented policies that would ignore any concerns for the workers and the poor.

In retrospect, given sensitivities in Latin America about being in the orbit of the U.S. economy and about past U.S. economic and political interference in their countries, maybe calling this the Washington consensus wasn't the best rhetorical choice. But it was just supposed to be a list of what people around the Washington area thought should be done. Looking over the list, there's really nothing in it to justify a high level of fervor opposing it. I mean, yes, it's a different path. It's not the Populist path. It's not the import substitution path. Maybe parts of it are incorrect or overemphasized, but really, it's not some crazed, radical, imperialist scheme.

In the 1990s, as it turned out, a number of elements of the Washington consensus were tried out because, after all, whatever people say under their breath about the Washington consensus—chuckle, chuckle—it really was the consensus of how to proceed at the time. You'll be relieved to know that I'm not going to run through all 10 points in eye-glazing detail, but let me focus on some of the key elements of what actually changed in Latin America, going through the 1990s.

The first step was a movement away from Protectionism. In quite a short period of time, from the mid-1980s up to the early 1990s, many major economies in Latin America took a long step back from Protectionism—that is, a long step back from shutting out imports. Broadly speaking, there are two ways of blocking imports. You can put taxes on imports and set charges associated with customs (which sort of works like a tax on imports), or you can use nontariff measures, like using licenses, or import quotas, or various prohibitions. But those can be converted into a monetary value by economists. In the mid-1980s, if you were in Brazil and you wanted to import something, the average rate of tariffs on the imports was about 75% of the value of the good. Then, if you added in a monetary value on all the nontariff barriers, that would add up to another 44% of the value of the good. Add those together, and the barriers to imports were more than doubling the cost of any imported good. That's really a very significant disadvantage for anything that's imported.

By the early 1990s, just a few years later, tariffs had come down from 75% to 17%. The nontariff barriers had come down from 44% to 14%. The overall level of barriers against imports had been 119% of their value, and it was down to 31% of their value. Now, 31% isn't nothing either, but it's an enormously big shift in a really short time. Perhaps not surprisingly, foreign trade began to increase. For example, in Brazil, foreign trade rose about 8 percentage points of GDP from the mid-1980s up to the mid-1990s.

There were also a variety of free-trade agreements and free-trade areas across Latin America. Even if they were hesitant about competing with the United States or European or Japanese firms, at least they were competing more with each other. Trade, after all, brings a pressure of competition. Perhaps even more important, it brings contact with new ideas, new management skills, and connections to the rest of the world.

The second big step in the 1990s was opening up somewhat to foreign investment. There was a time not that long ago when foreign investment really wasn't very welcome in Latin America because it implied foreign investors would have a say in what went on. It implied a loss of local independence and control. It was thought to imply dependence on other countries, not the "growth from within" strategy Latin America was trying to emphasize. In the 1990s, a recognition developed that not only is getting some foreign capital investment good, but having some foreign expertise and management behind it can be good, too. After all, in a lot of businesses, the most important question is not precisely who makes the decision but that the right decision gets made and that a lot of people in an organization understand that it should be the right decision.

By the mid-1990s, Latin America had recovered from its debt crisis of the 1980s and foreign capital flows to the region had resumed. By the mid-'90s, Latin America is getting maybe $50 or $60 billion a year in foreign capital. Very roughly, if you broke down the capital flows at this time, it would look like this: Maybe 40% of the inflows were debt, that is, borrowed money. Another 40% was direct foreign investment, that is, purchasing property, and plant and equipment, and management interests in countries. And maybe 20% was purchases of stock in Latin American firms, which doesn't necessarily imply direct managerial control.

Breaking this down matters because certain kinds of funds are more committed for the long term than others. If you have borrowed money, and it has been borrowed for the short term, like 30 days, that money can flee very, very quickly, which can cause real problems. Purchases of plant and equipment may lose value or they may be sold, but the material assets aren't going anyplace. Similarly, with a stock market investment in firms, folks can sell their stock, but the actual assets of the company are going to remain there. There's no guarantee people who sell their stock are going to be able to pull out the same amount of money they put in. Substantial shares of foreign investment were being committed to Latin America not just in the form of short-term loans but being committed for the longer term and, thus, couldn't be pulled out very quickly.

A third big step was privatization. Latin America began to privatize in the 1990s, to sell off to the private sector a lot of the publicly owned firms. From the late 1980s into the late 1990s, more than half of the privatizations in the world, by value, occurred in Latin America. One count was that from 1987 to 1997, Latin American nations privatized 279 companies and raised $90 billion in the process. By value, again, this was more than half of all the privatizations in the world at that time. It's not uncommon to privatize firms that were producing a really large share of GDP. For example, Chile and Peru both privatized firms that were equal to something like one-eighth of the entire economy of those countries.

This was really a big deal because the state-owned firms had become huge money-losers and were gobbling government subsidies. One study in Argentina found that state-owned firms were producing 6.2% of GDP, but they were making annual losses equal to 5.6% of GDP. In other words, the losses they generated were almost as big as the amounts that they were producing. In Mexico in 1982, the 1,200 or so state-owned companies received government subsidies equal to 13% of GDP. Think of it—just the subsidies to those firms were something like one-eighth of the whole economy.

After the change to privatization, management of these companies typically got much better. There were almost immediately strong improvements in productivity and efficiency. There is still a lot of this going on—lots of big, state-owned companies across Latin America—but not as many as there used to be. In particular, three of the very biggest firms in all of Latin America are still state-owned companies. I mean here the state-run oil companies in Venezuela, and Brazil, and Mexico.

A fourth change is greater financial development. Financial development to an economist conveys how well a country's financial sector is collecting capital from savers, or how common it is for savers to have their money in financial institutions, and then the banks can use that money to make loans to the private sector. One measure of financial development is the amount of credit extended from banks as a share of GDP. For example, Latin America had credit from banks that was equal to about 15% of GDP back in the 1960s. That had gone up to about 30% of GDP by the 1990s. This is genuine progress. For high-income areas, like the United States and Western Europe, bank credit is over 90% of GDP in the 1990s. For Latin America, it's only about 30%. While that's a gain, the levels in Latin America are really only a little bit above the levels that used to prevail in sub-Saharan Africa and in South Asia, like India. There are gains there, but there is considerably more to be done.

A fifth step is getting budget deficits under control. Many Latin American countries have had a problem with borrowing a lot of money and then defaulting. This didn't just happen in the 1980s but in a series of episodes going back through the 20th century and even back into the 19th century. The ratio of public debt to GDP in this region is around 50% in the mid-2000s. That's not so much change from what it was in the mid-1990s. Public debt is not getting a lot better. It's not getting a lot worse either.

In particular, public spending in Latin America seems to come in waves. The mid-2000s saw another wave of public spending. The debt crisis isn't as bad as it was in the 1980s; it's just a little troublesome. A sort of rough rule of thumb for how much debt is safe for governments like those in Latin America to take on, given the risks that might affect repayment, suggests that the debt should be somewhat lower than 50% of GDP, maybe roughly half as much.

A sixth step is slaying the inflation dragon. Brazil was the last of the big Latin American countries to get its inflation under control. That happened around 1995 and 1996. By 1997, the overall inflation rate in Latin America was about 12% a year. The shift from inflation rates that are hundreds of percent[age points] down to double digits is just a huge thing. By the 2000s, inflation was often in the high single digits or in the low double digits across most of Latin America. This may still seem relatively high, say, by U.S. standards. But believe me, 1% inflation per month is a whole lot different than 1% or more inflation per day, which is what they had before.

Various studies show that an economy can invest and function in a reasonable way with inflation down in the low double digits. Perhaps even more important, this lower inflation shows some lessons have been learned, some macroeconomic lessons. If your government runs huge budget deficits and passes out subsidies right and left, you're probably going to get inflation—so don't do that. If your central bank starts printing a lot of money, you're going to get inflation—so don't do that. Sure, inflation is going to rise and fall some in the future, but the lessons have been learned. The sort of gross macroeconomic mismanagement that let triple-digit and quadruple-digit annual inflation exist in Latin America seems to be behind us— knock on wood, I guess.

That's the list of market-oriented reforms that Latin America tried during the 1990s. How well have they worked? Actually, a debate has raged since the 1990s as to whether the market-oriented reforms have been working pretty well, or barely working, or were actually counterproductive. The source of this debate has been that economic growth in Latin America since the implementation of the market-oriented reforms has been spotty at best. There was modest but positive growth from 1991 to 1997 for the region as a whole, then really stagnant growth from 1998 to 2002, then a resumption of more positive growth from the mid- and into the late 2000s. In comparison to the 1950s and the 1960s, this record, frankly, just doesn't look very good. In comparison to the Lost Decade of the 1980s, of course, it looks just fine. But there's widespread disappointment that the economic reforms haven't accelerated the growth rate of Latin America further or more consistently.

Latin America has gone through this economic and philosophical convulsion in the early 1990s. It makes the big decision: Our long-cherished approach didn't work all that well. We've just had a decade in the 1980s of going backward. We're going to change our approach; we're going to become East Asian tigers. We're going to get that rapid economic growth. With great controversy, they make the change, and what are the results? They are lukewarm. Lukewarm, I guess, is better than a bucket of ice water but not by much.

Some of the dispute here over these results and the growth outcomes after the reform involves how to put them in some historical context. You're really asking yourself: Did Latin America go through all this reform and conflict for piddling little results? There are worries in the first decade of the 21st century that the recent growth in the region is all about just selling commodities at high prices all over again, just in the way Raúl Prebisch warned against back in the 1940s. A lot of the current prosperity for Latin America in the first decade of the 2000s is commodity-driven. Raúl Prebisch in some sense must be wriggling in his grave. Over time, no nation rides high commodity prices to prosperity forever and ever. As we talked about when we were discussing the Middle East, there's reason to be wary of Dutch disease, of how high exports of minerals and other commodities can actually drag your economy down over time.

But when one looks back and thinks about the right standard for comparison, even by the standards of the 1960s and 1970s, Latin America continuing to fall behind the tiger economies of East Asia at that time. It's continuing to fall behind now, as well. Maybe there hasn't been a big change. It's also true that those earlier policies of Populism and import substitution didn't end up working out all that well, given the Lost Decade of the 1980s. At some level, there has been a huge dispute over whether these reforms were worth doing or not worth doing.

One possible reaction to the slow growth is to decide that more time and further reform is needed. A second possible reaction is, the reforms have caused all the problems. A third reaction is that maybe the market-oriented reforms are really missing the main problems, and other things need to be done. Let me talk through each of these responses in turn.

Let's first talk about the case for additional market-oriented reforms. The case for additional reform goes something like this: Let's get a wee bit of realism here. We had 50 years or so of import substitution, with bouts of high inflation and debt problems. We had vastly uncompetitive industry across Latin America. We had a sort of "who you know" corporatism that often was shading into corruption. It wasn't only economic inequality but also social and political inequality that were being produced by that set of arrangements.

The reforms only started in 1991, this argument would continue, and we've seen some progress. Industries that have opened up to competition have increased their productivity. State-owned industries and industries that didn't open up to competition haven't seen the same kind of productivity increase. If one looks across Latin America, countries that have reformed more and have reformed more toward the market-oriented have seen higher productivity and economic gains. The most vivid example is Chile, which carried out market-oriented reforms more quickly and has had strong growth through most of the recent decades. There's some evidence from economic studies that the growth rate of the economy across Latin America is maybe 2% a year higher by the mid-2000s as a result of the economic reforms that were carried out.

To continue this argument: Sure, we've had some mediocre economic years since the reforms. We had a downright lousy decade before the reforms, too—the Lost Decade, as a matter of fact. No one said the reforms would be perfect. The big problem is that slow period of growth from 1998 to 2002, really, that was a global financial problem. It started off with the East Asian debt crisis that we talked about in an earlier lecture. There was major globalization of capital movements. Capital moves in and out, it can really shake up an economy. While those problems started in East Asia, international financial problems can be contagious, as global investors skitter around and try to figure out where to put their money. Those problems ended up getting Latin America, as well. But that's not the problem of the market-oriented reforms.

However, the argument would go on: We're now much better at addressing that kind of international economic volatility. We'll talk more about that in later lectures on financial globalization and exchange rates. In fact, you might say—you want proof things are actually better? In the late 1970s and 1980s, there were difficult, severe international financial pressures, and the entire Latin America economy went backwards for an entire decade and suffered hyperinflation besides. Now, with a new set of international financial pressures, we got stuck in place for four or five years. But in an odd sort of way, this qualifies as progress. The Latin American economy is perhaps more resilient to international financial pressures than it used to be.

The final ingredient to this argument for further reform would go like this: The economic reforms so far have only been partial. It's like doing three sit-ups a day for a month and then grousing about why you don't have six-pack abs. There are still lots of things to privatize. There is lots of state-owned industry. There hasn't been much done to modernize the tax system so it imposes low and transparent tax rates instead of having lots of obscure high taxes on a limited amount of economic activity. The government is still accumulating debt. Sure, we're more open to trade than we used to be, but compared to developing countries around the world, we're not really all that open. There are high regulatory costs for opening businesses. There is still an underdeveloped financial sector compared to high-income countries and lots of rules about employment that can make it hard for businesses to hire and to expand.

Bottom line: This all is the argument that says we should keep going with the market-oriented reforms. We should keep moving in that direction. It's time to quit grousing about how the reforms weren't a magic potion. It's time to move ahead.

The next set of arguments is the case for slowing or reversing the market-oriented reforms. I'll say in advance, I think this case is a little bit weaker, but that's all right. The case would be based sometimes on just a sort of nostalgia for the days that were the 1950s and 1960s. But among economists, even critics of the market-oriented reforms don't advocate going straight back to the past. Let me just take that kind of nostalgia and set it aside.

The more interesting objection goes something like this: The market-oriented reforms have been highly disruptive to industries across Latin America, and great disruption can be very difficult for economies. For example, we know from the earlier lectures on the Soviet Union and its transition to a market orientation that when you have a bunch of industries that suddenly have to shift their orientation, it can be extraordinarily disruptive and difficult for a sustained period of time. The alternative here, at least to me, isn't quite clear. Ideally, I guess, you get wonderful new management with no need to reduce production or have any transition. But back here on planet reality, that doesn't seem a likely outcome. Disruption is the price you pay for decades of inefficiency, and subsidy, and being closed off to the world's economy.

As governments have sought to keep their spending under control, however, there is an argument that governments across Latin America have tended to back away from important, long-term infrastructure projects. One complaint about the reforms is that they're making long-term investments in those economies suffer. Figuring out how to do infrastructure in Latin America is a hard question. You're not just going to lift U.S.-type plumbing, and electricity, and fiber-optic cable, and roads, and railways, and ports and just insert them into Latin America. Remember, the United States has maybe four times as high a per capita GDP. The infrastructure across Latin America is just going to look somewhat different. You do need to think about varying approaches and combining the public and the private sectors. This is a real complaint, I think, about how the reforms have been carried out. But in and of itself, it hardly seems a reason to me to overturn or go back to all the economic policies that were popular in the 1950s and 1960s. Some people do argue for a U-turn; I think that's a little bit overextended.

Here's a third argument, which I think is more interesting and, in some ways, persuasive. It suggests that the market-oriented reforms may have been, to some extent, irrelevant. Supporters of this view often start off with some of the same studies I mentioned a couple of minutes ago, studies that say the market-oriented reforms have generated maybe 2 or 3% a year in additional growth. When folks from this point of view read these studies, they have two reactions. One is they say: Okay, it's fine to have [this] extra 2 or 3% a year in growth, but it's not exactly getting us to growth rates like the East Asian tigers, or China, or India, is it? It doesn't seem like much. In fact—and here's another reaction—those same studies suggest that maybe half of the gain, that 2 or 3%, comes just from getting inflation under control. The gains from the market-oriented reforms are only half as big as the 2 or 3% overall gain.

In addition, this argument emphasizes that countries and regions have different legacies. The geography can be different both within a country and relative to other potential trading partners. Countries differ in their levels of social cohesion and education, income distribution, political institutions, and their economic institutions. If all countries across Latin America are starting from somewhat different places, it makes some sense that maybe they should have different priorities as they try to develop their economies. This argument holds that we should just be pragmatic about diagnosing the biggest priorities in each country and then trying to fix them. Don't take some one-size-fits-all template, especially not one called the Washington consensus, and try and jam it down the throat of every country in the Latin American region.

In recent studies about economic development, there's a lot of emphasis on the role of strong institutions, for example, an independent judiciary and a rule of law that is fair for everyone; a better quality of civil servants and government workers, so you don't have corruption and incompetence that makes it difficult for businesses to work; a better definition and enforcement of property rights; an independent central bank. It may be hard to do some of these things, and personally, it's really hard to measure them. I know how to measure what it means to have a lower tariff rate on imports, or to reduce a budget deficit, or to get more bank lending; I don't know exactly how to measure a better institution or a better rule of law. But, of course, just because I can't measure it doesn't mean that it isn't even more important.

These possibilities suggest that there's a choice between more reform or less reform or just alternative reforms. Of course, in the real world, these are not mutually exclusive. The real world has a lot of different dimensions. You could do more of some reforms and less of other reforms and focus on certain areas. It may be that there are a number of interrelated constraints to economic growth, and you need to tackle a few of them at a time—not just find the biggest problem, tackle that problem, find the second biggest problem, tackle that problem, and try and work your way down some list.

Also, there may well be feedback from one problem to another. For example, less government favoritism toward certain producers will tend to reduce the possibilities for corruption and political wheeling and dealing. Less corruption and political wheeling and dealing might improve the climate for business. If you have good export industries, there will be a political constituency for open trade, and certain kinds of rule of law, and improved transportation and electrical and communications infrastructure. Then, in turn, if you have improvements in open trade, and the rule of law, and physical infrastructure, that tends to improve your export industries, as well.

My point is that many of these proposals sort of blend into each other and can reinforce each other. This sort of new consensus about trying a variety of things and seeing how they reinforce each other is sometimes called the "augmented Washington consensus." You can just imagine how happy that label makes some of the fire-breathing critics of the original Washington consensus.

Overall, this question of what to tackle, in what order, is a slippery, difficult question. I'm sympathetic to the problem that you don't want to have some rote list of economic reforms that every country has to do, no matter what. I'm also sympathetic to the problem that you need to have some priorities. You can't just say you need a major overhaul of a dozen major economic and legal and social institutions all at once, and every change has to be the top priority. I'm sympathetic to the political problem that sometimes you go after what seems easiest to do, even when you know it's not the most important problem, because politically, maybe you can't address the most important problem just yet. All of this is a long, difficult way of saying, as I've been suggesting all along, that economic reform of Latin America's economy can be a really frustrating subject.

Further, economic reforms take some time. It takes time, probably decades, for any reforms to bring noticeable progress. But saying, in the political process, let's wait a decade or two and see what happens, is never going to be your best political stance. You can almost hear the critics saying something like: What are you saying? We do this for 20 or 30 years [and] we'll see 2 or 3% a year faster productivity? And all this time, we're growing relatively slower than China, and India, and East Asia? Who cares that it took Japan decades to catch up or the story of the East Asian tigers evolved over decades? We need a crash program. We need success now. If markets don't deliver it, dump the markets. Go with *my* plan. But the proposed plan, for those who are impatient, is typically a return to the Populism in the Latin America style. That is, they say: Blame the foreign investors and the big companies; promise big government subsidies; shut out trade. Really, those would be the worst sorts of steps to take.

Most economies of Latin America are fundamentally on a good track as the first decade of the 21st century runs its course. They do need further reforms; there is uncertainty about what political priorities to pursue. But perhaps the greatest danger is that old disappointments, and frustrations, and unrealistic expectations could combine to destroy the reforms that have already been undertaken.

Lecture Twenty-Three
Globalization in Goods and Services

Scope:

A simple way to measure globalization in goods and services is to look at the share of world output that is sold outside the national economy in which it is produced. In 1950, world exports were about 7% of GDP; now, world exports are about 25% of GDP. International trade generates economic gains in both direct and subtle ways. However, economic gains often come about through disruption of existing patterns, and trade is no exception. Trade reshuffles jobs between industries. It also leads to fears that regulations concerning workers and the environment may be circumvented by production in other countries. In the future, such issues may come into sharper focus as the practice of breaking up the value chain and trade in services increase.

Outline

I. The increase in global trade of goods and services in the 21st century looks fairly large compared to the past, but such trade is expected to grow even more in the future.

    A. A simple measure of the expanded trade in goods and services is the ratio of exports to GDP. By that measure, globalization has roughly tripled or quadrupled in both the world economy and the U.S. economy since 1950.

    B. Another way to think about how far globalization has proceeded is to think about how much trade might exist in a borderless world economy. In other words, to what degree do national borders still restrict trade?

        1. Studies have compared the amount of trade between regions within a country to trade between similar regions at similar distances across national borders. The amount of trade crossing national borders is usually only a fraction of the trade that takes place within a country.

        2. In a unified economy, competitive pressures mean that goods sell for similar prices in different locations. Goods cost generally the same across U.S. regions, but prices often differ considerably across national borders.

3. For producers, crossing national borders means dealing with differences in legal systems, language, currencies, transportation systems, and more; such differences add extra costs in selling across national borders.

II. Both real-world experience and well-developed economic theory suggest strongly that rising levels of international trade generate overall gains for an economy.

   A. Times of expanding trade tend to be times of growing economies, and countries with expanding trade tend to be countries with growing economies. There are no counterexamples in modern history of countries that managed strong economic growth while shutting themselves off from international trade.

   B. Gains from trade come from several sources.
      1. The classic economic theory of gains from trade is based on countries that differ in some ways. The theory states that if countries focus on producing where their productivity advantage is greatest or their productivity disadvantage is least, then all parties can benefit from trade.
      2. Much of the trade in the world, however, takes place between similar economies, with similar costs of production. For these countries, the gains from trade come from a combination of economies of scale, hyperspecialization, and variety.
      3. International trade brings greater competition and helps to spread knowledge and technology.

   C. Changes in prices of imports or exports can cause a shock to an economy. Although such changes in price may cause a redistribution of the gains from trade, they do not mean that trade has become an overall negative factor.

III. How will the globalization of goods and services affect workers?

   A. No evidence exists to support the idea that increases in trade systematically diminish the total number of jobs in an economy.

   B. Dislocation of workers often has no relationship with trade at all. The U.S. economy, for example, has a certain amount of job loss for a variety of reasons, including losses from domestic competition, bad management choices, and outdated products.

C. If trade increases overall productivity, then it will also increase average wages over time.

D. Trade affects some parts of economies more than others and, thus, contributes somewhat to inequality.

    1. The degree of inequality created by trade depends on the extent and effectiveness of economic institutions in an economy, such as unions, minimum wage laws, taxes, and government social programs.

    2. If inequality means that some are benefiting now but others will benefit in the future, it may not be such a bad thing.

IV. One concern about globalization is that it will pressure governments to reduce regulations that are intended to protect the environment or workers.

A. The theory of the "race to the bottom" holds that countries will seek to compete in world markets by reducing regulations. As some countries do so, others will be economically pressured to follow, and the result will be a worldwide diminution of such rules.

B. Globalization has been proceeding for decades, and the race to the bottom hasn't happened yet—not across U.S. states, nor in high-income countries, nor in other countries around the world.

V. Levels of world trade seem likely to rise in the future.

A. Increasingly, manufacturers will seek to slice up the "value chain," the steps involved in the assembly of a final product. The combination of cheaper transportation, ease of information flow, and increased practical experience in working with these kinds of arrangements will make slicing up the value chain even more practical in the future.

B. Trade in services has traditionally been much lower than trade in goods, but this pattern is shifting.

C. Our definition of trade may change in the future as our sense of products to be traded and product origins becomes more fluid, but most people seem to adapt rapidly to increased globalization of trade.

Suggested Readings:

Taylor, *Principles of Economics*. Chapters 3 and 6.

———, "The Truth about Globalization."

Questions to Consider:

1. Is globalization more likely to be a trend that is just starting or a trend that has almost run its course?

2. What are the arguments explaining why trade brings economic gains?

3. Identify some of the concerns over why increased trade may be injurious to an economy, and (whether you agree with the answers or not) identify some of the responses economists give to those concerns.

Lecture Twenty-Three—Transcript
Globalization in Goods and Services

The structure of this course up to this point has been to take a tour around the world economy. I confess it has been a brisk tour, kind of like those package vacations where you see nine countries in six days. But even a brisk tour can let you see many of the highlights and give you a sense as to what you would like to follow up on when you have more time to stay in a particular place. I hope that the tour of globalizing economy, moving between regions and countries, has served that function and widened your perspective beyond just the domestic issues of the U.S. economy. I hope you have a better sense of many of the important episodes, policies, trends, and issues around the global economy.

But now, the focus of the lectures shifts from a geographical structure to a topics structure. We're going to talk about things like the international flows of goods and services, capital, exchange rate markets, and international migration. We'll then move on to other broad topics, like population growth, poverty, urbanization, climate change, and others. Of course, the plan here is that in discussing these broader issues, we can draw on the knowledge, and insights, and examples developed throughout the earlier lectures.

Let's start by talking about globalization of goods and services. First question is: How far has globalization of goods and services actually proceeded in the first decade of the 21st century? A simple-minded answer, which often is a pretty good answer, is to look at some statistics, like exports as a share of GDP. In 1950, world exports were about 7% of GDP. In the first decade of the 21st century, world exports were about 25% of GDP. There's a similar general pattern for the United States. In 1950, U.S. exports were about 3% of GDP, and 60 years later or so, they're about 12% of GDP. In both cases, there has been a tripling or a quadrupling.

Notice that the U.S. level of exports to GDP is actually much lower than the world average. The reason is that the United States is a large country and a large economy with big oceans on either side. A lot of the U.S. economy happens within U.S. borders. If you have a smaller economy, surrounded by land borders, and maybe even a really big city or two right outside the borders of the country, then you'll tend to have less of your economy within national borders and more of it flowing across those borders. For example, Belgium, in the middle of

Europe, is going to have a much higher share of exports to GDP than the United States.

This explanation should make some intuitive sense, I hope, but it has an implication that U.S. citizens don't always recognize. On average, the U.S. economy is much less affected by global trade in goods and services than the average economy of the world. If we sometimes feel in the United States that economic globalization is out of control, other countries of the world have far more reason to feel that way and have had reason to feel that way for decades.

But instead of comparing the extent of economic globalization to the past, how about if we use a different standard? When people talk about globalization, they often talk about a borderless world, where goods and money zoom back and forth as if national borders don't exist. How close are we to a world where, from an economic point of view, national borders just don't exist? The perhaps surprising answer is that national borders really matter a lot for economic activity. Let me describe some of the evidence to you on that point.

One approach is to compare trade within countries and between countries. If national borders don't matter, then trade between, say, metropolitan areas, or states, or regions that are a certain size and distance apart should be about the same within a country as between countries. The border shouldn't make a difference. For example, you can look at trade from, say, Montreal to Vancouver and you can look at trade from Chicago to Seattle. Then, you compare Montreal-to-Seattle trade and Chicago-to-Vancouver trade. You see whether going across the border makes a difference.

If you do lots and lots of comparisons like this between lots of pairs of cities or regions, what kind of patterns do you find? One of the first kinds of studies like this looked at trade between provinces of Canada and states of the United States. It found that after adjusting for distance and for the size of local economies, Canadian provinces trade maybe 12 times to 20 times as much with each other as they do with comparable U.S. states going across the border. Studies that have looked at other high-income countries around the world—the United States, Canada, Europe, Japan, Australia—trade within the country is often 3 to 10 times as high as trade that goes across borders to similar destinations. The exact multiple depends on the study and what the study takes into account. The point is that it sure looks like national borders matter a lot.

Another test of whether national borders matter: Do things cost pretty much the same in different places? For example, tradable goods that are common across markets, like, say, televisions or cars or blue jeans, cost pretty much the same in different cities of the United States, like Minneapolis and Chicago and St. Louis, in part because if it cost a lot less in one city, it would be easy to buy up a bunch of stuff where it's cheap and sell it where it's more expensive. Eventually, this kind of trade would equalize prices across the cities. But would that kind of trade equalize prices across national borders? There are a lot of detailed surveys of prices across national borders, and they find wildly different prices for a lot of goods, like TVs and cars, that should be traded.

In fact, one way to see this point is to think about what happens when exchange rates shift. When an exchange rate moves, often, you see hardly any change in the price in, say, Japanese cars in the U.S. market. Eventually, maybe half the effect of the exchange rate filters through to the price paid in another market. When you compare prices across countries, you convert using an exchange rate. A jump in exchange rates means the price in Japan versus, say, the price in the United States has just changed a lot. This kind of change happens all the time.

Why is it that the quantity of trade is so much less across national borders? Why do prices for similar goods differ so much across national borders? It isn't that complex when you think about it. There are a bunch of good reasons. Transportation networks, for example, are usually developed with nations in mind, not to go across national borders. If you go across borders, you have to deal with two different legal systems, two different tax systems, sometimes different language and culture issues, sometimes different currencies, and remaining trade barriers, whether tariffs or nontariff barriers. If you add all these things together, they can easily add an extra 25% or more to the cost of shipping something across a national border. That's quite substantial.

The bottom line is: Globalization of trade and services is at an all-time high by the export-to-GDP ratio, but national borders still matter a lot. Some of these differences will recede over time. For example, transportation and communication networks are still being built and developed further. Lots of types of economic output with a lot of information content can be shipped over these networks.

Governments are still negotiating to reduce trade barriers, and firms are getting more experienced with international trade and learning how to deal with all the legal and financial and regulatory issues. But the lesson I take away from all this is that the global trade in goods and services has been rising and could easily go much higher. Right now, we are not yet close to a world where national borders don't matter to economic transactions.

The next big issue is: How has this increased trade helped to bring prosperity? I do think trade brings economic growth, and the circumstantial evidence is really pretty strong here. Times of expanding trade tend to be times of expanding economic growth. On the other side, times of contracting trade, like the 1930s, have been economically lousy. Countries with expanding trade tend to be countries with expanding economies. When we were looking around the world at all the different countries where economies have grown in a healthy way, you see expanded trade as a key part of the process everywhere. We're talking about Europe and the United States, about Japan, the East Asian tigers, China, and India since the 1990s, as well.

In other areas, where trade has been limited by government rules, the economy has sometimes grown over the short or medium run but not in the long run. You can think of the old Soviet Union with its limited trade, or India trying out self-sufficiency, or China from the 1950s up to the 1970s, or Latin America trying import substitution. You literally cannot name a country that has made strong and lasting economic gains while clamping down and avoiding international trade.

The World Bank published a study a few years back. They split the world into two groups, looking at data from the '80s and 1990s. [One] group they called the globalizers. Those countries are where the ratio of exports to GDP had doubled over those two decades. That includes China, India, Mexico, and most high-income countries of the world. The total there is about 3 billion people. For the globalizers' group, per capita GDP rose 5% per year in the 1990s. Another group is the non-globalizers, where the ratio of exports to GDP fell over those two decades. That includes much of Africa, the Middle East, and Russia. For the non-globalizers, per capita GDP fell an average of 1% in the 1990s.

Kofi Annan, who was for some years secretary-general of the United Nations—and he's certainly no raving free-market economist—said in his speech accepting the Nobel Peace Prize, "The main losers in today's very unequal world are not those who are too exposed to globalization but those who have been left out." I do think, though, that economists have been less good than they could be in explaining why there are gains from trade and putting those gains in some kind of perspective.

The classic economic theory of gains from trade, the classroom example, is based usually on countries that are very different in some ways. You grow wheat in the United States and you trade it for oil from Saudi Arabia. Clearly, the United States has better soil and climate for wheat; Saudi Arabia has oil reserves that are easy to get. Trade between those two countries will work in some way. The key underlying idea is that the fundamental constraint on any economy is the time workers have available. The goal should be to have high and growing productivity in an economy, more output per hour. If places are very different in some way, it will make sense to produce different goods in different places. The difference could be rooted in natural resources. It could be rooted in the skills of the workforce. But if certain tasks can be done in a more cost-effective way in certain places, then do those tasks in those places.

Those classic models of trade rely on countries being really different in some way. However, well over half of all world trade happens between countries that are economically very similar. The high-income countries of the world, in North America, Europe, and Japan, do about half of all world trade. Much of this trade involves buying and selling the same products to each other. That is, they import and export cars. They import and export computers and electronics; they import and export machine tools. A few years back in Britain and France, cars were the biggest export and the biggest import. It's not different countries selling different products; it's the same product being sold across national borders. A lot of the study of international trade, starting in the 1970s and 1980s, has focused on why this kind of trade might be beneficial.

Here are several of the reasons that come up: One is that you can take advantage of economies of scale. If you have a relatively small economy, like, say, France or the United Kingdom—compared to the United States at least—you could have a large car plant that can sell across borders, and that helps you get more efficiency. You can also do what's sometimes called "breaking up the value chain." You break up where a car is produced into lots and lots of different locations. As you do that, you're not re-exporting the car, you're exporting parts and pieces of the car, like the high[-tech] electronics, or the low-tech seat covers, or the assembly of the car, and all those kinds of bits and pieces. Or you might specialize in some particular kind of machine tool, or computer chip, or optic lens and trade it for other kinds of machine tools, or computer chips, or optic lenses. Finally, there's a gain from variety. If you have countries that trade a lot of the same product, you can produce just one or two kinds of the product in one country and then trade with other countries and get a lot more variety.

International trade not only brings greater competition, [but] it also helps to spread knowledge and technology. I'm not just talking about scientific discoveries here, like pharmaceuticals or electronics. But, for example, in Japan, they invented just-in-time inventory management, which the United States firms were then able to bring into our country. Other kinds of information and incentives and management move across national borders. One famous example of importing an idea that may not be true comes from the 14th century, when the great explorer Marco Polo went to China and brought back the idea of noodles, which later became the Italian pasta industry. He didn't bring back actual noodles; it was trade in ideas.

All of these different gains—the gains from scale, from breaking up the value chain and hyperspecialization, gains of variety, competition, and the spread of knowledge—are probably much more important to productivity than just trading, say, oil and wheat. But it's also a whole lot harder to model and measure those kinds of differences.

What about when trade causes negative effects? Doesn't it sometimes prove that trade must be having a negative effect on an economy? For example, when the United States imports oil and the price of oil goes up, doesn't that prove the U.S. economy was hurt by international trade? Actually, it doesn't prove that. The increase in the price of oil proves we're not benefiting as much as we were before, but presumably, we're still better off. If we weren't better off from buying the imported oil, then we wouldn't buy it, and we would do something else with the money instead. Think about, say, buying milk at the grocery. If the price of milk goes up, does this mean you are now actually a loser from buying milk? No, it just means the benefits to you from buying milk aren't as large as they were before, and you might end up buying less of it as a result. When I say trade is beneficial, I don't mean trade can't be disruptive. In fact, I'll argue later that often many things with economic benefits do involve some element of disruptiveness.

The bottom line is: The gains from trade are real, but the estimates of how big those gains are really squishy. To get big gains from trade or increases in the rate of economic growth over time, you need to bring in these ideas about trade in information and management, which are really hard to estimate precisely. In fact, probably the most important part of trade is what we can measure least.

It's also important to keep the gains from trade in some sort of a context. For example, how important is globalization for overall economic growth compared to, say, education and good health of the population; or physical infrastructure, like water, electricity, telecommunications; or keeping inflation low; or a lack of corruption in the rule of law; or a well-regulated financial system? In this mix of things that affect growth, trade obviously helps, but it's not the obvious be-all and end-all, the undisputed king. I wouldn't even put it at the top of the list.

The third big question is: How does globalization of goods and services affect workers? Let's start off by talking about how it affects the total number of jobs. Here, the evidence is actually fairly blunt. There is just no good evidence that trade will reduce the overall number of jobs in an economy. Perhaps the most vivid illustration of this point came during the arguments over the North American Free Trade Agreement back in 1994, when Ross Perot said there would be, if we signed this agreement, a giant sucking sound of jobs heading south if we signed that agreement with Mexico. But we did sign the agreement in 1994, and it was followed by seven of the best years for job growth in U.S. history.

More generally, globalization of trade in goods and services has been going on for decades now. If it was going to cause long-term mass unemployment, that would have happened, certainly, 10, 20, or 30 years ago. It should have been happening all around the world, right? But we aren't seeing mass unemployment in Europe, or Japan, or

China, or East Asia, or anywhere around the world as a result of the growth in globalization over recent decades.

A second issue about the labor force would be whether globalization disrupts workers' jobs, and this is a real issue. In the United States, for example, automakers and steelmakers in the 1970s and 1980s and other manufacturing industries, like textiles, have clearly been hurt by a surge of imports in their particular industry. This claim is certainly true, but it's worth keeping the disruption from international trade in some kind of perspective. The U.S. economy as a whole has a certain amount of dislocation in its job market for lots and lots of reasons. Sometimes, domestic competition creates winners and losers. Sometimes, there are bad management choices, or outdated products, or the workforce doesn't keep up for one reason or another, or there's a local natural disaster.

In any given year in the U.S. economy, about 1 in 10 jobs is destroyed, and another 1 in 10 jobs is created. Job creation is, in most years, a bit higher than job destruction, so the total number of jobs rises. Sometimes people move to new jobs directly; sometimes they're unemployed for a time in between. At any given time, about half of those who are unemployed find new jobs in six weeks or less. But as they find new jobs, they're generally replaced by others on the unemployment rolls, others who have just lost jobs.

An overwhelming amount of this churning in the labor markets in the United States has nothing to do with trade at all. In fact, I'm often baffled as to why people focus so much on trade. Somebody laid off is just as laid off, regardless of the reason. They need the same kind of help. It's not clear to me why those laid off because of trade deserve different help or more help than others who are laid off for other reasons that have nothing to do with trade.

Worker dislocation, worker job loss, is a real issue, and there are tools for dealing with it, tools that are better than trying to shut down foreign trade. Those tools include unemployment insurance, more job retraining, having a healthy economy that keeps generating more jobs, and giving assistance with job search. In general, the United States could do a lot more in all of these areas.

The third question about the labor market and globalization is how it affects average wages. If trade does increase productivity, as I've argued that it does, then over time, it will increase average wages.

The link between productivity and wages isn't always immediate, but over time, productivity really does determine what wages are going to be. A final effect could be trade affecting the inequality of wages. It's clear that trade affects some parts of economies more than other parts, and so it could contribute to inequality. It's worth remembering, though, that about two-thirds of the jobs in the U.S. economy don't compete much with trade at all. Many service jobs, for example, like jobs in law, health care, education, finance, child care, construction, and transportation—it's very difficult for those jobs to ever be traded. Tradable goods are just one slice of the economy.

Within the United States, there has been a big rise in inequality of incomes. It started some time in the mid- or late '70s and has extended into the first decade of the 21st century. The consensus among economists seems to be that while globalization can contribute to inequality, other factors have been much more important in creating this inequality. The big factor most economists focus on is the change in technology. The argument is that changes in information and communications technology have led to a massive restructuring of industries, often in a way that has magnified the earning power of the top manager. That top manager used to need three levels of middle management to keep track of, say, the sales force, but now that top manager can see the sales force instantly with computer software. As a result, that top manager can get paid more than [he or she] got paid before.

It's also true that inequality is determined by a lot of factors across an economy, like the power of unions, the level of minimum wages, tax levels on different income groups, and government social programs. The mainstream estimate would be that globalization might have caused maybe one-fifth of the increase in inequality in the United States. More generally, around the world, globalization has caused a lot less inequality in Europe. A likely reason for that is that Europe's economic institutions, like unions, minimum wages, taxes, and government social programs, are all geared at producing more equality than in the United States.

My final point about inequality is that inequality isn't always obviously bad. For example, in China there's more inequality because the rise of the rich coastal cities in the east has created inequality with the poorer inland areas of the west. You could also say, in Mexico, inequality is up because the northern regions most involved with U.S. trade have prospered, while the southern regions not involved with U.S. trade haven't gained as much. But it's not clear the best answer to that kind of inequality is to make sure nothing takes off at all. If the choice is keeping everyone equally poor or trying to build economic institutions to spread and share the growth, that second option seems a lot better.

The next major question about the effects of globalization is: How does it affect government regulatory power? There's a theory here called the "race to the bottom," and the theory works like this: To succeed in the world economy, corporations are going to try to produce at the lowest possible cost. They're going to put pressure on countries to reduce regulations, so they'll be able to compete in the world economy. But if some countries start reducing their regulations, others will follow suit, and the result will be a race to the bottom, lower and lower environmental standards, lower and lower rules about workers and wages.

This all sounds plausible enough, but we have empirical evidence on the point, and it doesn't suggest that a race to the bottom is actually happening. For a long, long period of time, you can have extensive trade between countries that have really different environmental standards or worker rules and very little pressure to equalize or race to the bottom. Think, for example, across U.S. states: They differ wildly in things like, say, workers' compensation, the level of welfare they pay, their state taxes, and even their environmental laws. I'm from Minnesota, a fairly high-tax, high-regulation state. We're right next door to North and South Dakota, which are fairly low-tax, low-regulation states. It has been this way a long, long time. It doesn't seem to have forced either state to change their laws very much.

Or look at Europe, an area that is extremely open to free trade across the continent and elsewhere. For decades, they've had very generous rules, like six weeks and more of vacation per year, generous unemployment benefits, and in many cases, tighter environmental laws than the United States We haven't seen Europe racing to the bottom. You can look all around the world over recent decades. Labor and environmental rules have gotten generally stronger, both in the United States and in middle-income countries, like Mexico, or in other countries, like China or East Asia.

Maybe it's true that progress on certain kinds of environmental or safety rules should be going along faster. But the idea that they've been racing to the bottom, lower and lower, is just wrong. Ultimately here, the biggest defense against the race to the bottom is that people around the world want environmental and labor protection. When multinational firms come into a country, they're very visible. They're very vulnerable to public pressure. Generally, multinational firms do a better job of complying with local environmental standards than the domestic companies do. They bring a lot of know-how in how to do things in a more worker-friendly or environmentally friendly way.

Our final big question is the prospects for rising levels of trade in goods and services in the future. It does seem likely to me that there will be a rise in trade of goods and services in the future, as there will be increases in various dimensions of trade. Let me talk about the particular ways in which I think trade is going to increase.

The first way involves slicing up the value chain. The "value chain" refers to the steps in production that create a final product. Many production processes involve slicing up this value chain into separate parts that happen in separate places. For example, I read an article about the Barbie doll a few years back. It reported that the plastic and the hair for the Barbie doll came from Taiwan and Japan. The cotton for the dresses came from China. The assembly was done in Indonesia, Malaysia, and China. The molds for the dolls and the paints came from the United States. Of the $10 price that the doll was sold for, basically $2 was for materials and assembly, $7 was for transportation, marketing, wholesaling, and retailing—mainly all costs in the United States—and $1 was profit to the manufacturer, Mattel.

It seems more and more true that, in the future, a car is not going to be made in one country. Bits and pieces of the car are going to be made all over, assembled into other larger parts all over, and eventually made into cars. These different bits and pieces may cross national borders many times. The combination of cheaper transportation and almost free cost flows of information and communication, along with increased practical experience in working out the kinks of these kinds of arrangements, is going to make this slicing up the value chain so much more practical in the future.

A second major increase in the kinds of trade I expect to see is more trade in services. Traditionally, there has been much less trade in services than in manufacturing, but this pattern is shifting. For the United States, trade in goods is now, toward the end of the first decade of the 21st century, about 2.5 times as large as trade in services. But more than half the U.S. economy and four-fifths of all the workers in the U.S. economy are in services. With changes in telecommunications and information technology, this may be changing.

Think, for example, about a big service industry, like health care. You might say: We need to provide that domestically, right? Because you have to provide it right to the people on hand. What about record keeping for health care? What about customer service for health care? What about specialists and workers who are trained elsewhere and then come to work in the United States? What about medical care technology products that are produced elsewhere?

I'm just suggesting that a lot of what we think of as health care services could be created geographically somewhere else. You can think of something similar relating to education—materials being produced overseas—or entertainment from overseas, and parts of financial or legal or marketing jobs being done in other countries, at other places. In an Internet world, the costs of transporting services around the world can really be extremely low. This is actually a really big opportunity for the U.S. economy because we have many producers who are really good in service industries.

A third big change I expect is a greater blurring of where something is actually made. As we slice up the value chain and spread things around to different locations, I suspect this will change the public's sense of what trade actually means. We're used to these ideas where the United States makes cars, Japan makes computers, and Saudis pump oil. But companies within certain nations are less and less likely to make complete products. They make little pieces of goods—the springs of the car, the assembly of the car seat. They do the record keeping, or the Web maintenance, or the call center. This can make a big political difference. When we think about protecting an industry, we say something like: We're going to protect the autoworkers who make cars. It's not clear to me that we're going to get equally excited about protecting a firm that does design services for new car seats or protecting a firm that provides consumer service calls for magazine subscriptions.

Still, I'm sure we'll have some moments with high political tension, but under the surface, it seems to me that most people are adapting very rapidly to a more global world and the decisions about what to buy and where to make it. There are going to be many more opportunities for slicing up the value chain, many more opportunities for trading services, and continuing declines in transportation and communications costs. I think we've seen the opening waves of globalization in recent decades, but a whole lot more is coming.

Lecture Twenty-Four
Globalization of Capital Flows

Scope:

In the 1990s, international capital flows became much larger. Broadly speaking, these flows can be categorized as either foreign direct investment, which involves taking a management interest in a foreign company, or portfolio investment, which involves only the purchase of a financial instrument. Economists debate the question of whether or how countries should proceed in allowing inflows and outflows of foreign capital. Many countries welcome inflows of capital, especially direct investment, which often brings with it management and technological expertise, as well as connections to markets in high-income countries. But too great an inflow or outflow of foreign capital can destabilize the banks and financial sector of low- and medium-income countries.

Outline

I. Flows of international financial capital are often divided into portfolio investment and foreign direct investment. Both categories have grown rapidly in recent years.

   A. "Portfolio investment" refers to financial investments that do not involve actually managing a firm and, thus, can often be sold quickly. Portfolio investment rose sixfold from 1997 to 2006, from about $5 trillion in 1997 to more than $30 trillion by 2006.

   B. Foreign direct investment involves taking a management interest in a company in another country.

      1. This kind of investment increased quickly in the 1990s, peaking at $1.2 trillion in 2000; fell back to about $550 billion in 2002; then rose back to $1.2 trillion by 2006.

      2. Direct investment is not as liquid as portfolio investment and is far more likely to involve transfers of technology or specialized skills or supplier relationships.

II. The potential costs of international capital flows are written in financial crises, such as the debt crisis in Latin America in the 1980s and East Asia's financial crises in 1997–1998. The potential benefits appear to be substantial but more subtle than one might expect.

A. International capital flows can threaten countries with two primary dangers, a debt crisis or a sudden stop, which can be interrelated.

    1. In a debt crisis, a country that has borrowed heavily from foreign investors may face extremely high interest payments and the possibility of defaulting on its debt.

    2. With a sudden stop, international capital first pours into an economy, then pours out, whipsawing the financial and banking systems in that country.

B. The classic argument in favor of international capital movement is to let capital flow from capital-rich to capital-poor economies. However, this outcome seems less important in the 2000s than some more subtle arguments about how international capital flows can share risk, allow intergenerational transfers of wealth, and build stronger economic institutions.

    1. The classic argument for international capital flows is based on the idea that some countries have greater numbers of good investment opportunities than they have domestic savings; thus, an inflow of foreign investment capital will raise their growth rate.

        a. The basic theory here implies that financial capital should flow from high-income to low-income countries. Although this pattern sometimes occurs, it is not currently the predominant pattern in the world economy.

        b. Just as investing in only one company would offer insufficient diversification to most investors, being limited to investing in one country limits diversification, too. Sharing risk across countries can have substantial advantages for those economies that are relatively small or heavily dependent on a few industries.

    2. Some degree of investment from middle-income countries in the stock markets of high-income countries can be explained by aging populations. Retirees in the United States and other high-income countries may have invested in financial assets that they are now looking to sell. Presumably, they will sell to younger workers who are looking to save for their own retirement. These younger workers can be found in such countries as Brazil, China, and India.

   3. For countries with underdeveloped financial markets, inflows and outflows of financial capital can be potentially dangerous. However, as countries improve their financial regulations and relevant legal practices, inflows and outflows of capital are more likely to be beneficial. Ultimately, a virtuous circle is possible, in which an expansion of international financial capital flows helps to improve economic institutions.

III. Most of the risks of international capital flows occur for receiving countries; either they encounter a debt problem from receiving so much capital, or they experience a disruptive sudden stop of capital flows. What policies can offer protection against such risks?

   A. Countries receiving capital inflows can take a number of steps to reduce their vulnerability to large amounts of debt and sudden stops.

   1. Capital inflows often arrive through the banking system. If banks are well regulated, they will look at their assets and liabilities, consider all the risks involved, and make plans to reduce those risks where possible.

   2. As we discussed in an earlier lecture, a country with large foreign exchange reserves is less vulnerable to a sudden stop. Since the 1997–1998 East Asian crisis, many countries have built up substantial foreign exchange reserves.

   3. Often, the reason for a country's debt problem is that the government runs large deficits. Governments need to be cautious about borrowing to their limits.

   B. Most international borrowing now is fairly simple at root: Money is borrowed, then repaid with interest. But more complex financial contracts are possible. For example, agreements can be written so that the amount of repayment automatically decreases if a country goes into recession or if the price of a key export falls. Such contracts would force lenders to share more of the risk.

C. International agreements or agencies can sometimes step in when international capital flows have gone bad. For example, the World Bank and the International Monetary Fund have run the Heavily Indebted Poor Countries (HIPC) initiative since 1996 to reduce debt burdens for deserving poor countries.

D. A common reaction from some non-economists and politicians is to try to avoid the potential costs of foreign capital flows by blocking inflows or outflows of financial capital. Such policies can be effective, but in eliminating the potential costs, they also eliminate potential benefits.

IV. The world economy remains some distance from being fully globalized. Capital does not yet move as easily around the world economy as it does, say, across the regions or states of the United States.

A. One measure of the extent of financial globalization is the investors' "home bias," that is, the degree to which people from a given country invest in assets from their own country rather than diversifying globally.

B. The relatively limited size of international capital flows used to be called "the mother of all puzzles in economics." After the increases of portfolio investment and foreign direct investment in recent years, this statement is not as true as it once was, but the potential exists for a great deal more expansion in international financial markets.

Suggested Readings:

Crook, "A Cruel Sea of Capital."

World Bank, *Global Development Finance: The Development Potential of Surging Capital Flows*.

Questions to Consider:

1. Why is foreign direct investment typically preferred by recipient countries over portfolio investment?

2. What are some reasons why an international flow of financial capital might benefit the world economy?

3. What policies might reduce the risks of ever-larger flows of international financial capital?

Lecture Twenty-Four—Transcript
Globalization of Capital Flows

International capital flows seem dark and mysterious and a little ominous to many people. We know international bankers are involved, of course, and multinational corporations, and in general, a foreigner is buying up companies and assets in other countries. The amounts are measured in hundreds of billions or even trillions of dollars, and occasionally, leads to a full-fledged economic disaster. I hope this lecture can demystify international capital flows. Sometimes, they do lead to economic crises, but many other times, they help serve perfectly plausible, and reasonable, and beneficial economic functions.

Let's start with some basic facts and distinctions. Flows of international financial capital are often divided into portfolio investment and foreign direct investment. Both of these categories have grown a lot over recent years. "Portfolio investment" refers to financial investments that do not involve actually managing a firm. For example, if an investor in China buys U.S. treasury bonds, that investor isn't going to manage any firms. In fact, in general, if people buy debt or they invest in mutual funds, that doesn't involve management of a firm in another country. Portfolio debt can typically be bought and sold very quickly.

There has been an enormous expansion in this kind of foreign investment in recent years. Portfolio investment rose sixfold, for example, from 1997 to 2006. It was about $5 trillion in 1997 and over $30 trillion by 2006. Let's put this another way, in the context of the world economy. Portfolio investment was equal to about 20% of world GDP in 1997. That is, it was equal to about 20% of total world production of goods and services. By 2006, portfolio investment was equal to about 70% of world GDP in that year. We need to talk about what this means and why it matters, but for now, let's just establish those basic facts and move on to foreign direct investment.

Foreign direct investment involves taking a management interest in a company that's in another country. This kind of investment was about $200 billion a year throughout the 1970s and up to the mid-1980s. At that point, it started rising quickly. It peaked at about $1.2 trillion in the year 2000 and then fell back to about $550 billion in 2002, in the aftermath of the U.S. stock market fall of 2001. That stock market fall both decreased foreign direct holdings by itself—just because all the stock was worthless—and it also scared investors off, to some extent, from those kinds of direct investments in companies. But by 2006, foreign direct investment in the world economy was back up to about $1.2 trillion a year.

This isn't just United States or European or Japanese firms investing in companies in other countries, which is maybe the stereotype of what we think of by foreign direct investment—high-income countries owning firms that are in low-income countries. But more and more and more, foreign direct investment involves firms from countries like China or India investing in other countries, or South African firms buying parts of firms in other parts of Africa, or Latin American firms buying firms in other parts of that region.

The numbers here are much lower than portfolio investment. Remember, that was multiple trillions of dollars, more than $30 trillion in 2006. But foreign direct investment has a different rule. Because it involves some level of management responsibility, it's more likely to involve management expertise. That means that the purchaser of the firm in another country is more likely to transfer certain kinds of accounting skills, legal skills, and financial skills. It's more likely to involve transfers of technology to some company that's being acquired. It's more likely to involve one firm acting as a supplier for firms in other countries or perhaps as a customer for firms in other countries. As a result of these kinds of differences, many nations feel a lot better about the economic benefits they might receive from foreign direct investment than about the economic benefits they might receive from portfolio investment, which could come and go much more easily.

With this distinction in mind, what are the dangers and the benefits of globalizing financial markets? There are two main dangers of international capital flows. They can be interrelated to each other. One is a debt crisis and the other is something called a "sudden stop." Let's talk about these in turn.

If a country ends up with very high levels of debt—debt that's borrowed from foreign investors—and it ends up facing extremely high payments on that—extremely high interest payments—and perhaps eventually defaulting on that debt, it can cause all sorts of economic problems. For present purposes, it doesn't really matter here much whether the fault for these high debts is on the borrower for borrowing too much, or it's on the lender for lending too much, or it's on economic circumstances for shifting in some way that maybe neither the borrower nor the lender could really anticipate.

The point is just that some country has massive debts; it can't pay them off; and it has really high interest payments that are soaking up a lot of the available funds that the government has. It means that country, because of those debt payments, can't invest as it might want to in, say, schools, or health, or infrastructure. It also means, often, that banks are not doing much lending to that country because the banks are worried about the debts not being repaid. Banks within the country may also well be bankrupt. They're unable to repay loans they've taken out, and so private borrowers in that country have very little access to finance. As a result, countries in that situation, in a debt crisis, can end up mired in a no-growth situation for years, and years, and years.

The classic example of this problem, discussed earlier in these lectures, was the Latin American debt crisis of the 1980s. You'll remember that decade was called the "Lost Decade" for its lack of growth. But you could also cite problems faced by the highly indebted economies of Africa in the 1980s and into the 1990s. Clearly, it's a potential cost of international financial flows that countries sometimes end up mired in debt and long-term recession or depression as a result.

The other major problem with international financial capital flows is the issue of a "sudden stop," when international capital first pours into an economy and then pours out, whipsawing the financial and banking systems in that country. Of course, the classic example here is the experience of East Asia's tiger economies with financial crises in 1997 and 1998, which we talked about in a previous lecture. Again, what happens in this situation is that international funds rushed into those countries. The banking systems, the stock markets in those countries weren't really ready to evaluate the risks involved. Outsiders kind of assumed these countries were growing well; the growth would go on forever. Then, when the economy turned a little bit sour, those same foreign investors who had poured the money in, then flooded out, at least for a few years. As they flooded out, that collapsed the domestic banking system of the country, made all the banks effectively bankrupt, and led to a period of recession and flat growth.

In the U.S. economy, we've seen these kinds of rushes ourselves, although they haven't quite had the same powerful effect on the economy. For example, a lot of the money that rushed into the Internet stock boom of the late 1990s and then rushed out again was international money. That's why foreign direct investment flows were so high in 2000 and dropped off by 2002.

As discussed in the earlier lectures, these debt and financial crises are real and severe crises. But by themselves, they don't prove that international capital flows are always a bad idea. It would sort of be like saying that some people pile up too much credit-card debt, so let's abolish credit cards. Or some mortgage companies and borrowers went crazy with subprime mortgages, so let's eliminate mortgages for everyone. Or saying poorly regulated banks can have financial problems, so rather than getting better regulations, we'll just get rid of all banks. It's true that financial markets can go bad in all kinds of ways, but let's look at the other side of the coin, concerning the potential benefits international financial lending can offer.

One potential benefit is providing capital for capital-poor countries. The sort of classic argument for international capital flows is based on the notion that there is, as economists would say, "diminishing marginal productivity" to capital investment. All that means is that countries with a lot of financial capital—high-income countries, like the United States—should have relatively low rates of return on investment. Because they already have so much capital invested, the additional capital should have a lower rate of return. Countries with little financial capital—tending to be lower-income countries—should have lots of opportunities for investments that provide a higher rate of return. Thus, financial capital should flow from high-income countries to low-income countries in search of higher rates of return.

This pattern has sometimes happened during world history. For example, Britain during the 19th century was a high-income country at the time and commonly had lots of investment abroad. In modern times, Germany and the United Kingdom also tend to have net investment abroad. On the receiving side, we've talked about how there were inflows to growing regions of the world economy, like East Asia, or Latin America, or even what may be happening with Africa in the first decade of the 21st century.

However, this pattern of high-income countries sending money to low-income countries has not been the predominant pattern in the world economy over the last decade or so. For many countries, the inflows and outflows of financial capital in their economies more or less balance each other. Looking at it from an international perspective, they aren't on net either sending investment abroad or receiving investment. They're doing both in an offsetting way.

Among the countries receiving financial capital from international investors, by far the biggest recipient nation through the 1990s and through the first decade of the 2000s is the United States. The United States is clearly a high-income country with lots and lots of financial capital by world standards. Conversely, some much lower-income countries, like China, are sending capital abroad. [Aren't] there great growth opportunities in China, with its rapid, rapid economic growth? To economists, this is kind of a puzzle. It's like water flowing uphill. Why should capital be flowing away from a low-income, high-growth country, like China, which seems like it could really use that investment capital, and toward a high-income country, like the United States, that already has a lot of investment capital? It's kind of like if Saudi Arabia started importing oil or Brazil started importing coffee. Don't you already have a lot of that in those countries? How are we explaining what we see?

One likely factor here is a process of risk sharing and diversification. One of the most important general lessons of investing is: Don't put all your eggs in one basket—diversify! If you invest all your savings, for example, in one company that expects to have a 7% per year return, the problem is that if that company goes south, you might lose everything. But if you invest in 100 companies that all expect a 7% rate of return, some will do better, some will do worse—it will mostly even out—and you are more likely to actually get that 7% return that you were expecting. It's much safer to diversify. It reduces risk.

That same lesson applies in general for economies. Imagine that you're a small country, and you depend heavily on a few industries, like copper, or coffee, or tourism. If you are only invested in your country, you're exposed to a lot of risk. The same holds true even for a big economy, like the United States, where you can go through an Internet stock bubble or a meltdown in the housing market. And maybe it's good to have investments both in countries that are oil importers, like the United States, and oil exporters. If you do that, then movements in the price of oil wouldn't help or hurt you too much; they would sort of be offset. Countries have recessions at different times. They face different risks, so it makes sense to diversify across them.

If you think about diversifying from a global perspective—where should we put our money—the U.S. economy has a real advantage. Compared to a lot of the rest of the world, the United States has well-developed financial regulators, and well-developed companies, and lots of ways to invest in those companies pretty easily, like mutual funds. One way to think about this is: The United States is really a world-class producer of marketable and easily transferable financial assets, where you can really be pretty clear about what you're buying and what you're likely to get. In a lot of the rest of the world, if you're trying to invest there, either it's hard to invest in practical terms or it's hard to know what you're getting when you invest or both.

Of course, professional investors have known about diversification for a long, long time, but it's really only in the last decade or two that financial markets around the world have become well developed enough that they can apply this lesson of diversification on a worldwide basis. A lot of the money flowing into the U.S. economy is clearly flowing here to diversify risks from other countries.

What's another big reason for these international flows coming to the United States? The United States and other high-income countries have aging populations. The retirees are going up as a share of their populations. Many of these retirees have saved up a fair amount of money for retirement. That's maybe a pension fund, or an IRA, or a 401(k), something like that. The retirees will want to sell off these assets as they start retiring. As retirees sell off these assets, who is going to buy them? Presumably, it's going to be younger workers, who are going to start saving for their own retirement. But in an aging country, where can you find enough younger workers who are willing to buy the assets that retirees are selling off? The answer is: You probably won't find them inside the country. You'll find them outside the country. You'll find a number of them in countries with younger workers, like Brazil, China, or India. That helps explain why you might see investors in those countries buying stock market investments and buying firms in high-income countries. There's nothing necessarily ominous in that pattern.

There's also an interesting gain for countries with underdeveloped financial markets. We know that inflows and outflows of financial capital can be potentially dangerous—Latin America in the 1980s, East Asia in 1997–1998—but, we also know that as countries improve in their financial regulations and their relevant legal practices, the inflows and outflows of capital are more likely to be beneficial over time.

When I talk about these regulations and rules, what do I have in mind? What I'm really talking about is rules about accounting, companies reporting audited financial figures that are publicly available to investors. I'm talking about regulating banks, so they don't take absurd risks. I'm talking about economies that have recognized financial contracts in standard forms and clear laws and rules about who owns what, who gets owed what, how money can be collected, straightforward bankruptcy procedures when those are needed, and an understandable and predictable tax code.

My point here is that there's sort of a virtuous circle which is possible. Imagine that a country allows some international financial capital flows. With those flows, they get some interest from foreign investors and managers and banks. They all want to know what's going on in that economy. That helps bring a development of these useful financial institutions. Studies over the last decade or so suggest that the inflows and outflows of financial capital in and of [themselves] might be less important, in a way, than their role in helping to develop this kind of invisible institutional infrastructure that makes financial markets work better.

International flows of capital have potential costs and potential benefits. Like a lot of economic situations, it's all costs and benefits. The question is whether there are policies or institutional frameworks that can make it more likely the benefits will be received and reduce the chance that the costs will be incurred. Most of the risks of international capital flows occur for the receiving country. Either the country is receiving so much capital that it causes a debt problem or it experiences a disruptive sudden stop of capital flows. What policies can a country undertake that would offer protection against these kinds of risks?

One set of policies would involve better risk management in the receiving countries. They can take a number of steps to reduce their vulnerability to large amounts of debt or sudden stops. For example, capital inflows often arrive through the banking system. That is, banks in a country borrow in a foreign currency, like U.S. dollars, and then the money is loaned out in local currency to the rest of the economy. If banks are well-regulated, when they take this kind of a process underway, they'll need to look at their assets and their liabilities and consider the risks in doing this—particularly the risks of the local economy turning bad, the risks of exchange rates shifting, and the risk of interest rates shifting—and plan ahead to reduce those risks, where possible, and to hold sufficient reserves so [the bank] wouldn't be so exposed to risk.

A related step, then, is these foreign exchange reserves, the additional reserves that could be held by governments. Since the '97–'98 East Asian financial crisis, lots of countries have been building up substantial foreign exchange reserves. For example, China had something over $1 trillion in foreign exchange reserves at the end of 2007. Korea had over $200 billion in foreign exchange reserves. India and Brazil had over $200 billion; Russia had about $400 billion. Mexico had $75 billion in foreign exchange reserves. Even the countries of Africa, if you take them as a group, have over $200 billion in foreign exchange reserves.

The great advantage of holding foreign exchange reserves in a fluctuating and volatile international economy is that if foreign investors decide they want to leave your country and start selling off your currency, your central bank can buy its own currency. It can buy it using the foreign exchange dollar reserves that it has accumulated. The fact that those reserves exist reassures foreign investors. They don't have to race for the exit. They don't need to panic. If they need to sell, they'll be able to do so. That helps prevent a sharp drop in the value of a currency.

Another step governments can take to manage their risks is to limit government borrowing. Sometimes, the reason for a country's debt crisis, a lot of the time, is that the government of the country has just been running large budget deficits. If money flows to the private sector, lenders tend to be pretty cautious. But with governments, sometimes lenders just assume that the government will find a way to repay the debt somehow. Also, in some countries—Brazil is an example—there are strong state-level governments that have the power to borrow, as well. If all the state-level governments start borrowing, they can get the economy of the whole country in trouble as a result. Governments need to be cautious about borrowing out to their limits and consider the risks involved.

Another broad category of steps that can reduce the chance of financial crisis is innovative financial instruments. Most international borrowing right now is fairly simple at root. You borrow money; you repay interest and principal. But more complex financial contracts are certainly possible. For example, you might have a financial contract that has interest payments, but the amount of repayment might automatically decrease if a country goes into recession, or it might automatically change if the price of a key export falls. Why not have a financial contract that automatically adjusts, linked to these kinds of outcomes?

You could imagine if you have some key export for your country, then you'd link repayment of your debts to the price of that key good. If the good goes up in price, you'll pay more. If it goes down in price, you'll pay less. It's all written into the contract in advance. Or, similarly, if your economy has been going up and down, up and down, like the economies of Latin America, have your debt contract [written so] that with higher GDP growth, you'll pay more; with lower GDP growth, you'll pay less. In fact, several countries during the first decade of the 2000s have sold GDP-linked bonds that worked just like that.

Such contracts are, of course, a tradeoff, like everything else. If risks go bad, the people who loaned you the money are going to share more of the risk. Because lenders know they are sharing more of the risk, they are likely to demand higher interest payments for these kinds of loans. In effect, a borrower is paying a little more in interest, but that could be a reasonable form of insurance, really, for avoiding the worst costs of an international financial collapse.

Another broad category that could help reduce the risks of international lending would be intervention from international institutions. Let me give you a couple of examples there. International agreements or agencies can step in sometimes when international capital flows have gone bad. For example, in 1996, the World Bank organized a program that was sometimes called the HIPC program. HIPC stood for "highly indebted poor countries."

The idea of HIPC was that if a low-income country with a lot of debt started following sensible economic policies—and we're talking here about low government borrowing, relatively low inflation, some focus on reducing poverty—then you would give that government some help in having some or all of its debts forgiven.

By 2006, 10 years later, 22 countries in Latin America and Africa had had debts forgiven under this plan. Examples of some of those countries would be Bolivia, Honduras, and Nicaragua in Latin America or, in Africa, Ghana, Ethiopia, and Uganda. There are a number of other countries that, in theory, would be eligible for this plan, but they haven't gotten their act together to do the kinds of economic reforms that could get their debts reduced. Examples would be Nepal, Sudan, Somalia, and others.

More generally, one main purpose of the International Monetary Fund is to step in when international financial flows go bad. What we're usually talking about, here, is something like a sudden stop. Imagine that foreign investors are racing to sell their stakes in a given country. There's a stampede to get out and it's causing all sorts of troubles—bankruptcies of banks, a collapsing exchange rate, all those kinds of issues. The International Monetary Fund could step in and offer the country a loan. That loan would help stop the rush to the exits. It would allow an orderly way of dealing with the economic problems of the country. We'll discuss in a later lecture some of the issues and problems that arise with the International Monetary Fund and these kinds of loans, but that's really its overall function and role.

Another common reaction, from some non-economists and politicians more than economists, is to try to avoid the potential costs of foreign capital flows by blocking the inflows of foreign capital or blocking outflows. It's not easy to make these policies work. If you're involved in international trade, for example, then you're buying and selling stuff across your national borders all the time. Money needs to flow across the border, too. If you have money flowing back and forth across the border, it's pretty easy to re-label various transactions in a way that lets funds flow in or out of the country. For example, an international company that has operations in many different countries could say: We're just going to charge what's happening in this country a little bit more or a little bit less, and that will let us move money in or out of the country through our internal bookkeeping as inputs and production moves between different countries.

If you cut a country off from foreign trade, then of course, you could also cut it off largely from financial capital movements, as well. India, for example, in the '50s and '60s, up until the late '80s, really did a lot of this. Of course, if you eliminate financial capital flows going in and out of the country, you're also going to eliminate any potential financial benefits you might have gotten from those flows. The real difficulty, or one of the real difficulties, with this step is that governments often choose just the worst possible time to decide it's the moment to control capital flows. They choose the moment when a crisis has already occurred.

Imagine you have this situation: All sorts of foreign investors are holding their breath. Do they all need to sell their assets in a certain country and flee? Is it going to happen? Will there be a panic? Right at that moment is the moment the ham-handed government says: Hey, maybe we'll pass a rule that will stop anyone from taking funds out of the country. Of course, as soon as the government says that, everyone panics and gets out as much money as they can, as fast as they possibly can. If you're going to try and control capital flowing in and out of your economy, probably the best way is a gentle way.

Chile for a time had certain rules and taxes, and their idea was, in a way, to discourage portfolio investment while not putting the same restrictions on foreign direct investment. These rules weren't suddenly imposed in an emergency. They were just in place over a sustained period of time. The idea was that Chileans liked foreign direct investment—with the management and expertise and new technology it tends to bring, the international business ties—but it wasn't so keen on portfolio investment that might be moved out in a big hurry. Research suggests that Chile's policies had a modest effect for a time in funneling more investment in Chile toward foreign direct investment and making it a little bit less susceptible to an outflow of portfolio funds.

Given the huge changes in financial globalization that have occurred, we can ask ourselves: Are we getting near a fully globalized capital market? What would that look like? I think the short answer is: The world economy remains some substantial distance from being fully globalized. Let me think about just what it would mean to have a fully globalized financial market.

Essentially, it would mean that an American, say, could invest just as easily with a firm in Japan or Germany, and with the same information about risks and returns, as that American could invest in a firm in, say, New York or California. It would be just as easy and, perhaps, [pose] similar risks to buy a U.S. state bond or a U.S. city bond as it would be to buy, say, a German bond or, for that matter, a bond from the government of Thailand. Certainly, the ease of these international financial transactions has gone up a lot in recent years. You can do a lot of things buying mutual funds over the Internet. But there's strong evidence that international capital markets are not really close to fully integrated just yet.

One measure of the extent of financial globalization is the extent of what's called "home bias," that is, how much people from a given country invest in assets from their own country instead of diversifying globally. Think about this for a moment. If the United States is, say, round numbers, 25% of the world economy, then you should have 25% of your investments in the United States and the rest diversified around the world. One study found out that at the end of the 1980s, U.S. stock market investors had 94% of their stock investments in U.S. firms. Japanese stock investors had 99% of their investments in Japanese firms. French, German, and Canadian investors had only 1% or less of their money in U.S. firms. In other words, all across the world, people weren't diversifying in a way that was fitting, given the size of different economies in the world.

There has not been a huge change in the United States. It's still true, by the mid-2000s, that about 90% of the financial assets of U.S. investors are still in U.S.-type assets. But in France and Germany, thanks to the euro making it so much easier to invest across Europe, home bias has dropped substantially in the first decade of the 21st century. Australia has seen a lot less home bias, too, I suspect because there are a lot more Australians who are investing in China and across East Asia. We're still a long way, however, from the diversification you would expect in a truly borderless world.

Another puzzle that shows something about the limited size of international financial investment is the relatively limited size of international capital flows. Remember, in most countries, domestic saving and domestic investment pretty much balance each other out. The total amount flowing in or out of a country on net is maybe 1 or 2% of GDP. This isn't true in national economies. In national economies, you get big swings of capital going across regions—money going to the U.S. South, or to California, or away from the Rust Belt. In the international economy, you don't see these kinds of enormous swings.

Back in 1980, two well-known economists wrote a paper where they said the lack of financial capital going across borders was, as they called it, "the mother of all puzzles in economics." After the really rapid growth in portfolio investment and foreign direct investment in the last decade or so, it really isn't the mother of all puzzles anymore, but it's still the cousin of all puzzles. There's potentially a lot more international expansion of financial markets that can happen.

The key thing to remember is that financial flows are different in some fundamental ways from flows of goods and services. Financial markets involve extremely large amounts that can be moved very, very quickly. Because it involves placing values on assets, you can see bubbles and fads from time to time that can seem destructive. But it's worth remembering that finance can also be an essential component for healthy economic growth.

My wife used to work as a stock market analyst for an investment bank before we had children and she made a career shift, for a few years, to being a stay-at-home mom. She used to talk about financial capital as an underground river. You can't usually see it directly, but where the great underground river of investment capital flows, economies and businesses bloom. Where that great river doesn't flow, economies and businesses wither. The globalization of finance, if managed in a wise institutional framework, can offer great benefits to the world economy.

Glossary

agglomeration: When economic activity is concentrated in a certain geographic location—includes both benefits and costs.

Bank of Japan: The organization that conducts monetary policy for Japan's yen.

biofuels: Fuels made from agricultural products, such as corn-based ethanol.

brain drain: The concern that low-income countries will suffer because many of those with the highest level of skills or education may choose to emigrate to high-income countries.

Bretton Woods agreement: An international agreement signed in 1944 that helped to keep major exchange rates largely fixed until the early 1970s.

capabilities approach: The argument that in thinking about poverty, income is less important than whether people have a fair chance to develop their own human capabilities.

central bank: The organization that conducts monetary policy, including the Federal Reserve in the United States and the European Central Bank.

Council for Mutual Economic Assistance (COMECON): This organization managed the trade relationships between the Soviet Union and the countries under its sphere of influence.

credit crunch: A situation in which it becomes difficult to get loans, even for those willing to pay the going interest rate.

Depression: The worldwide economic downturn that started in 1929 and lasted well into the 1930s (also called the Great Depression).

deregulation: Reducing the extent to which government controls decisions about price and output in certain markets.

Doha round: The name for the most recent round of international negotiations to reduce barriers to trade as part of the World Trade Organization.

dollarization: When another country chooses to use the U.S. dollar as its currency.

Dutch disease: the nickname given by economists to countries in which the economy seems to suffer slow growth as a result of having large exports of oil or other natural resources.

East Asian tigers: A nickname for fast-growing countries of this region, typically including South Korea, Taiwan, Indonesia, Malaysia, Thailand, Singapore, and Hong Kong.

European Central Bank: The organization that conducts monetary policy for the euro.

European Coal and Steel Community: The initial step toward European Union taken in 1951.

European Community: A predecessor of today's European Union.

European Economic Community: An early predecessor of today's European Union created by the Treaty of Rome in 1957.

European Union: An economic and political partnership across 27 European countries.

exchange rate: The rate at which one currency is exchanged for another.

exports: Goods produced domestically but sold in another country.

Federal Reserve: The central bank for the United States, which controls monetary policy for the U.S. dollar.

fiscal policy: Tax and spending policies.

fixed exchange rates: Exchange rates set by the government and requiring government intervention to stay in place.

flexible exchange rates: Exchange rates determined by market forces.

foreign exchange reserves: When a country or central bank holds reserves in a different currency, such as the Bank of China holding U.S. dollars.

General Agreement on Tariffs and Trade (GATT): An international agreement to reduce barriers to trade, started in 1947 and evolving into the World Trade Organization in 1995.

globalization: The process of the world economy becoming more intertwined through trade and financial flows.

Gosplan: The committee most responsible for state planning of the economy in the USSR.

Great Depression: The worldwide economic downturn that started in 1929 and lasted well into the 1930s (sometimes just called the Depression).

gross domestic product (GDP): A standard measure of the size of an economy in terms of total goods and services produced.

Heavily Indebted Poor Countries (HIPC): The name of an initiative started in 1996 to reduce the debts of low-income countries.

human capital: The skills and education of workers.

hyperinflation: Inflation at very high rates.

import substitution: A policy of economic development that seeks to produce manufactured and technology goods domestically, rather than importing them.

imports: Goods produced in another country and sold domestically.

industrial policy: A government policy of choosing and favoring certain industries.

Industrial Revolution: The period in the early 1800s when economic growth began to take off in the United Kingdom and the United States.

inflation: A general rise in the level of prices.

Intergovernmental Panel on Climate Change (IPCC): A group of scientists and government officials who put out the benchmark estimates for global warming.

International Bank for Reconstruction and Development (IBRD): One part of the World Bank.

International Monetary Fund (IMF): An international organization that seeks to minimize major exchange rate movements.

license raj: The nickname given to India's pervasive system of business regulation from the 1950s up to about 1991.

Lisbon agenda: A set of proposals to make Europe a more competitive, knowledge-based economy, arising out of a summit in 2000.

Malthusian: Referring to the arguments of the early 19th-century economist Thomas Robert Malthus that population growth would eventually outstrip food supply.

megacities: Cities with a population of at least 10 million.

MITI: Japan's Ministry of Economy, Trade and Industry, which often took a leading role when Japan's government wished to intervene in the economy.

monetary policy: Policies to affect interest rates and the supply of credit in an economy, thus influencing both inflation and real economic activity.

"new economy": A shorthand way of referring to the change in the U.S. economy since about 1995, when a surge of productivity growth based on information and communications technology began.

per capita GDP: GDP divided by population.

physical capital: Plant and equipment.

poverty trap: In development economics, the theory that because poor people in low-income countries are unable to save for the future, their countries will suffer low rates of investment and slow economic growth into the future.

privatization: Selling off state-owned firms to the private sector.

productivity: The amount produced per worker or per hour of work.

Protectionism: A desire to protect domestic producers from foreign competition by imposing tariffs or quotas on imported products.

purchasing power parity (PPP) exchange rate: The exchange rate at which the buying power of two currencies (measured in terms of internationally traded goods) is equal; an exchange rate often used for comparing the size of two different economies.

race to the bottom: The theory that countries will compete to attract international business by reducing their environmental and social laws and regulations.

stagflation: When a stagnating economy and high inflation occur at the same time; a term coined to describe the U.S. economy in the 1970s.

state-owned enterprises: Firms owned by the government.

sudden stop: The shorthand term for a situation in which a large amount of international financial capital has been flowing into a country, but the flow then reverses itself.

trade balance: Exports equal to imports.

trade deficit: Imports greater than exports.

trade surplus: Exports greater than imports.

Treaty of Rome: A 1957 treaty that established the European Economic Community, a forerunner of today's European Union.

unemployment: The situation that exists when workers who are willing to work for the wage that fits their skill and experience level are unable to find jobs.

urbanization: The historical process by which a higher percentage of people move to urban areas as an economy develops.

World Bank: An international organization that seeks to encourage development in low-income economies with loans and expertise.

World Trade Organization: An international agreement to reduce barriers to trade, started in 1995, evolving out of the GATT.

Bibliography

Abrams, Burton A. "How Richard Nixon Pressured Arthur Burns: Evidence from the Nixon Tapes." *Journal of Economic Perspectives.* Fall 2006, 20:4, pp. 177–188. Economists have long asked the question: Why did the Federal Reserve allow inflation to get out of control in the 1970s? Broadly speaking, there are two explanations. One holds that many economists and policymakers had come to believe in the late 1960s and early 1970s that the Fed either couldn't stop inflation or could do so at only a very high cost. The other explanation is that President Richard Nixon pressured the head of the Federal Reserve, Arthur Burns, to jumpstart the economy before the 1972 election—even though Burns strongly suspected that inflation would take off after the election. This article discusses and contrasts these arguments—both of which hold true to some extent.

Asher, David L. "What Became of the Japanese 'Miracle?' Economic Development in Japan: Economic Myths Explained." *Orbis.* Spring 1996. http://findarticles.com/p/articles/mi_m0365/is_n2_v40/ai_18338847/pg_1. Asher walks step by step through the creation and rupture of Japan's bubble economy. He discusses the elements of Japan's previous growth that seem true in retrospect and those that seem like myth. He also argues that economic developments in Japan will affect the role that country is expected to play in the world, both economically and politically.

Banerjee, Abhijit, and Esther Duflo. "The Economic Lives of the Poor." *Journal of Economic Perspectives.* Winter 2007, 21:1, pp. 141–168. http://papers.ssrn.com/sol3/papers.cfm?abstract_id=942062 (working paper version). Banerjee and Duflo take a detailed look at the economic lives of those who live on less than $1 a day around the world. Using survey data, they look at consumer spending, savings, possessions, jobs and migration patterns, borrowing, and more. They come to the interesting conclusion that even on $1 a day, there is some degree of flexibility in the economic lives of the very poor.

Bertuch-Samuels, Axel, and Parmeshwar Ramlogan. "The Euro: Ever More Global." *Finance and Development.* March 2007. 44(1). http://www.imf.org/external/pubs/ft/fandd/2007/03/bertuch.htm. Will the euro overtake the U.S. dollar as the world's primary currency? Although the euro gained remarkably widespread acceptance in its first decade or so, it remains primarily used for transactions related to Europe in one way or another. At least so far, the U.S. dollar is not being seriously challenged by the euro as the world's primary currency.

Bhagwati, Jagdish. "Borders Beyond Control." *Foreign Affairs.* January/February 2003. http://www.cfr.org/publication.html?id=5356. Bhagwati is an eminent economist who supports free trade in goods and services. In this article, he proposes a World Migration Organization that would help coordinate low-income and high-income countries to maximize the benefits and hold down the costs of international immigration.

Bloom, David E., and Jeffrey D. Sachs. "Geography, Demography, and Economic Growth in Africa." In *Brookings Papers on Economic Activity 2: 1998*, pp. 207–295. Bloom and Sachs lay out in detail the factors related to geography and climate that have hindered economic growth in Africa. In particular, the first part of the article (pp. 207–251) is accessible to any informed reader. The remainder of the article sets out a mathematical model and some statistical tests that are of greater interest to professionals and college students.

"Briefing: Business in South-East Asia: The Tigers That Lost Their Roar." *The Economist.* March 1, 2008, pp. 73–75. This article focuses on the question of why Southeast Asia has spawned so few firms that produce world-class products, despite the region's decades of economic growth. It discusses issues of corruption and entrenched elites and offers a sense of the challenges that these economies face in trying to make the transition from middle- to high-income nations.

"Briefing: Food and the Poor: The New Face of Hunger." *The Economist.* April 19, 2008, pp. 32–34. Sharply rising food prices pose an especially major problem for several billion of the poorest people around the world, who have little room in their budgets to adjust. Given that many of these poor people are also farmers, it is hoped that they will see their incomes rise as a result of higher food prices. But many low-income countries are trying to hold down food prices for the benefit of consumers, without regard for incentives to producers.

"Briefing: Food Prices: Cheap No More." *The Economist.* December 8, 2007, pp. 81–83. This useful article summarizes an amazing change in agricultural markets: the shift from several decades of cheap food to what looks as if it will be some years of expensive food. The primary reason for the change lies in demand for food—supply is actually quite high. The main drivers behind the demand are increasing needs in such countries as China and India and biofuels policies.

"Briefing: Russia's Economy: Smoke and Mirrors." *The Economist*. March 1, 2008, pp. 27–29. This article surveys the extent to which Russia's economic growth in the last 10 years or so has depended on higher oil prices. It also argues that Russia has experienced an eroding rule of commercial law over this time; thus, even though higher energy prices have made Russia's economic growth look strong, the underlying development of Russia's private-sector economy has not proceeded as well as it otherwise might have.

Burton, David, and Alessandro Zanello. "Asia Ten Years After." *Finance and Development*. June 2007, 44:2. http://www.imf.org/external/pubs/ft/fandd/2007/06/burton.htm. This useful summary reviews what has happened in the 10 years since the financial crisis of 1997–1998 in Asia. It also considers the economic to-do list for the region if rapid growth is to resume.

Buvinic, Mayra, and Elizabeth M. King. "Smart Economics." *Finance and Development*. June 2007, 44:2. http://www.imf.org/external/pubs/ft/fandd/2007/06/index.htm. This article offers an accessible introduction to the reasons why better opportunities and fairer treatment of women offer real economic payoffs. The same issue of the publication includes two other articles on gender inequality and development: "Getting All Girls into School," by Maureen A. Lewis and Marlaine E. Lockheed, and "Budgeting with Women in Mind," by Janet G. Stotsky.

Cardoso, Eliana, and Ann Helwege. *Latin America's Economy: Diversity, Trends, and Conflicts*. Cambridge, MA: MIT Press, 1992. This readable book discusses the evolution of Latin America's economy up to the late 1980s. It includes chapters on the long-term evolution of the economy through the 19th century and the first part of the 20th, a chapter on import substitution and trade liberalization, and chapters on the debt and inflation crises of the 1980s.

Christian Aid. "Fuelling Poverty: Oil, War, and Corruption." 2003. http://212.2.6.41/indepth/0305cawreport/fuellingpoverty.htm. This well-written report is from a nongovernment organization devoted to fighting poverty around the world. It summarizes much of the research literature and folk wisdom around the resource curse and offers specific examples of problems in Angola, Sudan, and Kazakhstan. The organization's Web site has a section on resource-related corruption, a problem that doesn't involve just oil but also copper and other resources.

Conte, Christopher, and Albert Karr. *An Outline of the U.S. Economy*. U.S. Department of State, 2001. http://usinfo.state.gov/products/pubs/oecon. This free online book offers an overview of many aspects of the U.S. economy. Chapter 3, "The U.S. Economy: A Brief History," discusses U.S. economic experiences after World War II, through the good years of the 1960s, to the stagflation and productivity slowdown of the 1970s, and thereafter. Chapter 7, "Monetary and Fiscal Policy," also offers insights about how inflation got started in the 1970s and was put to rest in the 1980s. Produced by two former reporters for the *Wall Street Journal*, the book is well written and aimed at a generalist audience.

Council of Economic Advisers. "Economic Report of the President." Various years. http://www.gpoaccess.gov/eop/index.html. The Council of Economic Advisers is an office within the White House. The three members of the council are usually academic economists who are in Washington for only a few years before returning to their institutions—which helps to keep them intellectually honest. Each February, the council publishes an annual report. The first chapter or two is always an overview of the U.S. economy in the previous year. Later chapters take on particular topics; for example, the 2008 report includes chapters on "Credit and Housing Markets," "The Importance of Health and Health Care," and "The Nation's Infrastructure." Readers sometimes have to put up with a mild level of pro–White House propaganda in the report, but it always includes a hefty dose of useful background facts and analysis. The report also includes basic statistical tables for the U.S. economy going back several decades.

Crook, Clive. "A Cruel Sea of Capital." *The Economist*. May 1, 2003. Crook is one of the best-informed and most thoughtful economics journalists. In one of *The Economist*'s middle-of-the-issue essays, he begins by pointing out that global financial markets have expanded a great deal. This expansion offers extraordinary access to private-sector financial capital for countries that have traditionally found it hard to access such markets, but it also brings a real risk that pressures from financial markets can lead to dislocations and disruptions of national economies.

———. "India's Economy." *The Economist*. February 22, 1997. Crook is one of the fine economic journalists of our time. In one of the middle-of-the-issue survey articles that *The Economist* does so well, he looks at the changes from economic reform in India just a few years after they took place. His discussion gives a useful sense of just how constricted India's economy was by the license raj before the reforms—and how the reforms of 1991 were really only a first step toward the broader economic changes India needs.

Das, Gurcharan. *India Unbound: A Personal Account of a Social and Economic Revolution from Independence to the Global Information Age.* New York: Alfred E. Knopf, 2000. Das is a journalist and columnist who, in various ways, grew up with India. He was a boy at the time of independence. His family moved to America in the 1950s. He attended Harvard, then went back to India to work as a business executive who has often crossed paths with top government and industry leaders. He tells the story of India from independence up through the 21st century in a way that mixes interesting anecdotes and episodes with economic facts and background. This immensely readable book conveys both the attraction of India's early policies and the disillusionment they later caused for many. Chapters 1–14 cover the period from India's independence to the reforms of 1991. Chapters 15–23 cover the first decade or so after the economic reforms of 1991.

Easterly, William. *The White Man's Burden: Why the West's Efforts to Aid the Rest of the World Have Done So Much Ill and So Little Good.* New York: Penguin Press, 2006. Easterly is a former World Bank economist and a foreign aid skeptic who knows as much about actual experience with foreign aid as anyone. He argues that the time has come to shun "planners," who have grand schemes to end poverty, and to rely more on "searchers," who help ensure that goods and services actually reach the poor. Easterly also argues that those who distribute foreign aid have used their financial resources to impose their own shifting visions of development policy on poor countries—policies that have often not worked well. For an argument favoring foreign aid, see the book by Jeffrey Sachs.

Eichengreen, Barry. *The European Economy since 1945.* Princeton, NJ: Princeton University Press, 2007. Eichengreen is one of the leading writers on international macroeconomic developments in the 20th century. In this book, he offers a readable history of developments in the European economy since World War II, both summarizing and drawing lessons from the research literature. Chapters 2, 6, and 7 are especially relevant to Lecture Four.

─────. "Old Europe on the Comeback Trail." *Milken Institute Review*. 1st quarter 2008. http://www.milkeninstitute.org/publications/review/2008_1/26-37mr37. pdf (free registration required for access). One often hears dire predictions for Europe's economy: aging workforce, too much government, too much vacation, too little Capitalism. Eichengreen recognizes all these issues but offers the useful reminder that Europe's economy has actually performed quite well over the last few decades. Europe is clearly a high-income part of the world with genuine economic strengths and, Eichengreen argues, a hopeful economic future.

Emmett, Ross B. "Malthus Reconsidered: Population, Natural Resources, and Markets." PERC Policy Series PS-38. November 2006. http://www.perc.org/pdf/ps38.pdf. Emmett undertakes several tasks in this useful essay. He offers an overview of Malthus's beliefs and puts them in the context of modern debates about overpopulation. He also makes the argument (somewhat controversially) that Malthus was not as dire in his predictions about the likelihood and consequences of overpopulation as he has been portrayed.

Ericson, Richard. "The Classical Soviet-Type Economy: Nature of the System and Implications for Reform." *Journal of Economic Perspectives*. Fall 1991, 5:4, pp. 11–27. Ericson offers an overview of how the central planners attempted to operate the Soviet-type economy, looking not only at goods and services but at such elements of the economy as money and banking and foreign trade. Given the extremely interconnected nature of central planning, Ericson believes that partial reform was bound to be difficult and that total replacement of the system was probably necessary.

European Union. "The History of the European Union." http://europa.eu/abc/history/animated_map/index_en.htm. For a basic if somewhat sketchy history of the start and evolution of the European Union, chock-full of dates and events, this Web site is a good starting point.

Federal Reserve Bank of New York. "The Basics of Foreign Trade and Exchange: Foreign Currency Exchange." http://www.newyorkfed.org/education/fx/foreign.htm. The New York branch of the Federal Reserve handles most of the U.S. government's foreign exchange transactions. This Web site offers an informative overview for the general public of how foreign exchange markets work, who participates in those markets, and the choices between fixed and floating exchange rates.

Fischer, Stanley. "Globalization and Its Challenges." *American Economic Review: Papers and Proceedings.* May 2003, pp. 1–30. http://www.iie.com/fischer/pdf/fischer011903.pdf. Fischer is one of the fine macroeconomists of our time. In this public lecture, he considers many of the issues surrounding globalization from the position of a cautious advocate. For example, he looks at whether poverty and inequality are rising or falling, whether globalization helps economic growth, whether the international financial system is too crisis-prone, whether international trade is fair, and at levels of foreign aid. Many of these subjects have been introduced throughout this course, and by the time you near the end of this lecture series, you should be primed for reading articles like this one.

Fogel, Robert W. "Capitalism and Democracy in 2040." *Daedalus.* Summer 2007, pp. 87–95. Fogel won the Nobel Prize in economics in 1995. His primary focus in recent years has been the study of economic growth. Here, he polishes up his crystal ball to take a look at the expected patterns of the world economy several decades into the future. No one can see the future, of course, but some people's predictions—like Lucas's—are more valuable than others

Gall, Norman. "Mending Brazil's Megacity." *Wilson Quarterly.* Summer 2007, pp. 14–21. http://www.braudel.org.br/en/noticias/midia/pdf/wilson_20072.pdf (Web site of the Braudel Institute). This readable article focuses on São Paulo in Brazil, which is the center of an urban area that includes perhaps 20 million people. It has had all the problems of megacities in low-income countries: urban slums, population growth outstripping public services, crime, pollution. But it also has a diverse and growing economy and many personal and business connections to the world economy. The local government is showing some ability to grapple with its problems.

"Global Economic Inequality: More or Less Equal?" *The Economist.* March 11, 2004. This useful article summarizes many of the arguments in the academic literature over how globalization is affecting inequality around the world. The ultimate answer seems to be that inequality is declining in recent decades, but issues of data and interpretation make the question more complex than it may at first appear.

Her Majesty's Treasury. *The Single Market: A Vision for the 21st Century.* January 2007. http://www.hm-treasury.gov.uk/

media/E/0/eer_singlemarket21_21.pdf. The first chapter of this report, "Past, Present and Future—An Assessment of the Single Market," offers a short and readable overview of what the single market has accomplished so far and what challenges are ahead.

Hill, Christopher T. "The Post-Scientific Society." *Issues in Science and Technology.* Fall 2007. http://www.issues.org/24.1/c_hill.html. Hill argues that the second half of the 20th century was a time of science-based economic growth, in the sense that such companies as AT&T, General Electric, and others were built on turning new scientific discoveries into useful products. He further argues that the 21st century is seeing the arrival of a post-scientific society, still very much based in science but in which many of the economic gains and transformations are more related to broad-based integration of knowledge and capacities.

Hoshi, Takeo, and Anil K. Kashyap. "Japan's Financial Crisis and Economic Stagnation." *Journal of Economic Perspectives.* Winter 2004, 18:1, pp. 3–26. The authors discuss in some detail the internal mechanisms of Japan's financial system and how, in the aftermath of the bubble economy, these institutions have combined to create severe problems for the Japanese economy. Even in 2003, these issues were far from resolved.

Ilzkovitz, Fabienne, Adriaan Dierx, Viktoria Kovacs, and Nuno Sousa. "Steps Towards a Deeper Economic Integration: The Internal Market in the 21st Century. A Contribution to the Single Market Review." 2007. http://ec.europa.eu/citizens_agenda/ single_market_review/docs/ecp271_en.pdf. This report from the European Commission provides a detailed and exhaustive but completely nontechnical overview of what the single market initiative has done in Europe and the main challenges that European economic integration still faces.

International Monetary Fund (IMF). "Climate Change and the Global Economy." Chapter 4 in *World Economic Outlook.* April 2008. http://www.imf.org/external/pubs/ft/weo/2008/01/pdf/c4.pdf. Analysts at the International Monetary Fund describe the macroeconomic and financial consequences of policies to address climate change. According to the authors, the overall effect on world growth of such policies, spread over several decades, would be relatively small, but the costs would also be unevenly distributed around the world. This chapter offers an overview of a number of economic studies of the costs and benefits of climate change and the policies for reducing carbon emissions.

————. *Regional Economic Outlook: Sub-Saharan Africa.* April 2008. http://www.imf.org/external/pubs/ft/reo/2008/AFR/eng/ sreo0408.pdf (or type the title into a search engine). This *Outlook* report typically comes out twice a year. The first section is an evolving report on the current situation of Africa's economy, usually with some perspective going back 5 to 10 years. Later sections of the report sometimes focus on particular topics; for example, the 2008 report discusses private capital flows to Africa and power-supply issues.

————."What Is the IMF?" September 30, 2006. http://www.imf.org/external/pubs/ft/exrp/what.htm. This essay offers an overview of the IMF, including why it was created, where its money comes from, how it decides on loans, and more. The page also has links to other fact sheets and history.

————. *World Economic Outlook.* Published twice each year; available at the IMF external Web site. http://www.imf.org/ external/index.htm (or type "World Economic Outlook IMF" into a search engine). This semiannual report always begins with an overview of the current state of the world economy, working its way around the regions of the world. It then offers several chapters on broader topics. For example, the October 2007 report has chapters on "Globalization and Inequality" and "The Changing Dynamics of the Global Business Cycle."

International Organization for Migration. *World Migration 2005: Costs and Benefits of International Migration.* http://www.iom.int/ jahia/Jahia/cache/offonce/pid/1674?entryId=932. The International Organization for Migration is a leader in the attempt to work out migration issues. It has more than 120 countries as its members. Every two to three years, it puts out a lengthy report that summarizes the current state of affairs on migration. This edition focuses on costs and benefits of migration but also includes discussion of other issues and detailed statistical tables.

Inter-Parliamentary Union. "Women in Politics: 60 Years in Retrospect." 2006. http://www.ipu.org/PDF/publications/ wmninfokit06_en.pdf. The Inter-Parliamentary Union is a small international organization headquartered in Switzerland, with about 140 member countries. The first few sections of this report are detailed, eye-glazing tables, country by country, about women in different parliaments. However, the sixth part of the report has some interesting discussion of the patterns of women in politics over time and their underlying causes.

Kuran, Timur. *Islam and Mammon: The Economic Predicaments of Islamism*. Princeton, NJ: Princeton University Press, 2004. This book collects six essays that Kuran has written on the relationship between Islam and economic development, along with an overview of his work. He is cautious about drawing connections but quite willing to do so with appropriate context. In some of the essays, Kuran reaches back to the interactions between Islam and economic institutions several centuries ago. In others, he looks at the practice of "Islamic banking"—which does not involve interest—in more recent times.

———. "Why the Middle East Is Economically Underdeveloped: Historical Mechanisms of Institutional Stagnation." *Journal of Economic Perspectives*. Summer 2004, 18:3, pp. 71–90. This essay summarizes some of Kuran's thinking about the interaction of Islamic law, economic institutions, and economic development. The focus is extremely long term—that is, how economies of the Middle East have evolved over the centuries.

Landsburg, Steven E. "Save the Earth in Six Hard Questions: What Al Gore Doesn't Understand about Climate Change." *Slate*. October 22, 2007. http://www.slate.com/id/2176156/. Landsburg has, for some years, written a lively and entertaining "Everyday Economics" column for the online magazine *Slate*. In this article, he poses six questions about facts and values related to global warming. He emphasizes the idea that, from an economic point of view, deciding on answers to these questions is the basic precondition for figuring out what and how much to do about global warming. These six questions represent the kind of arguments that economists and policy analysts should consider in looking at global warming.

Lardy, Nicholas. "China: Rebalancing Economic Growth." Chapter 1 in *The China Balance Sheet: 2007 and Beyond*. May 2, 2007. http://www.chinabalancesheet.org/Publication.html#CBS_in_2007. Lardy is an expert on China who was translating Chinese government economic plans for Western audiences back in the 1970s. He argues that China must shift its economy away from growth based on ultra-high levels of investment and exports and, instead, focus on growth rooted in consumption—which includes higher spending on education and health. The Web site includes a number of readable papers from a May 2007 conference on China's economic and political prospects.

Lee, Ronald, and Andrew Mason. "What Is the Demographic Dividend?" *Finance and Development*. September 2006, 43:3. http://www.imf.org/external/pubs/ft/fandd/2006/09/basics.htm. The authors are economists and demographers. They explain how the demographic transition has proceeded around the world and offer some graphs and examples. They also explain the "demographic dividend"—that is, the reasons why the decades when the birthrate is slowing down can be especially productive for economic growth.

Lincoln, Edward J. "International Economic Relations." Chapter 5 in *A Country Study: Japan*. http://lcweb2.loc.gov/frd/cs/jptoc.html. The Library of Congress has published a number of country studies that are available on the Web. These studies are not continually updated, so they are often not useful resources for the last decade or two. But they can be quite helpful as an overview of the political and economic development of different countries through the 20th century and back into the 19th century, as well. This chapter systematically works through Japan's patterns of international economic relations, including discussion of MITI subsidies for industry and trade policies.

Lindsey, Brink, and Aaron Lukas. "Revisiting the 'Revisionists': The Rise and Fall of the Japanese Economic Model." Cato Institute Trade Policy Analysis #3. July 31, 1998. http://www.freetrade.org/pubs/pas/tpa-003.html. The authors quote numerous sources who believed into the late 1980s and early 1990s that Japan's economic model was obviously superior to the U.S. economic model—and were quite brusque in dismissing anyone who believed otherwise. This essay was written after the bursting of Japan's bubble economy, when Japan's economy entered a period of stagnation. Politely but clearly, the essay reminds those who were sure that Japan's economic model would overtake that of the United States of just how wrong they were.

Meredith, Robyn. "The Elephant and the Dragon." *Milken Institute Review*. 4th quarter 2007, pp. 61–78. http://www.milkeninstitute.org (free registration required for access). Meredith's book of the same title compares the economic prospects of China and India. The excerpt reprinted here discusses the challenges facing India as parts of its economy begin to compete with advanced technology at the global level while other parts remain in some of the deepest poverty found anywhere in the world. The author is a senior editor for *Forbes*; thus, her writing has less pure economics but a lot of the lively snap-and-crackle of the well-chosen anecdote and well-posed question.

Metcalf, Gilbert E. "An Equitable Tax Reform to Address Global Climate Change." Hamilton Project Discussion Paper 2007-12. October 2007. http://www.brookings.edu/papers/2007/10carbontax_metcalf.aspx. This practical and detail-oriented paper lays out how a carbon tax that starts at $15/ton and increases over time would work to reduce climate change. Metcalf proposes that the revenue from the tax be used to reduce income taxes. As economists see it, the main alternative to a carbon tax is a "cap-and-trade" approach, which is advocated in the paper by Robert Stavins on this reading list.

Metraux, Daniel A., and Kellie Ann Warner. "The Character and Structure of the Economy." Chapter 4 in *A Country Study: Japan*. http://lcweb2.loc.gov/frd/cs/jptoc.html. The Library of Congress has published a number of country studies that are available on the Web. These studies are not continually updated, so they are often not useful resources for the last decade or two. But they can be quite helpful as an overview of the political and economic development of different countries through the 20th century and back into the 19th century, as well. This chapter systematically works through Japan's patterns of economic development, looking at workers, businesses, and government policy.

Ndulu, Benno, with Lopamudra Chakraborti, Lebohang Lijane, Vijaya Ramachandran, and Jerome Wolgin. *Challenges of African Growth: Opportunities, Constraints and Strategic Directions.* Washington, DC: World Bank, 2007. http://siteresources. worldbank.org/AFRICAEXT/Resources/AFR_Growth_Advance_Ed ition.pdf. A group of leading African economists gives a good overview of current thinking about Africa's economy. They review Africa's growth experience over the last 45 years or so and discuss key challenges and policies. They especially emphasize the importance of investment climate, infrastructure, innovation, and institutional capacity. Chapter 2 discusses "Africa's Long-Term Growth Experience in a Global Perspective," which offers a perspective back to about 1960. The first part of chapter 4, "Constraints to Growth," has some discussion of the fact that

Africa's geography and climate are not especially favorable to growth.

Oppenheimer, Andrés. *Saving the Americas: The Dangerous Decline of Latin America and What the U.S. Must Do.* Mexico: Random House Mondadori, 2007. Oppenheimer is a U.S.-based journalist who is one of the better commentators on Latin American affairs. In this lively and well-written book, he looks at Latin America in the context of the rest of the world economy—especially in comparison with East Asia, China, and parts of Europe. He offers chapters on events and issues in Brazil, Mexico, and Argentina. His theme is that Latin America is in danger of accepting a path toward reduced economic relevance as its destiny and that the United States does not recognize the costs and dangers associated with that outcome.

Organisation for Economic Co-operation and Development (OECD). *China in the World Economy: The Domestic Policy Challenges.* http://www.oecd.org/dataoecd/45/57/2075272.pdf. This 72-page summary of a much longer report discusses China's economic reforms from 1978 up to 2000. The fundamental argument is that by about 2000, China had achieved most of the possible economic gains from freeing up particular industries, such as agriculture, or allowing prices to vary. The report also reviews the changes that have been made and argues that looking ahead, China will need to deal with broader issues affecting the entire economy.

―――. "Exchange Market Volatility and Securities Transaction Taxes." Chapter 8 in *OECD Economic Outlook.* June 2002. http://www.oecd.org/dataoecd/38/26/1937989.pdf. For some time, policymakers have suggested that a tax should be imposed on all exchange rate transactions around the world. The hope is that such a tax might diminish the volatility of exchange rates, because those in financial markets who trade frequently would have an incentive to trade less. However, there are also concerns that such a tax is impractical and could end up imposing costs on low-income countries that often have the most need for international transactions. This chapter reviews the evidence on exchange rate volatility and discusses the pros and cons of a securities transaction tax.

―――. *OECD Economic Surveys: China.* September 2005. The OECD's membership in 2007 included 30 countries "committed to democracy and the market economy." Historically, this has meant the high-income countries of the world. In recent years, however, the OECD has started talks with Russia, India, China, and Brazil about joining, which suggests that its focus is broadening to include major economies everywhere. Reports from the OECD are a consistently high-quality source of outsider analysis on specific countries and economic issues that cut across countries. This report focuses in particular on reforming the business sector and government finances.

―――――. *OECD Economic Surveys: Russian Federation.* November 2006, vol. 2006-17. One of the OECD's well-done country studies. This overview of Russia's economy focuses on how to sustain Russia's economic growth with a focus on innovation, public sector management, and health care issues.

―――――. *The OECD Jobs Study: Facts, Analysis, Strategies.* 1994. http://www.oecd.org/dataoecd/42/51/1941679.pdf. The OECD is a Paris-based international think-tank that puts out reports on issues of particular interest to high-income countries around the world. This study lays out in detail what Europe's unemployment problem looked like in the mid-1990s: high unemployment rates, long term to a large degree and brought on by combinations of well-intended but poorly designed policies that reduced incentives to work and hire. This study crystallized a consensus and was quoted and referenced for years after it appeared.

Organisation for Economic Co-operation and Development and UN Food and Agriculture Organization (FAO). *OECD-FAO Agricultural Outlook, 2008–2017: Highlights.* 2008. http://www.agri-outlook.org/dataoecd/54/15/40715381.pdf. The second chapter of this report is called "Are High Prices Here to Stay?" It discusses the effects of rising demand because of higher incomes and biofuels policies and offers estimated prices for the next decade. This report is updated annually. The UN FAO also has a useful Web site with facts and reports about high food prices around the world at http://www.fao.org/worldfoodsituation/en/.

Perkins, Dwight. "Completing China's Move to the Market." *Journal of Economic Perspectives.* Spring 1994, 8:2, pp. 23–46. Perkins was probably the foremost Western authority on China's economy for years leading up to the reforms of 1978 and, thus, was extremely well placed to put them in context. In this essay, he emphasizes how changes in rural markets and foreign investment were crucial to the early stages of China's market-oriented reforms.

―――――. "History, Politics, and the Sources of Economic Growth: China and the East Asian Way." In *China in the Twenty-First Century: Politics, Economy, and Society*, Fumio Itoh, ed., pp. 25–41.

Tokyo: United Nations University Press, 1997. In this chapter, Perkins offers an overview of many of the issues facing China's economy from the 1940s into the 1970s—before the economic reforms started. Perkins gives a sense of the economic chaos of that period and of one transition—the shift to becoming a high-saving economy—that has turned out to be helpful in the recent decades of rapid growth for China.

Porter, Michael E., and Mariko Sakakibara. "Competition in Japan." *Journal of Economic Perspectives*. Winter 2004, 18:1, pp. 27–50. It is commonly believed that the competitive market environment in Japan is less subject to laissez-faire policies than that in the United States. For these authors, it is more accurate to state that some Japanese industries have fierce competition while others do not. In addition, those industries that experience fierce competition tend to be those that are most successful in international markets. Levels of competition in other areas are generally increasing in Japan.

Pritchett, Lant. *Let Their People Come: Breaking the Gridlock on Global Labor Mobility*. Washington, DC: Center for Global Development, 2006. http://www.cgdev.org/content/publications/detail/10174 (available for purchase or free download). In this very readable book, Pritchett lays out five irresistible forces leading to more migration, eight immovable ideas blocking greater migration, and six accommodations for politically acceptable, development-friendly migration.

Rajan, Raghuram. "The Future of the IMF and the World Bank." *American Economic Review*. May 2008. http://faculty.chicagogsb.edu/raghuram.rajan/research/Future%20of%20IMF%20and%20World%20Bank.pdf. Rajan is a distinguished economist at the University of Chicago who served for several years as chief economist at the International Monetary Fund. Thus, his discussion of the future of the IMF and the World Bank—written soon after he had returned to academia—comes from a deeply informed insider's perspective. He emphasizes the idea that the traditional roles of these institutions have become outdated and discusses how their core functions might be strengthened and preserved in a globalizing world.

Reid, Michael. *Forgotten Continent: The Battle for Latin America's Soul*. New Haven, CT: Yale University Press, 2007. The author is a journalist who has covered Latin America for decades, including for *The Economist* magazine for the last decade or so. Chapters 4 and 5 of this book focus on Latin America's political and economic development from after World War II until the debt crisis. Somewhat dense, the book covers a broad range of facts and events. The remainder of the book may be of interest as a supplement to Lecture Twenty.

Roberts, Alan. "Open Up: A Special Report on Migration." *The Economist*. January 5, 2008, pp. 1–16. *The Economist* regularly publishes wonderfully informative middle-of-the-issue survey articles. In this one, Roberts points out that rich countries do gain overall from migration, but the benefits are unevenly spread. He also discusses how the various immigration policy choices are working and might work, including blocking migrants, allowing more permanent migrants, or allowing more temporary migrants.

Roodman, David. "Macro Aid Effectiveness Research: A Guide for the Perplexed." Center for Global Development, Working Paper 134. December 2007. http://www.cgdev.org/content/publications/ detail/15003. This paper argues that although foreign aid has done a number of good things—prevented famines, ended diseases, and more—it is difficult to make a case that foreign aid has helped the overall rate of economic growth in recipient countries. Roodman reviews much of the recent economic literature on the effectiveness of foreign aid and discusses how to reconcile these conflicting findings.

Sachs, Jeffrey. *The End of Poverty: Economic Possibilities for Our Time*. New York: Penguin Press, 2005. Sachs makes perhaps the most powerful arguments of any economist in support of a vision of how greatly expanded foreign aid could lead to dramatic decreases in poverty. He is especially good at identifying specific examples of aid programs that could usefully be expanded. Much of this book represents something of a tour around the world economy, including stops in Latin America, Eastern Europe, Russia, China, and India. The last eight chapters have a particular focus on Africa and issues of foreign aid. For the counterarguments that take a skeptical view of foreign aid, see the book by William Easterly on this reading list.

Scheller, Hanspeter K. "The European Central Bank: History, Role and Functions." 2nd ed., 2006. http://www.ecb.int/pub/pdf/other/ ecbhistoryrolefunctions2006en.pdf. This report offers a helpful introduction to the basics of the euro system. The first chapter focuses on the lead-up to the euro and some of the failed earlier attempts to stabilize foreign exchange rates across Western Europe.

The second chapter is a legal and institutional description of the European Central Bank, and the third chapter is an overview of the principles that guide its policies. If you're interested in more detail about recent policies and economic evaluations of the European Central Bank, surfing around this Web site is a good place to start.

Sen, Amartya. "More Than 100 Million Women Are Missing." *New York Review of Books*. December 20, 1990, pp. 61–66. In this highly readable essay, Nobel laureate economist Sen lays out some grim facts showing that the number of women living in the world doesn't match up with basic facts on the number of women who were born. He then offers insight and informed speculation on what factors have led to women dying sooner at different stages of life.

Shleifer, Andrei. *A Normal Country: Russia after Communism*. Cambridge, MA: Harvard University Press, 2005. Shleifer discusses how Russia's economic transition took place, both in terms of the political constraints surrounding the choices made and the economic outcomes of those choices. He argues that Russia under Boris Yeltsin made enormous strides toward political and economic freedom. Warning: The exposition in this book sometimes involves economic graphs and statistical measures that will be easy to understand for readers with some background in economics or statistics but may prove difficult for readers without such background.

Shleifer, Andrei and Daniel Triesman. "A Normal Country." *Foreign Affairs*. March/April 2004. http://www.foreignaffairs.org/ 20040301faessay83204/andrei-hleifer-daniel-treisman/a-normal- country.html. Shleifer and Triesman discuss the evidence that the transition away from Communism perhaps caused less disruption than has been widely perceived. They point out that if Russia is compared to other countries around the world with similar levels of per capita GDP, then many of its restrictions on political and media freedom, much of its economic inequality, and the shaky practice of the rule of law end up looking relatively normal.

Stavins, Robert N. "A U.S. Cap-and-Trade System to Address Global Climate Change." Hamilton Project Discussion Paper 2007- 13. October 2007. http://www.brookings.edu/papers/2007/ 10climate_stavins.aspx. A cap-and-trade system would set a limit on emissions of CO_2 and other greenhouse gases. Permits would be issued for businesses whose processes lead to emission of such gases, and the permits could be bought and sold. The permits would also "shrink"—that is, they would require a gradual downward level of emissions over time. This practical paper describes how a cap-and-trade system could work in the United States. As economists see it, the main alternative to a cap-and-trade approach is a carbon tax, which is advocated in the paper by Gilbert Metcalf on this reading list.

Stern, Nicholas. "Stern Review on the Economics of Climate Change." London: Her Majesty's Treasury, 2006. http://www.hm-treasury.gov.uk/independent_reviews/stern_review_economics_clim ate_change/sternreview_index.cfm. Stern is an eminent economist who was asked by the British government to put together a white paper on climate change issues. The resulting elegant paper offers an overview of all the issues, from the science to the economics to international policy. The report shows a bias toward the case for current action in various ways, such as choosing implausibly low discount rates. Nonetheless, Stern does an elegant job of breaking down the overall problem into specific issues and laying out how differing views on those issues will affect an overall conclusion.

Stone, Mark, Harald Anderson, and Romain Veyrune. "Exchange Rate Regimes: Fix or Float?" *Finance and Development*. March 2008, 45:1. http://www.imf.org/external/pubs/ft/fandd/2008/03/ basics.htm. Three economists at the International Monetary Fund offer a crisp and concise overview of hard-peg (fixed), floating, and soft-peg exchange rates and the likely costs and benefits of each approach.

"The Sun Also Rises." *The Economist*. October 6, 2005. As one of the middle-of-the-issue surveys that *The Economist* does so well, this article argues that Japan has largely worked through the problems of the bubble economy that led to more than a decade of stagnation and is now ready to resume at least moderate economic growth. Some of the political discussion in the article is now outdated, but the economic analysis of how debt has been reduced and the economy has been made more flexible and deregulated offers useful background.

"A Survey of the Soviet Economy: Gorbachev's Gamble." *The Economist*. April 9, 1988. This middle-of-the-issue survey article was written at about the time that Mikhail Gorbachev was attempting to loosen up the centrally planned Soviet economy in a way that would encourage economic growth. Gorbachev's policies eventually did much more than he expected—indeed, they preceded the breakup of the Soviet Union. But this article gives a good sense of the dire situation of the Soviet economy in the late 1980s, after decades of central planning.

Taylor, Timothy. *Principles of Economics*. Freeload Press, 2008. http://freeloadpress.com. Some listeners might be interested in a more thorough, textbook-style treatment that explains the reasons for gains from trade and the arguments over import protectionism from an economic point of view. Chapters 3 and 6 of this book provide this kind of overview. The chapters of this book can be downloaded for free as PDF files, although there is a brief registration form to fill out, and the first page or two of your download will be advertising.

―――. "Thinking about a 'New Economy.'" *The Public Interest*. Spring 2001, pp. 3–19. http://timothytaylor.net/articles/public_interest_spr_2001.pdf. In this article, I discuss the importance of the shift to the "new economy," including the economic importance of the rise in productivity and the ways in which advances in information technology manifest themselves in higher productivity.

―――. "The Truth about Globalization." *The Public Interest*. Spring 2002, pp. 24–44. http://timothytaylor.net/articles/public_interest_spr_2002.pdf. In this essay, I argue that the overall effects of globalization are positive and worth defending. I also argue that both the benefits and the costs of globalization are often overstated and that globalization has much farther to go.

Transparency International. "FAQs for Journalists: Facts and Figures on Corruption." http://www.transparency.org/news_room/faq/journalists_faq. On this useful Web page, Transparency International takes a stab at offering short answers to many of the obvious questions journalists often ask about corruption. This is a good place to get quick answers to questions about whether corruption is increasing, the economic and noneconomic costs of corruption, whether corruption imposes outside standards on low-income countries, the successes of some countries in fighting corruption, and more.

―――. *Global Corruption Report 2007*. http://www.transparency.org/publications/publications/gcr_2007. Transparency International is one of the best-known organizations that argues and collects information on corruption. This annual report examines the effects of corruption in one area each year. In 2007, the focus was on judicial corruption; in 2006, how corruption affects health services; in 2005, corruption in infrastructure.

Trehan, Bharat. "Changing Productivity Trends." Federal Reserve Bank of San Francisco Economic Letter, 2007-25. August 31, 2007. http://www.frbsf.org/publications/economics/letter/2007/el2007-25.html. A short and readable introduction to current academic thinking about the causes of the productivity slowdown of the 1970s. The author discusses the strengths and weaknesses of some of the common explanations, including higher oil prices, information technology, and changes in the service sector.

United Nations. "The Millennium Development Goals Report 2007." http://www.un.org/millenniumgoals/pdf/mdg2007.pdf. This report, which comes out annually, is an easy-to-read overview of where the world stands with respect to the Millennium Development Goals. Because it is a summary report, it has a number of bar charts and short explanations and goes through all the issues in 20 pages or so.

———. *Population Challenges and Development Goals*. 2005. http://www.un.org/esa/population/publications/pop_challenges/Population_Challenges.pdf. This report offers an overview of demographic trends worldwide, including total population, as well as aging, fertility, death rates, and other issues, with breakdowns by region. It also has a section on population policies around the world.

———. *World Urbanization Prospects: The 2007 Revision.* "Executive Summary." February 26, 2008. http://www.un.org/esa/population/publications/wup2007/2007WUP_ExecSum_web.pdf For those who want underlying numbers and trends without a lot of fancy writing, this regularly updated and revised UN survey is the place to turn. This summary shows trends in urban and rural populations projected ahead several decades and divided by region of the world. It also shows projections for megacities and offers an overview of government dissatisfaction with the developing population patterns.

United Nations Development Programme (UNDP). *Arab Human Development Report 2002: Creating Opportunities for Future Generations*. New York: United Nations Publications, 2002. Available at a number of places on the Web, including http://www.ituarabic.org/hresources/Ar-Human-Dev.pdf. In this fascinating project, economists from the Middle East write more-or-less annual reports on factors that could help economic development. The reports have a political dimension—for example, they sometimes spend a paragraph or two recapping the Arab position in the Arab-Israeli conflict. But in their economic dimension, they often show some courage in delivering unpopular truths. This first report focuses on issues of governance, greater power for women, and access to knowledge. Later reports, available at the UNDP Web site, address other issues, such as the role of science and technology in the economies of the Middle East.

Varma, Amit. "Profit's No Longer a Dirty Word: The Transformation of India." February 4, 2008. http://www.econlib.org/library/Columns/y2008/Varmaprofit.html. Varma is a journalist who is highly knowledgeable about India. In this short article, he summarizes the historical context of India's reforms of the early 1990s. He also gives a sense of how the economy has evolved since that time and some of the country's current challenges.

Williamson, John. "The Choice of Exchange Rate Regime: The Relevance of International Experience to China's Decision." A lecture at a conference on exchange rates organized by the Central University of Finance and Economics in Beijing, September 7, 2004. http://www.iie.com/publications/papers/williamson0904.pdf. Williamson is one of the top experts on the practical policy side of exchange rates, and he is also a lucid expositor. In this lecture, he reviews the general issues of exchange rate policy, then offers advice that China should not (and probably cannot) seek to keep its exchange rate fixed at levels as low as occurred in the mid-2000s.

———. "Did the Washington Consensus Fail?" Outline of a speech at the Center for Strategic and International Studies, Washington, DC. November 6, 2002. http://www.iie.com/publications/papers/paper.cfm?ResearchID=488. In this short article, the economist who coined the term "Washington consensus" offers a reminder of what the term originally meant. He points out that the policies themselves can be debated, but they should be discussed on their merits, not that many of them are little more than economic common sense.

World Bank. "About Us." http://web.worldbank.org/WBSITE/EXTERNAL/EXTABOUTUS/0,,contentMDK:20046292~menuPK:51123588~pagePK:50004410~piPK:36602~theSitePK:29708,00.html (or type "World Bank" into your browser and click on "About Us"). This part of the World Bank Web site describes the institution. If you follow the links, you will find a short history of the World Bank, organizational charts, descriptions of workers, descriptions of the agencies within the bank, and links to other publications and research.

————. "Avoiding the Resource Curse." Oil and Gas: Petroleum Sector Briefing Note #3. May 2007. http://siteresources.worldbank.org/INTOGMC/Resources/cambodia_ oil_gas_newsletter_3.pdf. This essay describes the policies that four resource-rich, low-income countries have taken. In Nigeria, oil wealth seems to have made the economy worse off. In Indonesia, Malaysia, and Botswana, oil wealth seems to have helped the economies.

————. "East Asia and Pacific Update: 10 Years after the Crisis." April 2007. http://siteresources.worldbank.org/ INTEAPHALFYEARLYUPDATE/Resources/550192- 175629375615/EAP-Update-April2007-fullreport.pdf (or type "World Bank" and the title of the article into a search engine). Twice a year, the World Bank publishes this "East Asia and Pacific Update." This particular update has a chapter devoted to events since the financial crisis of 1997–1998 and includes a discussion of China. Of course, you can also look up more recent reports for updates on the region as a whole.

————. *The East Asian Miracle*. Oxford University Press: New York, 1993. This report is the canonical starting point for thinking about the growth experience of East Asia. To offer a sense of the contents over roughly 350 pages, here are the chapter titles: "Growth Equity and Economic Change," "Public Policy and Growth," "Macroeconomic Stability and Export Growth," "An Institutional Basis for Shared Growth," "Strategies for Rapid Accumulation," "Using Resources Efficiently: Relying on Markets and Exports," and "Policies and Pragmatism in a Changing World." The report is written in a fairly readable manner, with jargon and professional details pushed back into some chapter appendices that are easy to skip.

————. *Global Development Finance: The Development Potential of Surging Capital Flows*. 2006. http://econ.worldbank.org/ WBSITE/EXTERNAL/EXTDEC/EXTDECPROSPECTS/EXTGDF/ EXTGDF2006/0,,menuPK:2344945~pagePK:64167702~piPK:6416 7676~theSitePK:2344908, 00.html. (or type "GDF 2006" into a search engine). This report appears annually. In the back of the report are statistical tables on international capital flows. The first chapter provides an overview of events in the previous year, and later chapters look at a particular subject. Thus, the 2006 report focuses on the conditions under which capital flows can assist development, while the 2007 report is subtitled *The Globalization of Corporate Finance in Developing Countries*. The 2007 report is available at the following Web site: http://econ.worldbank.org/ WBSITE/EXTERNAL/EXTDEC/EXTDECPROSPECTS/EXTGDF/ EXTGDF2007/0,,menuPK:3763156~pagePK:64167702~piPK: 64167676~theSitePK:3763080, 00.html (or type "GDF 2007" into a search engine).

————. *Global Economic Prospects*. Published annually. Available at the World Bank Web site at http://web.worldbank.org/ WBSITE/EXTERNAL/EXTDEC/EXTDECPROSPECTS/GEPEXT/ 0,,contentMDK:21021075~menuPK:51087945~pagePK:51087946~ piPK:51087916~theSitePK:538110,00.html (or type "Global Economic Prospects World Bank" into a search engine). This annual report begins with an overview of the world economy, and the back of the volume has a useful appendix on "Regional Economic Prospects" that works its way around the main regions of the world in an approach similar to the structure of these lectures. Each annual report also focuses on a particular topic, usually related to economics.

————. "Governance as Part of Global Monitoring." Part II in *Global Monitoring Report 2006*, pp. 121–192. http://web.worldbank.org/WBSITE/EXTERNAL/EXTDEC/ EXTGLOBALMONITOR/EXTGLOBALMONITOR2006/ 0,,contentMDK:20810084~menuPK:2199415~pagePK:64218950~ piPK:64218883~theSitePK:2186432,00.html (or type "Global Monitoring Report 2006" into a search engine). Chapter 5 of this report discusses approaches to measuring governance, including the Transparency International report, but also a number of others. Chapter 6 discusses ways of fighting corruption at lower levels of government through various kinds of monitoring and transparency. Chapter 7 covers international agreements to fight corruption. Informative examples are liberally sprinkled throughout the discussion.

————. "India: Inclusive Growth and Service Delivery: Building on India's Success—Development Policy Review." May 29, 2006. http://siteresources.worldbank.org/SOUTHASIAEXT/Resources/ DPR_FullReport.pdf. This report is written at a time when the faster growth in India's economy can be taken for granted; thus, the focus is on how to help that growth extend through space to reach more of the population and how to lay a basis for extending the growth through time. Much of the emphasis is on the failure of India's government to provide adequate basic public services.

―――. "Oil and Gas: A Blessing or a Curse?" *Oil and Gas: Petroleum Sector Briefing Note #2.* April 2007. http://siteresources.worldbank.org/INTOGMC/Resources/cambodia_ oil_gas_newsletter_2.pdf (or type "World Bank" and the title of the article into a search engine). This four-page note does a nice job of summarizing the evidence on how oil and gas resources affect an economy—that is, sometimes for better but often for worse. The difference seems to depend on the society's institutions for spreading the oil and gas wealth across the economy as a whole and on whether the economy can develop a healthy non-oil sector, as well.

―――. "Overview: The Making of a Miracle." In *The East Asian Miracle.* Oxford University Press: New York, 1993, pp. 1–26. This "Overview" chapter offers a readable summary of the arguments concerning the economies of East Asia during their period of rapid growth, from about 1965 into the early 1990s. For details about specific countries and information on investment, education, export promotion, macroeconomic stability, and much more, dip into the chapters in the rest of the report.

―――. "PovertyNet: Understanding Poverty." http://web.worldbank.org/WBSITE/EXTERNAL/TOPICS/EXTPOV ERTY/0,,contentMDK:20153855~menuPK:373757~pagePK:148956 ~piPK:216618~theSitePK:336992,00.html (or type "World Bank" and the title of the Web page into a search engine). The World Bank maintains this Web site as a place to gather together information about global poverty. This page offers an introduction to such issues as measuring poverty, trends in poverty rates, and policy responses to poverty. You can also surf and click the many links from this page to find more detailed discussions and data.

―――. "Promoting Gender Equality and Women's Empowerment." Chapter 3 in *Global Monitoring Report 2007: Confronting the Challenges of Gender Equality and Fragile States.* http://www-ds.worldbank.org/external/default/WDSContentServer/WDSP/IB/20 07/04/11/000112742_20070411162802/Rendered/PDF/394730GMR 02007.pdf > (or type "Global Monitoring Report 2007" into a search engine). Greater gender equality is one of the Millennium Development Goals set by the United Nations. This chapter spells out why greater gender equality is important, summarizes some of the relevant evidence, and gives a sense of how gender equity should be measured and evaluated.

―――. *World Development Report 2008: Agriculture for Development.* http://econ.worldbank.org/WBSITE/EXTERNAL/ EXTDEC/EXTRESEARCH/EXTWDRS/EXTWDR2008/0,,menuP K:2795178~pagePK:64167702~piPK:64167676~theSitePK:2795143 ,00.html (or type "World Development Report 2008" into a search engine). The *World Development Report* is one of the annual flagship reports of the World Bank. Each year, the report covers a particular topic, drawing on a combination of academic research and the World Bank's experience around the world. The 2008 report is on the role of agriculture in development; it details the struggles of countries around the world to adjust to rising food prices.

"The World Goes to Town: A Special Report on Cities." *The Economist.* May 5, 2007. This special 14-page, middle-of-the issue survey begins with the fact that the world's urban population has now outstripped the rural population. It offers a brief overview of cities throughout human history, then focuses on issues of infrastructure and governance and the idea that cities must continually reinvent themselves.

World Trade Organization (WTO). *The Future of the WTO: Addressing Institutional Challenges in the New Millennium.* 2004. http://www.wto.org/english/thewto_e/10anniv_e/future_wto_e.pdf. On the 10th anniversary of the establishment of the WTO, an outside committee was appointed to look at the long-term future of the organization. The committee's report includes a number of interesting comments about trade agreements in a world of globalization, ongoing issues with national sovereignty, dispute resolution, and more.

―――. "What Is the WTO?" Updated in February 2007. http://www.wto.org/english/thewto_e/whatis_e/whatis_e.htm. This page offers links to various documents that give a basic overview of the WTO. "What Is the WTO?" discusses the evolution of the agreements over time, the negotiation process, the Doha round, and more. Also on this site are short pamphlets on "10 Benefits of the WTO Trading System" and "10 Common Misunderstandings about the WTO," along with links to a few educational videos.

Zachary, G. Pascal. "Trends: Africa Overreaches." *Milken Institute Review.* 2nd quarter 2008, pp. 6–13. This article discusses the surge of increased education across Africa in the last decade or so, with some emphasis on the experience in Uganda. The article sets forth a number of provocative facts about the increase and discusses some possible parallels to mass education in East Asia and the United States. It also points out that Africa has a long way to go and that education pays off in more economic growth only over decades, as children become young adults and enter the workforce, not in a few years.

Zettlemeyer, Jeromin. "Growth and Reforms in Latin America: A Survey of Facts and Arguments." IMF Working Paper WP/06/210. 2006. http://www.imf.org/external/pubs/ft/wp/2006/wp06210.pdf. This paper reviews some consistent patterns in the economy of Latin America: a lack of openness to foreign trade, macroeconomic instability, and high levels of inequality. It then discusses different views of why the economic reforms of the early 1990s have not led to greater improvement in economic growth.

Notes